OXFORD STUDIES IN POST

The *Oxford Studies in Postcolonial Li*
and accessible introductions to defi
regions within the rapidly diversifying field of postcolonial literary studies in English.

Under the general editorship of Professor Elleke Boehmer, the *Studies* in each case elucidate and explicate the informing contexts of postcolonial texts, and plot the historical and cultural coordinates of writers and of the leading movements, institutions and cultural debates situated within those contexts. Individual volumes reflect in particular on the shaping effect both of international theory and of local politics on postcolonial traditions often viewed as uniformly cross-cultural, and also on the influence of postcolonial writing on the protocols of international theory. Throughout the focus is on how texts formally engage with the legacies of imperial and anti-imperial history. Other titles in the Series include *The Indian Novel in English, West African Literatures*, and *Pacific Islands Writing.*

OXFORD STUDIES IN POSTCOLONIAL LITERATURES

The Indian Novel in English
Priyamvada Gopal

Australian Literatures
Graham Huggan

Pacific Islands Writing
Michelle Keown

West African Literatures
Stephanie Newell

Postcolonial Poetry in English
Rajeev S. Patke

OXFORD STUDIES IN POSTCOLONIAL LITERATURES IN ENGLISH

GENERAL EDITOR: ELLEKE BOEHMER

POSTCOLONIAL POETRY IN ENGLISH

Rajeev S. Patke

OXFORD
UNIVERSITY PRESS

OXFORD
UNIVERSITY PRESS

Great Clarendon Street, Oxford OX2 6DP

Oxford University Press is a department of the University of Oxford.
It furthers the University's objective of excellence in research, scholarship,
and education by publishing worldwide in

Oxford New York

Auckland Cape Town Dar es Salaam Hong Kong Karachi
Kuala Lumpur Madrid Melbourne Mexico City Nairobi
New Delhi Shanghai Taipei Toronto

With offices in

Argentina Austria Brazil Chile Czech Republic France Greece
Guatemala Hungary Italy Japan Poland Portugal Singapore
South Korea Switzerland Thailand Turkey Ukraine Vietnam

Published in the United States
by Oxford University Press Inc., New York

First published 2006

British Library Cataloguing in Publication Data
Data available

Library of Congress Cataloging in Publication Data
Data available

Typeset by SPI Publisher Services, Pondicherry, India
Printed in Great Britain by
Biddle's Ltd., King's Lynn

ISBN 0–19–927564–5 978–0–19–927564–9
ISBN 0–19–926340–X (Pbk.) 978–0–19–929888–4 (Pbk.)

1 3 5 7 9 10 8 6 4 2

For Nikish, Meghan, and Varsha

The carpet is glad to have sat in the sunshine
and rain
Glad to have taken to the air
time and again

PREFACE

I was mired in attachment
[...]
So I mastered new rungs of air

Seamus Heaney, 'The First Flight'

This book introduces readers to a body of poetry whose unique relation to language and history gives it a dual role in contemporary societies. On the one hand, this poetry bears witness to the residual force of colonial histories; on the other, it shows how that force may be turned to new forms of linguistic and cultural empowerment. Many books with 'postcolonial' in their titles ignore or marginalize the genre of poetry. Others address it within the boundaries of a single nation or region. Their insights leave room for another kind of project, which establishes connections between contemporary poetry and colonial history, and provides comparisons between the literary decolonization of societies linked by a colonial language, while remaining alert to the features that distinguish one society and poet from another. In addressing these aims, I have tried to contextualize poetry in terms of historical developments, supplement broad outline with salient detail, and balance exposition with analysis, while grounding ideas and concepts in their capacity to clarify the experience of reading poetry.

The field covered by this book is held together by three factors. The first is the global community constituted by English. The second is the set of creative possibilities wrested by poets from a combination of assimilation and resistance to English as a language and a culture. The third is a pattern of development shared between regions with a history of twentieth-century decolonization. Poets writing before and after the end of colonial rule tackled challenges and accessed opportunities that created local traditions; these went through a series of transformations, from imitation and dependency to varying degrees of cultural self-confidence. This book is an attempt to introduce, narrate, and analyse these transformations, treating differences in cultural predicament and poetic strategy as equal in significance to commonality.

The book is divided into three parts, corresponding to the three tasks it undertakes: introduction, narration, and analysis. Part I introduces the relation between poetry and postcoloniality in terms of common perspectives, historical contexts, and a method of analysis that relates colonial literary formations to the goal of achieving poetic individuation and authority. Part II narrates the historical development of local traditions: first, with reference to the colonized zones of Asia, Africa, and the Caribbean, and then with reference to the settler colonies, whose shared features are highlighted through comparisons. Part III analyses a set of preoccupations central to the themes and techniques of postcolonial poetry. These include the problems of self-representation for minorities marginalized by ethnic difference; the cultural politics of gender, modernism, and postmodernity in the specific context of postcolonial societies; and the entire gamut of experience from migration to self-exile that poetry renders through the metaphor of translation between languages, cultures, and values.

Any account of how poetry is formed in the aftermath of Empire is a large undertaking for a small book. A few concessions are therefore in order. The relevance of poetic developments in America is noted, but references to its influence are attenuated, in recognition of the fact that after independence American poetry took a path that divagates from the one trodden by other former British colonies. It would be ideal if one could read Anglophone poetry in conjunction with other genres and in the context of all the languages promoted or displaced by colonialism, but that aspiration remains outside the present scope. I have had to omit reference to much that is of postcolonial or poetic interest, with regret. If specific texts or topics fail to get the attention they deserve, that is because any selection of material is spoilt for choice. I have tried to make space for poets to speak for themselves, even if briefly, so that the poetic text is not altogether displaced by paraphrase and commentary. I hope that the limitations of this undertaking will encourage readers to explore for themselves, closer to the ground, territories here mapped from a middle distance.

ACKNOWLEDGEMENTS

It is a pleasure to acknowledge the debts of gratitude accumulated in the course of writing this book: to Elleke Boehmer, for the invitation to join the project, and for her advice throughout the writing of the book; to Ruth Anderson for seeing it through its early stage; to Tom Perridge, Jacqueline Baker, and Christine Rode for seeing it through the press; to Matthew Brown for his care and attention to detail in preparing the final typescript; to the National University of Singapore for study leave during 2003; to its Faculty of Arts and Social Sciences, for a research grant (R-103-000-042) during 2003–2004; to the staff of its Central Library, for their unfailing support in acquiring materials; and to the Department of English Language and Literature, for its support in countless ways, over many years.

Inevitably, a book that works its way across such vast terrains must build on the work of others. I am grateful to the numerous poets and readers of poetry whose writing has made mine possible. Several friends and colleagues—Walter Lim, Philip Holden, Gwee Li Sui, and John Whalen-Bridge—read the book in part; Susan Ang, Anjali Kadekodi, and Kirpal Singh read a draft in full. I am grateful to them for their comments and suggestions. The responsibility for all the sins of omission and commission inevitable to such an undertaking remains, ruefully, with me.

I am grateful to the following for permission to quote copyright material:

A. K. Mehrotra, for a quotation from 'Dream-figures in Sunlight', *The Transfiguring Places* (Delhi: Ravi Dayal Publishers, 1998);

Eavan Boland and Carcanet Press, for 'In Which Hester Bateman . . .', *Code* (Manchester: Carcanet Press, 2001);

Kamau Brathwaite and Oxford University Press, for quotations from *The Arrivants: A New World Trilogy* (Oxford: Oxford University Press, 1973);

Nourbese Philip, for quotations from *She Tries Her Tongue, Her Silence Softly Breaks* (London: The Women's Press, 1993), and *Zong!* (forthcoming);

Nuala Ní Dhomhnaill, and The Gallery Press, for 'The Language Issue', *The Pharaoh's Daughter* (Loughcrew: The Gallery Press, 1990);

Peter Wilhelm, and Jonathan Ball Publishers, for 'A Very Short Story', *Poetry South Africa: Selected Papers from Poetry '74* (Johannesburg: Ad. Donker, 1976);

Soonoo Kolatkar, for Arun Kolatkar, 'Pictures from a Marathi Alphabet Chart', in D. Weissbort and A. K. Mehrotra (eds.), *Periplus: Poetry in Translation* (Delhi: Oxford University Press, 1993);

Vinay Dharwadker, for 'The Alphabet', in V. Dharwadker and A. K. Ramanujan (eds.), *The Oxford Anthology of Modern Indian Poetry* (Delhi: Oxford University Press, 1994).

In order to keep the list of references to manageable proportions I have listed publications which are quoted in my text, but not the sources of my epigraphs, nor all the publications that proved useful in the writing of this book.

CONTENTS

PART I INTRODUCTION

PART II THE DEVELOPMENT OF LOCAL TRADITIONS

PART I
INTRODUCTION

1

Poetry and postcoloniality

For me, the *post* in post-colonial does not just mean *after*, it also means *around*, *through*, *out of*, *alongside*, and *against*.

Albert Wendt, *Nuanua: Pacific Writing in English since 1980*

. . . a borrowed voice sets the true one
Free

A. K. Mehrotra, 'Borges'

Overview

The first section of this opening chapter defines the conditions under which the notion of 'postcolonial poetry' serves a meaningful function in literary and cultural studies. It describes the historical preoccupations and linguistic strategies that constitute the central link between poetry and postcoloniality. It also indicates how the method and organization of this book takes account of some of the pitfalls associated with the term 'postcolonial'. The second section provides a condensed account of the spread of English in the British Isles, and the ambivalence with which this was met from Scotland, Wales, and Ireland. The significance of this motif is developed in section 3, which provides a reading of two poems about the relation between Ireland and England. These readings prefigure the analyses in Chapter 2, where the issues surveyed in the first chapter are extended to cultures and societies outside Britain.

1.1 Terms, contexts, and perspectives

Have you no language of your own
no way of doing things

> did you spend all those holidays
> at England's apron strings?
>
> E. K. Brathwaite, 'The Emigrants'

In the most literal sense, any poem is postcolonial which happens to be written from a place implicated in colonial history, by a person whose access to language has colonial associations. In a more dynamic sense, postcolonial poetry shows awareness of what it means to write from a place and in a language shaped by colonial history, at a time that is not yet free from the force of that shaping. The most interesting Anglophone poetry from the regions settled or colonized by Britain grapples with this awareness with an acute sense of the difficulties encountered, and the resolutions accomplished, in the pursuit of poetic freedom. This book is dedicated to an account of that pursuit. It uses the term 'postcolonial poetry' to sustain a stereoscopic perspective on the dialectical play between assimilation and resistance, or dependency and the will-to-autonomy, which constitutes the fundamental relation between poetry and postcoloniality. Based on this definition, the reading method used in this book looks to poetry for three kinds of synergy: between assimilation and resistance to colonial culture, between being shaped by and giving new shape to the colonial language, between the will to community and the will to modernity in an era of asynchronous decolonization.

Critical awareness of the force exerted by colonization is not confined to the former colonies. It can come from within Britain, even from poets not directly involved in the colonial experience, as in 'A Short History of British India', a sonnet sequence by Geoffrey Hill (b. 1932, UK), which acknowledges the guilt of 'fantasies of true destiny that kills | "under the sanction of the English name"' (1994: 193). The self-righteousness of the colonizer is here deflated in retrospect with a sombre sense of how British pride at colonial rule was complicit with violence against the colonized. Hill's sentiments qualify the kind of presumption enshrined in the title of a poem by Rudyard Kipling (1865–1936), 'The White Man's Burden', which was written in 1899, during the heyday of Empire, as a response to the American takeover of the Philippines. Kipling promoted a view of Western imperialism that downplayed its exploitative intent. The critique to which this view is vulnerable can be indicated through a remark from Margaret Atwood (b. 1939, Canada), who defines 'colony' laconically, as a place 'from which a profit is made, but not by the people who live there' (1972: 35–6). The positions exemplified by Kipling and Hill suggest that a study of postcolonial poetry can begin with the recognition that British cultural imperialism was met by a small but resolute element of resistance within the British Isles. Brief examples of this resistance are given in the second section that follows.

Subsequent chapters show how the notion of 'postcolonial poetry' acquires currency because the collapse of the modern European empires did not put an end to the derivativeness that prevailed, and in many cases persists, in cultural productions from the former colonies. 'Postcolonial' thus covers the gap between political self-rule and cultural autonomy. The process of political decolonization took place over a large expanse of time, from the declaration of independence by America (1776) to self-government in the settler colonies: Canada, 1867; Australia, 1901; New Zealand, 1907; South Africa, 1910; and the Irish Free State, 1921. The dissolution of the British Empire became a sweeping reality during the period from 1947 to the early 1960s, when large parts of Asia, Africa, the Caribbean, and Oceania became politically independent. The latest event in this process was the reversion of Hong Kong to mainland China in 1997. The six counties of Northern Ireland remain, in their unique way, the first and last region colonized by England, even if the Irish, like the Scots and the Welsh, also participated in the establishment of the British Empire.

This book is organized around a single question that can be stated simply: what is the relation of Anglophone poetry to the cultural aftermath of Empire? The answer takes many forms. The first concerns language, and shows awareness, as noted by the Sri Lankan linguist Arjuna Parakrama, that 'despite all disclaimers to the contrary', the 'standard' forms of language often 'discriminate against minorities, marginal groups, women, the underclass and so on, albeit in different ways' (1995: 41). John Agard (b. 1949, Guyana) gives lively expression to the logic of resistance in 'Listen Mr. Oxford don':

I ent have no gun
I ent have no knife
But mugging de Queen's English
Is the story of my life

(Petersen and Rutherford 1988: 134)

This degree of candour and self-awareness was slow to take hold in poetry. Colonial writing was committed to the premise that British English could be used creatively without being constrained by its distance from Britain. Poets from the colonies chose to write in English either because they were settlers of British descent, or because they were drawn to its expressive resources. In either case, mastery over English was aligned to its role as an instrument of modernity, progress, and cultural self-empowerment.

However, colonial poets soon found that the poetic resources of English were ruled by a set of traditions governing diction, form, and style that were tempting to emulate but difficult to reproduce with conviction in societies outside Britain. Early attempts to do so led to various forms of mimicry, incongruity, and ineptness. In this respect, as the chapters comprising Part II will show, no one colony or settlement was more fluent or less derivative than any other. The predominantly monolingual cultures of the settler colonies developed sooner than in non-settler colonies, where access to English was confined to a minority, and its use in writing competed with numerous local languages that already possessed their own well-established oral and written traditions. Many colonial poets used English as if they lived in an England of the mind; others learned to accommodate European models to the inflections of the vernacular. Their example proved the more useful for later generations.

Over time, reliance on traditional features of diction, syntax, rhythm, and prosody made way for alternatives to the British legacy. The search for poetic idioms closer to local speech rhythms gathered momentum first in American poetry, where the self-affirmative example of Walt Whitman (1819–92) was followed by a vigorous call to indigenization, which took the development of American poetry in a direction of its own. The very titles of early twentieth-century prose works such as *In the American Grain* (1925) by William Carlos Williams (1883–1963), and *Make It New* (1934), by Ezra Pound (1885–1972), are typical of a process that postcolonial poets in other former colonies of Britain have sought to emulate in respect to their cultures. Pound's recognition, 'To break the pentameter, that was the first heave' (*Canto* LXXXI, l. 54), found common cause with postcolonial poetry.

Though stanzaic and metred verse is written in all the former colonies, postcolonial poets also show a marked preference for free verse. It exhibits all the features that Marjorie Perloff (1998) associates with American poetry of the first half of the twentieth century. They include (1) avoidance of recurrent patterns of stress and syllable, (2) dominance of the image, (3) regulated syntax based loosely on the spoken idiom, (4) linear movement, (5) relatively unobtrusive sound structure, and (6) visual presentation on the printed page that is not too different from conventional metred verse, except in its use of variable line length.

The postcolonial predilection for free verse needs to be placed in two contexts. The first is the cautionary advice offered by T. S. Eliot (1888–1965, USA/UK) in 'Reflections on "Vers Libre"' (1917): 'the ghost of some simple metre should lurk behind the arras in even the "freest" verse; to advance menacingly as we doze, and withdraw as we rouse. Or, freedom is only truly freedom when it appears against the background of an artificial limitation' (Perloff 1998: 86–7). The semblance of 'freedom' promised by free verse needs another contextualization, which Perloff underlines from the French historian of modern prosody, Henri Meschonnic. Her translation from his *Critique du rythme* (1982) offers a reflection that is significant for postcolonial poetry: 'freedom is no more a choice than it is an absence of constraint, but the search of its own historicity' (89). This book traces the many routes taken by postcolonial poetry in grasping its own historicity.

A study of this body of writing demonstrates that alertness to language and form provides new orientations to experience and history. How this works, and why certain poems or poets manage it with greater conviction and authenticity, provides the ground for a comparative approach to the reading of postcolonial poetry. Sometimes the same poet can illustrate the difference between expressing sentiments that are sincere but banal, and dramatizing speech acts in which language and rhythm translate sincerity into authentic critique, as in the case of the aboriginal writer Kath Walker (1920–93, also known as Oodgeroo Noonuccal). In 'Let Us Not Be Bitter', she exhorts her community, 'Away with bitterness, my own dark people | Come stand with me, look forward, not back' (1992: 20). This is sensible as ideology, but bland poetry, especially when compared with the rhythmic poise shown by the same poet in 'No More Boomerang':

No more boomerang
No more spear;
Now all civilized—
Colour bar and beer.
[...]
Lay down the stone axe,
Take up the steel,
And work like a nigger
For a white man meal.

(1992: 54–5)

The poem is sharp at the level of cultural insight, alert in rhythm, direct and simple in address. Utterance becomes ballad-like: as a parody of the white man's notion of aboriginal speech rhythms, but also as a way of returning the aborigine to the element of song natural to her culture. The polarization of stone and steel alerts the reader to the power of stereotypes. The primitive is kept in place by the allegedly 'civilized' through sheer force of technological advantage and thick-skinned self-interest, shorn of tradition and accoutrements, and domesticated to the humiliations of segregation and cheap drunkenness. Pathos and anger are held in check so that a disarming simplicity can dissemble enormous sophistication of insight and social intelligence. Protest is kept alive in how the injustice of hard labour is pointed up through the equation of aborigine and 'nigger'. A 'white man's meal' still remains the ironic reward, always just out of reach. A poem like this accomplishes the task of post-colonial critique, making poetry part of what Homi Bhabha calls 'a mode of living, and a habit of mind' for those 'who have been displaced or marginalized on the grounds of their cultural, civilizational, or, as it is often described, moral and spiritual backwardness' (2000: 370). Chapter 7 gives further attention to the poetics of the marginalized.

The second answer to the question of how poetry relates to the aftermath of Empire concerns the will to localism, which committed poetry to various forms of ecological mimeticism. Colonial poets applied themselves to the challenge of representing new realities, at first in borrowed idioms, but as old forms and conventions proved incongruous in the face of new physical realities, poetry registered a sense of place as an affirmation of living in the here and now. One of the most successful transpositions of a British style to the harsh but bracing aspects of a new environment can be found in the work of Isabella Valancy Crawford (1850–87, Ireland/Canada). It animates the blank verse of the long narrative poem 'Malcolm's Katie' to incandescent effects of imagery, as in

> Torn caves of mist walled with a sudden gold—
> Resealed as swift as seen—broad, shaggy fronts,
> Fire-eyed...
>
> (1972: 198)

and:

> ...the scouts of Winter ran
> From the ice-belted north, and whistling shafts
> Struck maple and struck sumach, and a blaze
> Ran swift from leaf to leaf, from bough,
> Till round the forest flashed a belt of flame,
> And inward licked its tongues of red and gold
> To the deep-crannied inmost heart of all.
>
> (1972: 199)

Crawford's vivid energy was rare for the nineteenth century, and indicative of what could be accomplished by poets endowed with linguistic vigour and a sharp eye for detail.

The chapters comprising Part II show how the colonial aim of representing the natural environment soon joined forces with the drive towards cultural nationalism. The process was gradual and cumulative. At its worst, it was prone to insularity, parochialism, and the fallacy of national mimeticism (discussed in section 1.2 below). At their most robust, however, colonial poets established traditions of localism that continue to subsidize the postcolonial domestication of English. Thus Nissim Ezekiel (1924–2004, India), in 'Background, Casually', refers to his urban home of Bombay as 'My backward place' (1989: 181). The 'backward' is proffered disarmingly and tongue-in-cheek, since the poet celebrates his location on the margins of the former Empire as the true centre of his poetics.

The third answer to the question of how poetry relates to postcoloniality concerns the dynamic relation set up by poetry with colonial history. Poets revisit history as a zone of imaginative recovery and recuperation, like Orpheus trying to win back Eurydice from Hades. They solicit and raid history in order to understand how the colonial past led to their predicaments in the present. For them, poetry is an attempt to construct knowledge about how the past, the present, and the future interrelate for societies and individuals yet to free themselves from colonial formations. For example, Olive Senior (b. 1941, Jamaica/Canada) invents a delicate allegory to describe the workings of colonialism through the lifecycle of 'Plants':

> The world is full of shoots bent on conquest,
> invasive seedlings seeking wide open spaces,
> material gathered for explosive dispersal
> in capsules and seed cases.
>
> (1994: 61)

Her imagery invites the reader to fall in with the idea that human expansionism is part of a natural process to which there are analogies in the vegetable kingdom. The effect is complex: 'shoots bent on conquest' appears bizarre, even funny. That an innocuous shoot might nurse rapacious intent is startling and salutary. The allegory achieves a double purpose: it naturalizes human conquest, while humanizing natural expansionism. Each is rendered more starkly than we might have imagined, because each is presented as amoral yet natural.

Other poets recover a sense of the free-wheeling aspect of early colonial exploration. In 'Landfall in Unknown Seas', Allen Curnow (1911–2001, New Zealand) commemorates the 'discovery' of New Zealand by Abel Tasman in 1642 with the sardonic recognition that 'Simply by sailing in a new direction | You could enlarge the world' (Bornholdt *et al.* 1997: 401). In 'Album Leaves', A. R. D. Fairburn (1904–57, New Zealand) enumerates the motley crowd that participated in the transformation of exploration and trade into settlement:

> offshoots, outcasts, entrepreneurs,
> architects of Empire, romantic adventurers;
> and the famished, the multitude of the poor;
> crossed parallels of boredom, tropics
> of hope and despair...
> sprouting like bulbs in warm darkness, putting out
> white shoots under the wet sack of Empire.
>
> (Bornholdt *et al.* 1997: 430–1)

A poem from the 1960s, 'Stanley meets Mutesa' by David Rubadiri (b. 1930, Malawi), dramatizes an encounter between the European explorer and an African tribal chief as symbolic of the fateful intrusion of Europe into Africa. Poetry becomes the vehicle for a form of retrospective understanding of how the past remains immanent in the present:

> The tall black king steps forward,
> He towers over the thin bearded white man
> Then grabbing his lean white hand
> Manages to whisper
> 'Mtu Mweupe karibu'
> White man you are welcome.
> The gate of polished reed closes behind them
> And the west is let in.
>
> (Senanu 1988: 141)

Another poet from Africa, Niyi Osundare (b. 1946, Nigeria), broods over the consequence: 'Africa's truth has always been at the mercy of the fiction of others' (2002: 22). A more agitated bitterness at the damage done by Empire to its colonies is given voice by Lakdasa Wikkramasinha (1942–78, Sri Lanka) in 'Don't Talk to Me about Matisse':

> Talk to me instead of the culture generally—
> how the murders were sustained
> by the beauty robbed of savages: to our remote
> villages the painters came, and our white-washed
> mud-huts were splattered with gunfire.
>
> (Thieme 1996: 772)

The fourth perspective on the relation of poetry to postcoloniality concerns the centrifugal force of diaspora, exile, and self-exile. It treats individual and collective displacement as part of the lasting fallout of Empire in a contemporary world that has replaced the 'colonial' dimension of experience with the 'cosmopolitan' or the 'global'. Diasporic predicaments are emblematic of the transition from the global consequences of Empire to the realities of neocolonialism and globalization. Chapter 9 illustrates the ways in which poetry seeks to mitigate the negative effects of alienation, isolation, and dispersal through the literal and symbolic activities of translation. The fragmented sense of self, the frailty of survival, the persistence of hope, the wariness of the new, are all represented with sharp precision by Ania Walwicz (b. 1951, Poland/Australia), in 'New World':

> I'm first mark on my page. I get just born. I'm new here. I do my first year. I'm first spring. I'm dawn light. I'm early morning. I leave my hospital behind. I just get out of prison. I meet different people. Mister New is my name. I'm new. I get new clothes for my new life. I live now. I live now. I'm alive now. Yesterday I was heavy with me...
>
> (Petersen and Rutherford 1988: 88)

Postcolonial poetry bears witness to the nomadic dimension of contemporary existence. The shifting temporariness refracted by poetry has another, more distant application. Poetry recognizes that 'postcolonial' alludes to histories held together by a provisional term that must anticipate its own obsolescence. 'Postcolonial' is premised on the assumption and hope that the former colonies are intent on maximizing their potential for literary autonomy. Where, and when, the potential for poetic and cultural autonomy is maximized, one can expect the term 'postcolonial' to become redundant and obsolete. The final stanza of a poem by A. K. Mehrotra (b. 1947, India), 'Dream-figures in Sunlight', gives an image for that anticipated futurity:

> Years from now, may the sap-filled bough
> Still print its shadow on running water,
> And a dusty March wind blow its leaves
> Towards a page of Kipling, a home-grown page.
>
> (1998: 22)

Seen in this light, it is understandable that most poets are impatient with the term 'postcolonial', and resist its application to their work and aspirations. They argue that the term perpetuates dependency, homogenizes difference, simplifies complexity, misdirects reading, practises a form of nominalist colonization, and pushes literary uniqueness into a ghetto where academics fight over intellectual property while professing to bring writers from the margins closer to the metropolitan centre.

Poets are not the only people who worry about 'postcolonial'. Commentators have urged several types of critical awareness. For Aijaz Ahmad (1991), 'postcolonial' imposes a perspective that exaggerates the degree to which colonialism and its demise preoccupies writers. Poetry from the various former colonies is inconclusive about this claim: Asian poetry is not as often preoccupied with colonialism as African or Caribbean poetry. Anne McClintock (1992) notes that a 'postcolonial' perspective tends to emphasize the hierarchical relation between a colonized and a colonizing culture, thus subordinating relations between postcolonial cultures. Part II of this book tries to avoid this likelihood: Chapters 3, 4, and 5 provide regional surveys for parallel traditions of poetry, and Chapter 6 brings together for comparison developments in poetry from all the settler cultures. Part II thus promotes a lateral rather than a hierarchical approach to poetic cultures. Ella Shohat (1992) raises another anxiety: that the term 'postcolonial' is confusing in its reference, since it can be applied to the colonizer, the colonized, and the hybrids produced by their interaction. I have tried to avoid ambiguity by marking every shift in reference explicitly, as in the discussion of South Africa before and after apartheid (Chapter 5), ethnic minorities (Chapter 7), and the analogy between colonialism, racism, and male chauvinism (Chapter 8).

Any survey of the relation between poetry and postcoloniality must also take account of the mechanics and politics of the production, circulation, and reception of poetry as cultural capital. Publishing was a Western technological invention whose dissemination was part of the modernity brought to the colonies by the British. The publishing of poetry remained centralized in London for a large part of colonial history. Approbation remained local if a poet was admired only in the colonies; it became global when endorsed by the metropolis. The paternal aspect of metropolitan publishing was never easy to separate from its power as patron. Nevertheless, local canons, in all the settler and non-settler colonies, were invariably put together by local poets, and the small pamphlet or the anthology established itself as the principal means of circulating poetry and establishing reputations in postcolonial societies.

The subsequent absorption of 'Commonwealth' and 'Postcolonial' literatures into the academic canon opens a wider potential readership for poetry, though this is curtailed in practice by the tendency to equate 'postcolonial literature' with narrative prose. The relative neglect of postcolonial poetry was not redressed until the publication of works such as the *Routledge Encyclopedia of Post-Colonial Literatures in English* (1994), Radhika Mohanram and Gita Rajan's *English Postcoloniality* (1996), and Jahan Ramazani's *The Hybrid Muse* (2001).

Meanwhile, the opportunities for publishing poetry locally and internationally have improved steadily in most postcolonial societies (with the possible exception of Africa). The scope for gaining new readers from the general reading public and the academic market is linked to how poets capitalize on the endorsement of discerning or empowering audiences. Questions such as who empowers endorsement, what constitutes discernment, who awards recognition, which criteria come into reckoning, and how recognition translates into canonicity constitute the cultural politics of the literary profession within which postcolonial—and all other—poetry is read.

Regardless of the cultural politics of endorsement, it can be safely said that poetry enriches the connotations of 'postcolonial' by keeping us close to the energies inherent to language and form, while also showing how postcolonial preoccupations bring the aesthetic dimension of poetry closer to its cultural, political, and ethical implications. The conjunction sharpens awareness of the role played by words, rhythms, idiom, and style in the translation of cultural dependency into cultural self-confidence. It also brings readers closer to what C. P. Surendran (b. 1959, India) calls 'a regime of muted justice and order within language' that enables poets to share with readers 'the discovery of a validating experience outside the arbitrariness of the social universe' (1999: xv).

1.2 English in Britain: assimilation and resistance

That Albion too, was once
A colony like ours, 'part of the continent, piece of the main'
Nook-shotten, rook o'erblown, deranged
By foaming channels, and the vain expense
Of bitter faction.

Derek Walcott, 'Ruins of a Great House'

The narrative of Anglophone postcolonial poetry is not confined to writing from societies colonized or settled by Britain. It begins with the spread of English as a language and culture within the British Isles, and stretches to the condition of British society today, whose people, language, and literary productions are the outcome of a complex process of linguistic, cultural, and ethnic hybridization.

Benjamin Zephaniah (b. 1958, Jamaica/UK) reminds the readers of *Too Black, Too Strong* (2001): 'From being totally uninhabited Britain has constantly taken in new visitors, be they Picts, Celts, Angles, Saxons, Chinese, Jamaicans, Huguenots. All of them with the possible exception of the Romans can be classed as refugees of one type or another' (10–11). The contemporary Asian version of the refugee experience in Britain is represented as wary and edgy by Satyendra Srivastava (b. 1935, India/UK) in 'The Resolve':

> Chanting Rule Britannia
> And Pakis go home
> I see them polishing their helmets
> Oiling their bikes
> Dusting their gloves
> Sharpening their knives
> Demonstrating their kicks on a piece of brick
> While looking at me
>
> (1994: 76)

The British were the most successful colonizers of modern world history. As a nation, they were themselves the outcome of successive settlements and colonizations (Talib 2002: 3). The processes of annexation and cultural domination that characterized the growth and consolidation of the British Empire in the eighteenth and nineteenth centuries were at work on the British mainland well before its inhabitants became actively involved in reproducing them elsewhere on a bigger scale. A large part of the British mainland was occupied by the Romans from about 43 BC to AD 410. Christian missions from Rome came to the region after AD 597. Latin eventually became, and remained for a long time, the staple language of religious practice, law, medicine, science, and education. The next major change arrived with the Norman Conquest of 1066, which made Norman culture the dominant new influence in the British Isles until 1362. The formation of early modern England was the result of layered interactions between several cultures, ethnicities, and languages (Crystal 1995).

Literature in England came to maturity during the fourteenth century in poetic writing of great originality and power written in various dialects of Middle English. William Chaucer (*c.* 1343–99) was the first poet to turn away from the unrhymed accentual rhythms of Anglo-Saxon poetry. His writing assimilated Norman influences and created a new poetic language that shaped the subsequent development of poetry in early modern English. The changes brought about by Chaucer's example extended to every aspect of writing, from vocabulary and metre to cultural values and assumptions. Kamau Brathwaite (b. 1930, Barbados) points out in *History of the Voice* (1984) that once the pentameter had established itself through Chaucer, its power prevailed for more than four centuries, and it took the example of Whitman, and later poets in America, and elsewhere, to break its hold over the language. Derek Walcott (b. 1930, St Lucia) also recognizes Whitman as the first poet to practise a form of 'forgetting, which has to be deliberate and must not be irresponsible' (1997: 239).

The growth of an energetic literature in early modern English during the fifteenth and sixteenth centuries was accompanied by the steady decline of the Celtic languages in Wales, Scotland, and Ireland. This process was accelerated by numerous forceful English incursions into Celtic territories. Meanwhile, the defeat of the Spanish Armada in 1588 consolidated a central role for England among European nations. A large part of the identity of the nation was shaped over the next four hundred years by the colonization of overseas lands and peoples.

The role of English as an instrument of acculturation can be inferred from the attitudes of poets to overseas English expansion in the early days of colonialism. The etymology of 'colony', like that of 'culture' and 'civilization', derives from the Latin word for farming, as when the English poet Edmund Spenser wrote of the reign of Henry II, in the twelfth century, as the time when Ireland was first 'planted with Englishe' (1934: 19). In *A View of the Present State of Ireland* (1596), he used the form of prose dialogue to promote one of the earliest English examples of a colonizing argument, the need to civilize the native: 'reducinge that salvage nacion to better gouerment and cyvillitie' (1934: 3). The use of force against 'a nation ever acquainted with warrs' (7) is justified with the argument that 'thorough wisdome' the Irish 'maye bee maistred and subdued' (4). Ireland is admired for its natural beauty—'sure yt is yet a most bewtifull and sweete Countrie as any is vnder heaven' (25)—but despised on account of the 'salvage bruttishnes and [loathlie] fylthyness' of its people (70). Pride in conquest is given expression by Sir Walter Ralegh (1552–1618) in *The 11th: and last booke of the Ocean to Scinthia*: 'To seek new worlds, for golde, for prayse, for glory' (1972:

43). At the very beginning of the British colonial enterprise, a poem by Samuel Daniel (1562–1619), *Musophilus* (1599), reveals a more sober anxiety about how England and the English language would fare overseas:

> And who in time knowes whither we may vent
> The treasure of our tongue, to what strange shores
> This gaine of our best glorie shal be sent ...
> What mischiefe it may powerfully withstand,
> And what faire ends may thereby be attain'd.
>
> (1950: 96–7)

Resistance to English was minimal in Wales, sporadic in Scotland, persistent in Ireland. By the end of the seventeenth century, Scots occupied a secondary position in Scotland, even though it subsidized a tradition of writing that fostered pride in local culture, from the poems of Allan Ramsay (1685–1758) to Robert Fergusson (1750–74), and Robert Burns (1759–96). The forms of written English continue to dominate administration, law, and education, while Scots is still spoken widely, and Gaelic survives, though in reduced numbers. The use of Scots and Gaelic in literary writing, folklore, and humour can seem to adopt an aggressive-defensive tone in its representation of regional issues or in its attitude to English culture.

The mixed quality of such linguistic resistance is illustrated by the 'Lallans' ('Lowland') Movement of the 1920s and '30s, which was led by Hugh MacDiarmid (1892–1978, real name Christopher Murray Grieve). This movement was dedicated to fostering a new Scottish Renaissance using a synthetic variety of Scots (that is, a literary dialect artificially put together rather than actually spoken quite that way by Scots people). MacDiarmid's long and lively satirical poem, *The Drunk Man Looks at the Thistle* (1926), is animated by an often bitter, and sometimes funny, anger at the degeneration of Scottish culture:

> I widna gi'e five meenits wi' Dunbar
> For a' the millions o' ye as ye are).
>
> I micht ha'e been contentit wi' the Rose
> Gin I'd had ony reason to suppose
> That what the English dae can e'er mak' guid
> For what Scots dinna—and first and foremaist should.
>
> (1987: 620)

MacDiarmid's friend Sydney Goodsir Smith (1915–75) also wrote spiritedly in Scots, as did Robert Garioch (1909–81), who invokes an Edinburgh forebear in the poem 'To Robert Fergusson':

> But truth it is, our couthie* city (*comfortable)
> has cruddit in twa parts a bittie* (*curdled)
> and speaks twa tongues, ane coorse and grittie,
>   heard in the Cougait
> the tither copied, mair's the pitie,
>   frae Wast of Newgate ...
>
> (Dunn 1992: 87–8)

Among others of the circle, Ian Crichton Smith (1928–98) wrote in both English and Gaelic, while Sorley MacLean (1911–96) wrote in Gaelic. An essay by Smith, 'Real People in a Real Place' (1986), voices an acute sense of displacement that is characteristic of writers from the Celtic regions who became reluctant members of the English domain:

> I know that my own life has been a snake pit of contradictions, because of an accident of geography and a hostile history. I envy, for instance, those poets who have developed in a stable society, who can start from there and are not constantly analysing the very bases of their art.
>
> (Morgan 2000: online)

The regional spirit of the 'Lallans' movement continues to enlist contemporary loyalists who write in Scots and Gaelic, and attempt to redress the negative connotations of 'provincial' dialects by refusing assimilation into English literature. Their resistance to the force of its cultural imperialism joins common cause with contemporary writing in Irish. Marginalization thus acquires what Robert Crawford describes as 'a devolutionary momentum', which prompts writers from various parts of the world other than England 'to use the English language and its varieties to enunciate a cultural identity that is not that of the traditionally dominant London-Oxbridge English cultural centre' (1992: 7). The resistance to English offered by poets in Scots and Scottish Gaelic does not find a counterpart of comparable energy in Welsh, except in R. S. Thomas (1913–2000), who wrote in English, taught himself Welsh as a guilt-ridden adult, and lamented the diminishment suffered by Wales at the hands of the English people and language. 'The Old Language' is representative of his mortification:

England, what have you done to make the speech
My fathers used a stranger to my lips,
An offence to the ear, a shackle on the tongue
That would fit new thoughts to an abiding tune?
Answer me now . . .

(1993: 25)

Wales and Scotland were annexed; Ireland was colonized. Ireland was the first territory to be settled overseas by England, a process that started with Norman incursions under Henry II in the twelfth century: 'Norman French and English became established as vernacular languages, though their speakers gradually crossed over to Irish' (Paulin 1984: 178–9). The foreign presence took permanent shape in the form of settlements during the sixteenth century. The initial settlers adapted readily to local customs, but after the establishment of the Church of England under Henry VIII, new settlements polarized the difference between underprivileged Catholic Celts and privileged Protestant English. This pattern was reinforced through the forceful suppression of Irish resistance during the reign of Elizabeth I, increased colonization under James I, and the brutal military suppression of resistance to English rule carried out by Oliver Cromwell in 1649–50. In 1800, an Act of Union formalized the inclusion of Ireland in the United Kingdom. In 1921–22, resistance to rule from London eventually brought partition to the island, with England retaining control over the six counties of Northern Ireland, while the South became independent.

The poetry of William Butler Yeats (1865–1939) provides the earliest and grandest model for a decolonizing impulse in colonial poetry that assimilates the dominant poetic tradition, but uses it to forge a poetic version of a local culture (cf. Patke 2000a). Yeats believed for a while in what the American poet and critic Yvor Winters (1900–68) describes as a romantic error in the context of Whitman's relation to America: 'the fallacy that the poet achieves salvation by being, in some way, intensely of and expressive of his country' (1947: 441). Yeats promoted the ideals of the Celtic Revival at the end of the nineteenth century as a way of creating a distinctive poetic identity for himself, and as a way of conferring cultural value upon the Irish. Many years later, writing in support of the 1950s anti-colonial struggle in Algeria, Frantz Fanon (1925–61) warned against the temptation to glorify a mythical past. Fanon diagnosed such sentiments as symptoms of 'the secret hope of discovering beyond the misery of today, beyond self-contempt, resignation, and abjuration, some very beautiful and splendid era whose existence rehabilitates us both in regard to ourselves and in regard to others' (1963: 210).

In light of such reservations, Yeats's considerable influence over subsequent poets from the colonies is ironic, since his ideal of the Irish nation flourished independent of the Irish language. Yeats used English because it was the natural medium for an Anglo-Protestant of his background. The language also had the advantage of a large potential readership, and a rich poetic tradition whose example could liberate a poet from the provincial, provided he could avoid being overpowered by the weight of its Englishness. Yeats's response to the language question was to abandon belief in an intrinsic link between a people's language and their culture, while insisting that culture had to take on a nationalizing function.

The opposite view was argued in 1900 by his friend George Moore: 'That a nation should express itself in the language fashioned by the instinct of the race out of its ideas and spiritual aspirations is, I think, certain' (Storey 1998: 158). Since the 1970s, writers from different parts of the formerly colonial world have revived this argument. The Kenyan novelist Ngugi wa Thiong'o (b. 1938, Kenya) abandoned English for his native language Gikuyu, arguing that a national culture could not be based on the language of the former colonizer, since it placed the native in a position of permanent derivativeness. The Marathi novelist Bhalchandra Nemade (b. 1938) offers a similar argument from India. Yeats's example endorsed the opposite principle. He functioned as the patron saint of all colonial and postcolonial writers who took to English regardless of its historical provenance, willing to relinquish local languages for the enticements of English. Yeats's confidence in English was not shared by all his Irish successors. Thomas Kinsella (b. 1928) felt that 'An Irish poet has access to the English poetic heritage through his use of the English language, but he is unlikely to feel at home in it, or so I find in my own case' (Deane 1991: 1313).

Other problems that recur in postcolonial poetry found focus in Yeats's life and writings: the national culture he celebrated was a product of his imagination as much as it was a legacy from the Irish past. His commitment to Revivalism tried to dignify the Celt through the recovery of a lost heroism, but produced a 'Celt' that merely inverted the unflattering typologies generated from France in the mid-nineteenth century by Ernst Renan and consolidated by Matthew Arnold. John Rickard describes this composite Celt as 'antiscientific, antimaterialist, highly sensitive, spiritual, pantheistic, and politically ineffectual' (1997: 98). Yeats's perpetuation of this image can be juxtaposed with the self-image of the colonized Indian as described by the sociologist Ashis Nandy:

> Colonialism replaced the normal ethnocentric stereotype of the inscrutable Oriental by the pathological stereotype of the strange, primal but predictable Oriental—religious but superstitious, clever but devious, chaotically violent but effeminately cowardly. Simultaneously, colonialism created a domain of discourse where the standard mode of transgressing such stereotypes was to reverse them: superstitious but spiritual, uneducated but wise, womanly but pacific, and so on.
>
> (1983: 72)

Yeats anticipated the attempt to attach anti-colonial values to ethnic identity, as in the Negritude movement of the 1930s. Its Francophone members, Aimé Césaire, Léon Damas, and Léopold Senghor, hoped to redress the ethnic disparagement that accompanied colonialism by fostering racial pride in the 'negro'. The movement was the precursor of various forms of cultural nationalism, which gave the Black Diaspora from Africa an alternative to the dream of returning to a real or symbolic African homeland.

Yeats wanted to revive a common poetic tradition for the Irish while deriding the Catholic way of life, but no ideal of cultural unity could be sustained for long when grounded solely in Anglo-Protestant sympathies. Yeats was one of the earliest postcolonial writers fixed on projecting an idea of nation onto societies divided by language, religion, and ethnicity. Contemporary opinion among the Irish remains divided about whether the history of their island lends itself to the discourse of postcoloniality and the 'Third World' narrative of relatively undeveloped contemporary nations. Edna Longley prefers to read it in the context of a dynamics of power 'centering on land, religion, culture and the locus of authority', in which 'tensions between province and capital(s)' link more plausibly to European balkanization (1994: 30–1). Both perspectives recognize the fact that British rule in Northern Ireland continues to remain a source of fierce internal strife. Tensions between the Catholic and Protestant factions erupted in violence during 1968, and sectarian politics continues to ravage the North.

When the English editors of *The Penguin Book of Contemporary British Poetry* (1982) included Seamus Heaney (b. 1939, N. Ireland) in their notion of 'British', he reacted with *An Open Letter*:

> As empire rings its curtain down
>   This 'British' word
> Sticks deep in native and colon
>   Like Arthur's sword.
>
> (1983: 23)

In 2001, Heaney developed the point more temperately in the context of the poet W. R. Rodgers (1909–69, Ireland/England/USA), and his use of the Ulster locution 'through-otherness', to evoke the significance of

> the triple heritage of Irish, Scottish and English traditions that compound and complicate the cultural and political life of contemporary Ulster. For Rodgers, it wasn't a question of the otherness of any one part of his inheritance, more a recognition of the through-otherness of all of them.
>
> (2002: 366)

The mixed heritage invoked by Heaney assumes the obsolescence of the native language. Irish Gaelic was in a state of decline even before the abolition of the Irish parliament and the Union with England in 1800. In the twentieth century, the number of people bilingual in Irish and English in the Republic has grown slightly, due to periodic attempts since 1922 to make the teaching of Irish a part of the educational system. Those who speak Irish as their first language constitute a small proportion of island's population, and the Irish language remains an endangered species. However, a sturdy body of writing has grown in resistance to this danger, supported by the State through language policy, and by local publishers through the circulation of bilingual editions of poetry.

The continued survival of poetry in Irish can be placed in a broader context by examining the implications of the notion of 'minor literature' as developed by Gilles Deleuze and Felix Guattari in *Kafka: For a Minor Literature* (1975/1986). They argue that one may speak of Kafka, a Jew using a dialect of German in Prague, as creating a 'minor literature'. Their use of 'minor' sheds the connotation of belittlement in order to promote the claim that such writing constitutes a form of resistance to the dominant culture and its linguistic norms. This argument has been described as a misappropriation by Stanley Corngold (2003). He argues that Kafka's 'Prague German' was not a dialect, and that its relation to the dominant traditions of 'High German' did not constitute a form of revolutionary literature.

However, it is possible to separate Corngold's implied equation between 'minor' and 'minority' from the sense of 'minor' as a potential within a 'major' language, which a writer can develop in order to promote nuances repressed or denied by the 'major' tradition. The Deleuze–Guattari hypothesis provides a method for recognizing how writers, whether drawn from a minority or not, work within a 'major' language to make space for themselves in relation to an established metropolitan tradition, as in the cases of the Irish self-exiles James Joyce (1882–1941) and Samuel Beckett (1906–89). We can also speak of poetry written in Irish as negotiating space for itself while accommodating to the dominance of English by obliging or inducing English to give recognition to its 'minor' role through translation.

1.3 Local themes, global applications

> 'The language in which we are speaking is his before it is mine', but 'You talk to me of nationality, language, religion. I shall try to fly by those nets.'
>
> James Joyce, *A Portrait of the Artist as a Young Man*

To make English take notice is the precise achievement of the Irish poems of Nuala Ní Dhomhnaill (b. 1952, UK/Ireland). A number of leading Irish poets who write in English have honoured her in translation. Yeats renounced Irish as a language, but invoked for his art the magical role given to the poet in Irish culture. Dhomhnaill's writing shows a dual relation to the Yeatsian legacy. Like him, she upholds a magical conception of art, and a romantic view of the relation of art to history. However, while Yeats could be overbearingly masculine in the swagger of his verse, her art is intensely feminine. It encompasses a wide tonal range, from the ironic to the sublime, from the blunt to the delicate.

The simplicity of the following narrative supports and uncovers a complex intention based on the story of the infant Moses. The Orthodox Judaic version of the story is narrated in *The Talmud*, which states that the mother of Moses placed him in an ark of bulrushes in the brink of the river, where he was found by the Pharaoh's daughter, who adopted him and brought him up as a Prince at the Egyptian Court. The same story is also narrated in Exodus: 'And when she could not longer hide him, she took for him an ark of bulrushes, and daubed it with slime and with pitch, and put the child therein; and she laid [it] in the flags by the river's brink (*King James Version*, Exodus 2: 3). Dhomhnaill's poem is titled 'Ceist na Teangan' in Irish. It was translated by Paul Muldoon as 'The Language Issue':

I place my hope on the water
in this little boat
of the language, the way a body might put
an infant

in a basket of intertwined
iris leaves,
its underside proofed
with bitumen and pitch,

then set the whole thing down amidst
the sedge
and bulrushes by the edge
of a river

only to have it borne hither and thither,
not knowing where it might end up;
in the lap, perhaps,
of some Pharaoh's daughter.

(1990: 155)

The allegory is managed with deftly underplayed suggestiveness, whose power grows as the reader dwells on its relation to the tale of the infant Moses. The child is an Irish futurity both fragile and full of potential for growth. The bitumen and pitch allude to the earthiness of an Irish origin. The 'hither and thither' speaks of the uncertainty of progress and survival. The lap of a Pharaoh's daughter remains a hope. In a personal account, 'Why I Choose to Write in Irish', the poet comments on the mother's choice: 'She took what under the circumstances must have seemed very much like *rogha an dá dhiogha* (the lesser of two evils) and Exodus and the annals of Jewish history tell the rest of the story' (1997: 55). If Irish is like the infant Moses, and if English in Ireland allows it co-existence and patronage, the vulnerable language could grow into a Moses, influence the British Pharaoh, and lead the Irish Israelites out of diminishment and exile. The apparent acceptance of English as an imperial language is subtly counteracted by hints of incipient resistance to its dominance, and by the intense desire to survive.

Dhomhnaill describes herself as a white female aborigine. The hope nourished by her poetry gives gendered embodiment to earlier, largely male attempts at perpetuating Irishness. Her conception of the role of poet is romantic and vatic. It is also grounded in an earthy sense of the relation of poetry to common experience, showing how the first and last colony of the English nation and language survives and flourishes in more than one tongue. Another poem of childbearing, laden with metaphorical intent, is worth invoking in the genealogy of postcolonial poetic births. 'In My Name', by Grace Nichols (b. 1950, Guyana/UK), voices the experience of a Caribbean girl who gives birth to a child in a banana plantation, calling it 'my tainted | perfect child | my bastard fruit | my seedling | my sea grape | my strange mulatto | my little bloodling' (1983: 56):

for with my blood
I've cleansed you
and with my tears
I've pooled the river Niger

now my sweet one it is for you to swim

(1983: 57)

As in Egypt, so in Ireland, and Guyana: it is thus that a hybrid muse is engendered.

For a second example of Irish ambivalence we can turn to a poem by Eavan Boland (b. 1944, Ireland), 'In Which Hester Bateman, 18th Century English Silversmith Takes an Irish Commission':

Hester Bateman made a marriage spoon
And then subjected it to violence.
Chased, beat it. Scarred it and marked it.
All in the spirit of our darkest century:

Far away from grapeshot and tar caps
And the hedge schools and the music of sedition
She is oblivious to she pours out
And lets cool the sweet colonial metal.

Here in miniature a man and woman
Emerge beside each other from the earth,
From the deep mine, from the seams of rock
Which made inevitable her craft of hurt.

They stand side by side on the handle.
She writes their names in the smooth
Mimicry of a lake the ladle is making, in
A flowing script with a moon drowned in it.

Art and marriage: now a made match.
The silver bends and shines and in its own
Mineral curve an age-old tension
Inches towards the light. See how

Past and future and the space between
The semblance of empire, the promise of nation,
Are vanishing in this meditation
Between oppression and love's remembrance

Until resistance is their only element. It is
What they embody, bound now and always:
History frowns on them: yet in its gaze
They join their injured hands and make their vows.

(2001: 11)

The poet contemplates a spoon made by a silversmith. We note in passing that 'an Irish Commission' is noncommittal about whether the client was an English settler based in Ireland or someone native to Ireland. The silver was 'chased' and 'beat' into shape by a woman. The poem implies affinity between that woman, working her metal two hundred years ago, and the poet who is woman and 'wordsmith' at the end of the twentieth century, chasing her thoughts, beating them into shape around this token from the past. The poem also implies a tension between the silversmith, who was English, and the poet, who happens to be Irish. The significance of the time that has passed, for the Irish and the English, since the spoon was made, overshadows the act of making with a contemporary reckoning.

Silver is cool and hard to touch, but malleable under heat and pressure. When the silversmith 'lets cool' the metal, the idea of the art-object as something wrought on the anvil of passion is qualified by distancing it from heat, which allows for the hardening that gives shape to the raw material. When the poem says the silversmith 'pours out', the phrase allows us to see selectivity as a principle of omission as well as inclusion. It would appear as if Hester Bateman left no room for the whiff of 'grapeshot' and 'tar caps' from Ireland on her English ware. However, the poet insinuates the opposite sense: the silversmith was perhaps oblivious to the violence of the world she lived in, but her art retains an impression of its shaping power. The spoon may be wordless. However, the images and inscription congealed in its silver, like the full moon of the cursive script used by Hester on the 'mineral curve' of the ladle, now seem like an unconscious expression of awareness. The poet practises her own violence on the spoon: she treats it as a form of symbolic language, which she now decodes for herself and for the reader. It is a knowledge made in the poem, as if it had been found in the spoon. The silversmith produced a lasting impression on metal; likewise, her countrymen left their indelible impression upon Ireland. Now, the Irish poet elicits recognition of her involvement in that double impression.

Who or what is included in 'our darkest century'? The poem will not leave the silversmith free of complicity in the English brutalization of Ireland. A woman beating at an intractable metal is perhaps an allusion to a poem by Sylvia Plath (1932–63), 'Blackberrying', in which the sea striking the side of a hill makes, 'a din like silversmiths | Beating and beating at an intractable metal' (1981: 169). That might seem far removed from the harsh 'music of sedition' that defined the land from which Hester's commission came. However, the poem suggests, her 'craft of hurt' mirrors several types of tension between violence and love. The violence with which the spoon was made is an echo of the violence with which the English forced Ireland to the shape of their will. Likewise, the spoon can be said to mirror the violence practised by art on history, as well as the love with which art gives form to its material. The spoon was beaten into shape for an Irish wedding, silverware for some Ulster planter and his future generations. It depicts in miniature the forms of a man and woman arising from the earth, as from a 'deep mine' and 'seam of rock'. The spoon and its symbols now serve as an ironic token of the enforced union that sent English wares to the Irish market, and empowered and enriched the English on Irish soil. The silver was part of the economic, social, and political reality that tied England and Ireland together. That is a relation which binds. So is the ceremony of marriage that the spoon commemorates.

The violence of that shaping may now be tasted by the connoisseur—and the reader of Boland's poetry—as 'sweet colonial metal', driving home the point that marriage too, like colony, is a relation held together by power and design. The phrases of the poem circulate the flow of their drift through the layered ironies of craft, marriage, and colonialism. In the spoon, the celebration of marriage goes hand in hand with the subjection of metal by force. In Ireland, the space between the 'semblance of empire' and the 'promise of nation' is filled with resistance, Irish metal/mettle taking the force of English hammering. An 'age-old tension' is thus slowly brought to light: in art, in marriage, and in the relation between the two lands. The poem makes the silver speak of that tension as a form of retrospective knowledge. The reader is left to brood on her relation to all the ties that bind hurt to remembrance. The poem is a way of making sense of history, and of craft. It deals with a complex experience in which 'colonial' interacts with how the past remains implicated in the present. The poem is 'postcolonial' in reference and significance in that it refers to a predicament in which individual experience is overshadowed by the experience of communities marked by colonization, resistance, displacement, and relocation.

2

Back to the future

> Articulating the past historically does not mean recognizing it 'the way it really was'. It means appropriating a memory as it flashes up in a moment of danger.
>
> **Walter Benjamin, 'On the Concept of History'**

Overview

This chapter introduces the central issues that have preoccupied postcolonial poets in English across the twentieth century—language, history, locality, and displacement—through a reading of three volumes published during the period 1989–2002. Recent poetry is used as a vantage point from which to begin mapping the contours of the large and variegated territory of poetic concerns addressed in Parts II and III. Each volume undertakes a radical revision of the poet's relation to her own historicity in poems of striking force, precision, and originality. Such writing demonstrates the responsibility undertaken by poets towards the practice of a vocation that is energized rather than disabled by the traumas of a colonial past.

2.1 English as a 'foreign anguish': Nourbese Philip

> I did not go to Africa looking for my 'roots'. These are very deeply embedded in the black earth of the West Indies. But my much maligned ancestors came from Africa. I wanted to stand where they might have stood. I did.
>
> **Claire Harris, *Fables from the Women's Quarter***

Marlene Nourbese Philip (b. 1947) writes poems, plays, and fiction. She was born in Tobago, and lives in Canada, where she studied and practised law before becoming a full-time writer. She has published four volumes of poetry from Canada: *Thorns* (1980), *Salmon Courage* (1983), *She Tries Her Tongue, Her Silence Softly Breaks* (1989), and *Looking for Livingstone* (1991); a fifth, *Zong!*, is forthcoming. The early poem 'Sprung Rhythm' recognizes the power of syncopated rhythms to both split and bridge verse lines: 'kneading, distorting, enhancing | a foreign language' (1980: n.p.). The short poem 'No More' gathers its power from a simple inversion of syntax, beginning with 'Don' feel like a woman | no more', and ending 'like a woman | no more | goin' feel' (1980: 11).

The cohesion of Philip's writing is based on recurrent concerns: the indelible impression left on people of African descent by colonial history; the pain to be met, overcome, and accepted in using language (which resembles the pain of giving birth); the closeness of language to the physicality of blood and the body; the enormity of the silence breached by poetry. Of the colonial relation, Philip writes in the essay 'Managing the Unmanageable', 'The African's encounter with the New World was catastrophic and chaotic: how does one and how ought one to manage such an experience in poetry or in writing? How does one make readable what has been an unreadable experience?' (1990: 298). She answers the question by exploring history as the geography of silence.

She Tries Her Tongue, Her Silence Softly Breaks (1989/1993) consists of nine sections, followed by a prose essay on 'The absence of writing'. The first section, 'And Over Every Land and Sea', begins with a contemporary adaptation of Ovid's account of how Proserpine was abducted by Hades from her mother Ceres. The poem offers a poignant rendering of the loss inherent to diasporic scattering:

> Where she, where she, where she
> be, where she gone?
> [....]
> She gone—gone to where and don't know
> looking for me looking for she;
> is pinch somebody pinch and tell me,
> up where north marry cold I could find she –
> Stateside, England, Canada – somewhere about...
>
> (1993: 2, 4)

Girl separated from mother, mother searching for girl, become emblems for what has been lost or taken. The broken syntax explores the expressive function of linguistic opacity. The poet reacts against the colonial imperative of 'You better know your place' by making her language 'unmanageable', 'giving in to the urge to interrupt the text' (1990: 298). Tremulous hesitancy becomes expressive almost despite itself. The Caribbean migrant making a new home in the northern cold of Canada is lit by the classical myth of a girl picking flowers, whose bond to the underworld provides a poetic account of the seasonal change to winter. The story of the mother who served as wet-nurse to a King's child, where she turned a Prince into a lizard with a grim look, is transposed to the new life in which 'lizard headed | I suckle her | sucking me' (6). The cold is her Hades, the birth into new being 'a blooded hibiscus' (7).

The second section commemorates the 'Cyclamen Girl', 'black girl white dress' (12), who is evoked from a photograph circa 1960, hailed through the ancestral presences of Aphrodite, Mary, Atebey, Orehu, Yemoja, Oshun (17), initiated into adulthood by menstrual blood, 'my badge of fertility', 'my badge of futility' (18), dropped into life by a 'stone-bird mother', like 'Pebbles of blood and stone' (19). The genealogical succession from mother to daughter, each crossing the threshold of her own pain, links the first two sections, myth narrowed to focus on personal history, personal recollection resonating with myth to include 'all cyclamen girls' (18).

The next two sections consist of single poems inspired by specific artifacts. The third derives its elegiac inspiration from a collection of African sculpture donated to the Art Gallery of Ontario by a Canadian benefactor in 1981. The poet broods on the fact that so-called 'primitive' African art provided part of the impetus for Modernist art such as that of Braque, Picasso, and Brancusi. She finds it ironic that an African culture rich in the concrete was mined by artists from another culture for its 'abstraction' (punning on 'making abstract', 'abstracted, as in distracted', and 'pulling out'), giving us the bland cosmopolitanism of 'you plus I equals we' (22). The fourth section takes a slightly different angle on the ambivalence of the contemporary by asking a question that applies to many kinds of heterogeneity and hybridity:

In whose language
Am I

Am I not
Am I   I am yours
Am I not   I am yours
Am I   I am

If not in yours
            In whose
In whose language
                  Am I
If not in yours
            Beautiful

(27)

The struggle over language becomes the dominant theme through the remainder of the volume. 'Discourse on the Logic of Language' is a *tour de force* which juxtaposes four parallel texts. The first runs vertically down the left margin, so that one has to hold the book sideways in order to read it. The oblique relation of this discourse to the rest is signaled visually. It describes a mother who has given birth to a girl. She first licks the afterbirth, then opens her mouth, touches tongue to tongue, and blows the words she has inherited from all the mothers before her into the child's mouth. The passing on of the mother tongue is thus enacted in a literal ritual. In the next text, printed 'normally', (we infer) the daughter speaks, and what she utters is 'the foreign anguish' of speaking in 'english', which is not her mother tongue (32).

The two remaining texts act as marginalia and gloss respectively, each adopting a different register. The third provides a pair of edicts used in the Caribbean by slave owners who adopted the policy of mixing slaves from different language groups in order to minimize the likelihood of rebellion, and forbade the use of the mother tongue by a slave under threat of having the tongue removed from the mouth by force. The fourth gives a formal anatomical description of the regions of the human brain that are responsible for language, followed by a description of the human tongue as an organ of taste and speech, and 'the principal organ of oppression and exploitation' (33). Mother, child, slaver, and anatomist are thus used to assemble a stylistic collage, in which the complexity of language is captured within four vectors of force.

The sixth section, 'Universal Grammar', adopts a similar strategy of textual juxtapositions. Disparate registers bear upon the complexity of grammar, first to show how language can be broken down to its constituent elements, and then to exemplify significance built up from those elements, as in 'The tall, blond, blue-eyed, white-skinned man is shooting' (37, 39), cited in several European languages. The poem as visual performance is arranged as two sets of text facing one another. The left-hand side analyses words in terms of grammar and diction, dramatizing a form of knowing that is inert to the feeling that accompanies utterances like these: 'The smallest cell remembers O' (36), or 'fragments tremble ex man again' (38). The right-hand side provides the affect absent from analytic discourse.

The entire collage subjects the context-free conventions of analysis to a form of painful irony, which is mindful of the colonial residue that the postcolonial struggles to put together. The routine activity of 'parsing' is transformed into 'the exercise of dis-membering language into fragmentary cells that forget to re-member' (40). The words used to illustrate language also highlight gender, and the physicality of words: thus 'raped' (40) illustrates active and passive voice, and the actions of 'Suck Slide Play Caress Blow' (41) illustrate the role of the tongue in utterance. Making a language one's own becomes, figuratively speaking, one of 'Mother's Recipes' for 'How Not to Get Raped' (41).

The next section reinforces the connection between language and power: language poses a question; power is the answer. The vowel sounds of English are exemplified by a loaded selection of words: 'lose, look, boat, brawn, lot, shroud, coin' (44). Each is placed in a sentence touching upon some aspect of the life of Caribbean slaves. The facing page highlights their history in terms of the question 'how did they "lose" a language', and the answer: 'the word | that in the beginning was |—not his', used to 'smash | the in-the-beginning word | centre' (45). The exhortation 'Make it New', associated with the American poet William Carlos Williams, has an uncertain application in a predicament 'floundering in the old' (45). The poet alludes to the marginal or secondary nature to which the postcolonial is consigned, still smeared with the anxiety that produces the wrong emphases, limited to the kind of recognition conferred by

this chattel language
babu english
slave idiom

nigger vernacular
coolie pidgin
wog pronunciation

(47)

How words collect historical responses is borne out by speculations about the experience of the Middle Passage: 'By holding on to the meaning of life, did the slaves unconsciously limit it—or merely the word?' (48). The banishment and death of the Word, as in the Red Queen ordering heads to be chopped off in Lewis Carroll's *Through the Looking Glass* (1871), prepares for it to rise and live again.

The antepenultimate section consists of a single poem in six parts, 'Testimony Stoops to Mother Tongue'. The first part unleashes 'the promise || in ugly' (52). How people are described is determined by the connotations accumulated in a language by a people using them to describe others. The African has been imaged as having kinky hair, a flattened nose, thick lips, prognathous jaws, and a shrunken brain (52). The point made by the poem is that such imaging is an attribute of language use. The physical traits bespeak the culture they come from, not the culture they profess to describe. 'From whose perspective', the poet asks later, 'are the lips of the African thick or her hair kinky? Certainly not from the African's perspective' (86). The second part of the poem invites the reader to inhabit 'the beyond of pale', to 'touch tongue to tongue' (53). The third part laments that the English language wraps, squeezes the mind 'round | and around':

this/
fuck-mother motherfuckin-
this/
holy-white-father-in-heaven-
this/
ai! ai!
        tongue

(53)

The fourth part declares that the poet would like to pull out the tongue (the English tongue, the tongue using English): it is like a Gorgon head full of snakes. The fifth offers a more constructive alternative: to feed these snakes 'milk | from black breasts | (stroke and caress into | lactate)' (54–5), to breed a new 'warrior race | of words' (55). The sexual and the maternal are always latent within the aggressive–defensive dimension of experience, just as language is never free of the ethnicity and gender of its user. The poem ends with the heroic image of a black female Perseus, who has mastered the snaking Medusa of English, cohabited with this strange 'father's tongue' in order 'to revenge the self | broken | upon the word'. Philip thus joins the host of writers from Britain's former colonies who mix metaphors of revenge with incest, grapple with its power of paternity over their creations in order to 'engender by some alchemical practice a metamorphosis within the language from father tongue to mother tongue' (90).

The title sequence invokes the idea of metamorphosis from Ovid. The poet is 'loosed from the catapult pronged double with history' into 'a future biblical with anticipation' (58). As elsewhere in the volume, the sequence alternates between the registers of verse and prose. Two ideas—the poem as the poet's utterance, the poem as built, magpie-like, from aptly chosen quotations—make two texts resonate in unison. The prose quotation comments abstractly on issues handled more personally by the verse, as in advice on horticulture ('transplanting is always a painful process', 59), or a description of the human limbic system ('Memory is essential to human survival', 61). Forgetting and remembering are like uprooting and replanting, both linked to the specificity of languages, sharing the common ground where one utterance meets its sibling.

One of the most powerful effects in Philip's work is her ability to break language down to its bare elements, and use these with a musicality and rhythmic propulsion that does away with many conventions of syntax. Such poetry does more than allude to performance: it jumps off the page, the printed word asking to be heard as sound and pulse. Broken syntax doubles other kinds of breakdown: between thought and feeling, feeling and word, word and sense, sense and memory. At the same time, the bruised language becomes in itself a new expressive device, at once injury and anodyne. That is how 'the harsh husk of a future-present begins' (62), as in the partial overlap in the following series of nouns from alternate verse lines:

> oath   moan   mutter   chant
> [. . .]
> babble   curse   chortle   sing
> [. . .]

praise-song   poem   ululation   utterance

(64)

The sequence shifts focus to the African in a colonial environment. The verse dramatizes alternate bouts of self-loathing and resentment as the Afro-Caribbean descendants of slaves struggle to reconcile the loss of native cultural values with the acculturation into a European religion and language. Their roots feel like the 'blackened stump of a tongue' (66). They are like a child touched by a stranger who the mother will therefore not suckle (67). The proselytizing power of Christianity sits uncomfortably on the Afro-Caribbean. On the one hand, it merges with the paternal aspect of English as a 'father tongue', teaching the colonized a form of self-abnegation that persists into postcolonial times: '*I am not worthy so much as to gather up the crumbs under thy table*' (68). On the other hand, it leaves the formerly colonized wondering, 'Is it in the nature of God to forgive himself' (69).

Philip foregrounds the debilitating effect of words severed from their source (70). Poetry and history share one burden: memory. Just as there can be no history without memory (71), poetry can come into being only when it remembers that languages have been lost, taken, and forgotten. Therefore, if the poet is to sing again, like Philomela, she must undergo the metamorphosis that changed the raped woman without a tongue into a nightingale (72). If the pool is to be replenished with fish for the coming winter, the skeleton of the season's first salmon must be put back ritually into the water (73). In the re-membered death of an ineluctable past, the present begins to realize its future.

The final section of the book consists of a prose essay, which reiterates and expands on the ideas, feelings, and arguments suggested by the preceding poems. Philip coins the term 'i-mage making' (79) to refer to the power of the imagination to create powerful image-symbols in words. In the Caribbean, the autonomy of this power was withheld from slaves and their descendants during the colonial era. Later, it found expression in vigorous forms of popular culture such as calypso and reggae. Its 'Afro-centric' potential has a very brief history. However, the essay ends on a note of careful optimism. In contemporary times, the poet notes, the 'experience of the African in the Caribbean and the New World' is 'as much a part of the English collective experience as England is part, for better or worse, of the African experience' (86).

The same concerns animate *Looking for Livingstone* (1991). Its mixture of prose and verse narrates a symbolic voyage in which the poet's persona voyages to meet Dr Livingstone, and realizes that the explorer discovered not a continent but the continent's silence: 'discovered it, owned it, possessed it, like it was never possessed before' (1991: 20). Meanwhile, the traveller makes her own discovery: 'your word—engorging itself on my many, yet one, silence' (27). The process of going back in time to meet and confront 'Dr. Livingston—I presume' becomes an allegory for re-discovering the ability to articulate the silence of a fictive origin. Silence is that which the European snatched from the African, and replaced with the power of his word. Speech and silence are complicit with power and desire: 'HIS WORD SLIPPING IN AND OUT OF THE WET MOIST SPACES OF MY SILENCE' (25).

Livingstone pursued Africa, and Stanley pursued Livingstone. In the poem, both are taught in poetic hindsight, 'while you thought you were discovering Africa, it was Africa that was discovering you' (62). Silence is both noun and verb, a sentence that cannot be appealed but must be broken (70–1). To split silence is to release the enormous energy held captive within. Philip's gendered fiction of a voyage to an ancestral home far back in time and space shows how the poetic resource of the symbolic voyage, first explored by older poets from the Caribbean, continues to serve later generations.

2.2 'no darkie baby in this house': Jackie Kay

> Now
> what could consonance or assonance or
> even rhyme do to something like that?
>
> William Wantling, 'Poetry'

The title-sequence of Jackie Kay's first volume of poetry (after *Four Black Women Poets*, 1984), *The Adoption Papers* (1991), is described on the cover as telling 'the story of a black girl's adoption by a white Scottish couple—from three different viewpoints: the mother, the birth mother and the daughter'. The sequence is a remarkable achievement in a number of ways. It foregrounds the tension between ties of blood and those of upbringing through what we might describe as the principle of plural empathy. It makes room for what the two very different mothers are imagined to feel, at different times of the adopted child's conception and growth, while also leaving room for what the poet shows the daughter (the poet's persona) to learn about herself in relation to her two mothers. The time of writing is thus laden with the other viewpoints and lives that contributed to the daughter's (and poet's) growth into self-awareness. In this volume, to be 'postcolonial' is to be born to one race, but call another 'mother'.

The sequence foregrounds what we might call the principle of polyphonic cohesion. The daughter's development is traced through an alternation of three voices. The technique has a literary antecedent in 'Three Women' (1962), a poem by Sylvia Plath, in which the experience of giving birth is refracted through three perspectives: a woman who has a normal delivery, another who has either a miscarriage or an abortion, and a third woman who delivers an unwanted child. In both sequences, 'telling' is renovated by 'showing'. Verse autobiography is not restricted to a single narrative viewpoint. The use of fragmentary dramatic monologue frees the sequence from the limits of the lyric genre; at the same time, the assimilation of alternating voices into a complex polyphony enables the sequence to sustain the unity of consciousness that is central to the lyric genre.

The sequence also foregrounds the tension of the inter-racial by focusing on the social unit of the adoptive family. The relation between mother and child becomes a concrete instance that proves the capacity of need, care, and love to accept and transcend racial distinctions without recourse to the sentimental or the platitudinous. The daughter's circumstances illustrate how migration from former colonies has brought contemporary Britain to a forced negotiation with the possibility of a multi-racial society. The sequence transforms familial identification from an abstract notion about ethnicity to a demonstration that bonds developed through association and nurture can heal the damage caused by the severance of the bonds of nature.

The demonstration has implications for a society in which prejudice based on skin colour and ethnic origin is often at conflict with the weak liberalism of 'live and let live'. The idea of multiculturalism often appears too frail to sustain more than the semblance of uneasy neighbourliness, but in the sequence, the relation between black child and white parent gives sturdy proof that a much greater degree of closeness is possible insofar as the unit of the family can predicate a society that can deal robustly with issues of racial difference. It is worth noting that Kay's book is dedicated to Helen Kay, the adoptive mother, and the old lady who began her acquaintance with her new granddaughter with the remark, 'There'll be no darkie baby in this house', is given eventual recognition by the child as 'My Grandmother' (1998b: Track 1).

The persona of the birth mother develops in alternation with that of the adoptive mother. Neither is given a full poem to herself. This produces a composite effect. Motherhood and femininity are a series of often divergent frames of mind. The first poem shows the effectiveness of a technique based on an alternation of voices. The woman who gets pregnant cannot get over the surprise of how easily it happened, how unexpected it was, and by implication, how unprepared she finds herself to deal with what has happened. In contrast, the woman who will later adopt the child is shown as urgent to inhabit the role of motherhood, keen for her body to go through all the physical experiences of pregnancy. Five years of failure to conceive have prepared her for all the feelings that a birth mother might go through. The antiphonal structure of the poem is able to enact a simple and powerful recognition: the double irony of a woman who conceives without being ready for the role, and a woman ready for the role, but unable to conceive. The child is conceived in the gap between a body that wants, and another that does not want, a baby.

The sequence is arranged to resemble a narrative in three parts, the first covering the period from before conception to early childhood, the second taking up the story of the girl's life between age six and eighteen, the third bringing the narrative to the point at which the poet-persona begins writing the sequence. The daughter makes her entry in the second poem, where she is at the centre of a complex irony. The girl wants to secure a copy of the original birth certificate. Who one is depends on one's textual history. Whatever she may have thought she was, up to that point, will have to be revised depending on what the document reveals about her birth and origin.

At this point, the poet slips back into the past, into the mind of the girl who managed to get pregnant at nineteen, and now feels the stitches of what must have been a difficult and unwanted birth. Calmly, the poet's persona surveys the involuntary mother's options:

> I'll suffocate her with a feather pillow
>
> Bury her under a weeping willow
> Or take her far out to sea
>
> (13)

By the third night, the birth mother's attitude undergoes a change, she now wills the frail child to live. Meanwhile, the woman who cannot conceive turns to adoption agencies for an alternative way of becoming a mother. At the fifth port of call, when she declares that they do not mind the colour, a solution is at hand. The reader shares in the daughter's first discovery of her birth mother: age, height, place of work. The poet carries the reader through a series of intersections between three separate chronotopes—Mikhail Bakhtin's term for a unique conjunction of a specific 'here and now' (1981: 250).

Up to this point in the sequence, the language used by the poet, on the printed page, is colloquial Standard English. The poet distinguishes between the several voices of the poem by using different fonts for the daughter, the adoptive mother, and the birth mother. The Scottish accent and intonation that we encounter immediately when we listen to the poet reading her work enters the printed page as local variations of diction and rhythm characterizing the adoptive mother's speech as she prepares the house to receive the child:

> I thought I'd hid everything
> that there wasnie wan
> giveaway sign left
>
> (14)

The sense of who one is, as reflected in how one's speech derives from a specific place, time, and community, makes its own oblique but firm affirmation of belongingness. The adoptive mother is eager to welcome the child, and works hard to make the house look suitable as a home for a baby. The social worker is won over by evidence that the childless couple is active in causes like a nuclear-free world.

The birth mother makes her train journey back to Aberdeen, rationalizing the giving up of her baby to adoption. The adoptive mother has to wait anxiously for the baby to show signs of good health before the papers can be signed. The frailty of the newborn child is an issue that concerns more than physical health. The child lives without the physical closeness of the birth mother, without a home or a family that will claim her as theirs. The pathos of a plight that the daughter is too young to be aware of is thus dramatized by the poet as shareable, in retrospect, with the reader. The couple is pleased and proud after visiting the baby in an Edinburgh hospital, a 'darling' even before she can be legally claimed. The birth mother signs away her right to the baby, it passes the health requirement, and the adoptive parents now have two days in which to ready themselves for their responsibility: less time, but more readiness than what the birth mother received and found within her.

As for the birth mother, the waitress who returns to her solitary home in Aberdeen, the kissing and saying sorry that works in novels will not do for her. She is as empty as winter air. Once home, she conducts an odd and painful burial: the clothes she had bought for the baby are buried in the back garden in a ritual of farewell, grief, shame, and self-recrimination. At night, she dreams:

> she came in by the window,
> my baby Lazarus
> and suckled at my breast.
>
> (18)

The directness and plausibility with which the poet ventriloquizes every detail of either mother's frame of mind at a time when she, the daughter, was too young to know, makes the poem intuitive and humane in its emotional impact. The Wordsworthian sentiment that the child is the true parent, and binds the family in a form of natural piety, is realized in Kay's sequence by the compassion shown by the child towards either mother. The daughter proceeds with her search for the birth mother. Meanwhile, as if in a dream, the adoptive mother imagines a visit from the birth mother: the visitor appears as a spitting image of the baby, dressed oddly in tweed, and white in appearance, like lightening, or a ghost.

Part Two moves forward to when the daughter is six:

> She says my real mammy is away far away
> **Mammy why aren't you and me the same colour**
> But I love my mammy whether she's real or no
>
> (21)

The daughter is scared for a while that this mother will disappear or disintegrate, but soon forgets the fear amidst childhood routines. What is less easily forgotten or dealt with is the racism of children her age. To them, she is '*Sambo*' and '*Dirty Darkie*' (24). The daughter is pugnacious and fights back. The adoptive mother is firm in her affirmation that colour and 'racialism' can be resisted, just as she is firm in her dismissal of the notion that a child must have a umbilical connection with the mother for the relation to be real.

Clichés about blood and race recur throughout school life. The daughter is assumed to be able to dance the Cha Cha and the Black Bottom because 'you people had it in your blood' (25). The media proffer white figures from the world of music and cinema that the girl cannot hope to imitate. The birth mother re-enters the sequence with a recollection of the peat-coloured man who was the father. His name was Olubayo, and he never saw his daughter, although she would like to imagine his eyes looking back at her through the eyes of the baby in her hospital cot. Meanwhile the growing daughter takes up 'FREE ANGELA DAVIS' (27) as a slogan. We can interpret the slogan to have an application closer to home, while it grounds the cause of the radical Black American activist in the mundane racism of children at school and play.

Part Three catches up with the decade that brings us to the poet's present. The birth mother is imagined as living in desolation, never forgetting the child she gave up. Voices from her past echo like a pneumatic drill in her head. She reckons that her daughter must now be nineteen, the same age at which she arrived at her involuntary motherhood. Meanwhile, the daughter grows up, having to face the fact that her adoptive parents are not 'of the same tree' (29), that she has no direct knowledge of her blood relations, no tie between her own body and the blood of her ancestors. The poem alternates between the voice of the mother who cannot imagine what her girl looks like, and the voice of the daughter who wishes desperately that she could have a sense of the birth mother's physical presence, just as she has the sense of Scotland as 'the soil in my blood' (29).

Finally, efforts to bring daughter and birth mother together begin moving to a climax. The sequence ends with their meeting. Each is slightly surprised that the other is slightly different from how she had been imagined. Each recognizes an inevitable anticlimax to the long-awaited reunion:

> One dream cuts another open like a gutted fish
> nothing is what it was;
> she is too many imaginings to be flesh and blood.
> There is nothing left to say.
> Neither of us mentions meeting again.
>
> (33)

The fictive self conjured by each for the other in the twenty-six years of separation is too powerful to be displaced by a meeting with the person of flesh and blood. Absence has bred a reality of the mind that we the readers participate in through the poem. This reality of imagined encounters and experiences has become more 'real' to mother and daughter than the desolation they have lived in the other's absence. Their actual encounter only brings them closer to the desolation of lives not lived together, not liveable together. It is time to move on, time to begin again.

Like every ritual of initiation, and every *bildungsroman* that surveys the past from a point of vantage that also shows the path toward a future, the sequence marks a turning from (though not, by any means, a turning away from) the tie of nature to the tie of nurture. Without every getting didactic or preachy, the sequence manages to imply a lesson that we can adduce from Paul Gilroy when he writes of the need, in our times, for 'conviviality', which makes nonsense of 'closed, fixed, and reified identity and turns attention toward the always unpredictable mechanisms of identification' (2004: xi). The sequence lays a strong foundation—not for ethnic identity—but for identifications based on family and community. It empowers the poet to tackle race relations in contemporary Britain (and from the past, as in a poem that voices the feelings of the Hottentot Venus exhibited all over Europe in the nineteenth century) with a combination of passion and compassion. Above all, it enables Kay, in the other poems from this volume, and in *Other Lovers* (1993) and *Off Colour* (1998), to show how conviviality can be sustained in contemporary society without losing sight of the need for justice tempered with empathy. It makes for a poetry that is alert to avoid and expose blandness, hypocrisy, and bad faith.

2.3 'the invisible mending of the heart': Ingrid de Kok

> Too near the ancient troughs of blood
> Innocence is no earthly weapon.
>
> Geoffrey Hill, 'Ovid in the Third Reich'

From 1948, South Africa institutionalized the extreme form of racism known as apartheid, which lasted until 1994. The political and ethical fallout from apartheid continues to affect contemporary poets in South Africa, where the racial dimension of violence has tended to blur the distinction between colonial and postcolonial predicaments. The 1970s were the heyday of protest against apartheid. The black South African poet James Matthews (b. 1929) declared that the function of poetry was to 'record the anguish of the persecuted' (Bunn 1989: 53). From neighbouring Zimbabwe, Chenjerai Hove (b. 1956) invoked the English poet Wilfred Owen (1893–1918), who had reacted to the carnage of World War I, in which he lost his life, with the maxim 'The poetry is in the pity' (Wild 1988: 36). By 1990, in South Africa and neighbouring countries, the cost of pity was reckoned as too high. The white poet Stephen Watson (b. 1954) remarked of 'Soweto poetry' that 'Like the photograph of the girl in Philip Larkin's poem, the poetry itself grows smaller and clearer as the years go by' (1990: 82–3). He argued that the notion of a 'black aesthetic' remained as remote and unformulated in the 1980s as in the 1970s. Some of these issues are developed further in Chapters 5 and 6, which give a fuller account of the impact of apartheid on poets from black Africa and African settler communities respectively.

Watson wrote at a time when young poets like Lesego Rampolokeng (b. 1965) and Seitlhamo Motsapi (b. 1966) had not yet made their impact. White poets in the 1990s continued to face the difficulty of dealing with violence as a theme for acknowledgement, responsibility, complicity, guilt, and reconciliation, while having to avoid the appearance of indifference, blandness, or hypocrisy. In 1988, Ingrid de Kok (b. 1951) expressed the view that the tradition of the personal and relatively private lyric as derived from Europe was 'beleaguered' in South Africa (Bunn 1989: 55). She suggested that white poets could learn to adapt their practices to the performative modes opened up by protest writing, but worried that protest can neglect artistic rigour. How does a poet keep the edge of protest alive, without letting poetry succumb to considerations that dismiss or marginalize the aesthetic dimension? We will return to this question in Chapter 5. In South Africa, the challenge continues to preoccupy black poets, as in 'Lines for Vincent', in which Rampolokeng broods over the death of a cousin who was savagely tortured, and reiterates the responsibility of language to suffering:

> i know i might encounter the death
> of speech
> but it's said memory is a long road
> made worse by the heavy load
> of violence
>
> (1999: 13)

In 1976, de Kok left South Africa for Canada, from where she wrote, 'South African writers with rare exceptions and regardless of whether they were politically engaged or not, lost sense of a wider context of artistic engagement. In formal terms poetry stultified, xenophobia reigned' (1997b: online). She returned to her birthplace in 1984, determined to put in practice what she had learnt from poets like Robert Frost, Elizabeth Bishop, and Seamus Heaney about her interest in 'the formal representations of the furies, of grief, violence and anger and how they play themselves out, are reordered, in the delicacies and constraints of quite formal work' (1997b: online). 'Mending', from her second volume, *Transfer* (1997), shows how poetry can negotiate between form and the furies. The poem implies a domestic context of feminine suffering, in which the mundane activity of needlework acquires larger resonance, stanzaic neatness holding together a passion that aspires to healing:

> The woman plies her ancient art,
> Her needle sutures as it darts,
> scoring, scripting, scarring, stitching,
> the invisible mending of the heart.
>
> (1997a: 35)

The need to heal suffering without ignoring any part of violence becomes the central preoccupation of her third volume, *Terrestrial Things* (2002). The title alludes to 'The Darkling Thrush', a poem written by Thomas Hardy (1840–1928) from England during the gloomy days of the Boer War. Simon Lewis remarks of the allusion that the 'ecstatic caroling' of the 'blast-beruffled' thrush becomes a token for Hardy, and by implication for de Kok, 'that despite all the evidence "written on terrestrial things" there might still be "some blessed hope" ' (2003: online). In the 1980s, the black intellectual Njabulo Ndebele (b. 1948) called upon South African writers to avoid the 'spectacular' for the 'ordinary'. Maya Jaggi, in her review of Ndebele's *The Cry of Winnie Mandela* (2003), reminds us that from exile, Ndebele 'called for intimacy and introspection to be restored to a literature dominated, in his view, by the spectacular and exterior, by heroic contests between the powerless and the powerful' (2004: online). One of the chief merits of de Kok's volume is that in South Africa after apartheid, she manages the difficult feat of balancing the impulses toward the spectacular and the ordinary.

Terrestrial Things comprises four sections, of which I shall allude only to the dozen poems from the second in any detail. The first comprises poems from a visit to Europe, the third and fourth evoke childhood memories. The first explores a wider world seen through eyes overshadowed by what has been learnt and experienced back home. Childhood memories embed the familial in the social. The sensory realm of unforgotten sights, sounds, smells, and sensations is combined with recollection of persons, events, and modes of thought and feeling that are too exact to become sentimental, too sharp to serve as mere anecdotal social history. The volume is at its most resilient in tackling 'the spectacular' through a series of intense but modulated responses to the public drama of hearings, trials, and inquiries into human rights violations. One decade after the end of apartheid, the South African legacy of injustice remains both irresistible and problematic, asking for past suffering to be given present hearing, as the nation begins the tentative effort of reconcilement and a new beginning. De Kok described the poets' dilemma in a 1997 interview:

> I don't know how you can write in South Africa and not reference this major revelatory complex mixture of truth and lying in some way. Yet it also seems impossible, invasive, to do so. The only way I can is to acknowledge the moral torment involved, and then set it aside, or inside.
>
> (1997b: online)

'Parts of Speech', from *Terrestrial Things*, gives testimony to the humility and care with which the poet approaches her contemporary reckoning with violence: 'at this stained place words | are scraped from resinous tongues' (21). The 'stained place' can be read as a punning reference to the courtrooms where public inquiry into past crimes is recorded, and the spaces of art in which pain, suffering, and silence are to be inscribed. The poet practises self-abnegation. Can anyone dare to suppose that language will be adequate for what is now being revealed as an inquiry into the 'truth' of what happened to those who were killed, tortured, brutalized, and forgotten in the recent South African past?

> Why still imagine whole words, whole worlds:
> the flame splutter of consonants,
> deep sea anemone vowels,
> birth-cable syntax, rhymes that start in the heart,
> and verbs, verbs that move mountains?
>
> (21)

In 'How to mourn in a room full of questions', the language is diffident about what it can hope to do, but forceful in how its metaphors wrestle with the emotional force of what is being recounted:

> Old sorrow holds down anger like a plug.
> And juridical questions swab the brains and blood off the floor.
>
> (23)

The gap between the conventions of courtroom ritual and the kind of speech that suffering permits is starkly pointed up:

> 'Do you promise to tell the truth,
> the whole truth and nothing but the truth?'
> [. . .]
> The gull drags its wings to the lighthouse steps.
> 'That's the truth. So help. Whole. To tell.'
>
> (24)

The poem 'what kind of man are you?' focuses on the question addressed to an officer who was responsible for various acts of brutality, such as mounting a woman to suffocate her with a wet bag, and roasting meat while a man burned on a pyre near by. The officer merely echoes the question back: 'I ask myself the same question.' The poet reflects on the wider implications of the question he evades:

This kind, we will possibly answer,
(pointing straight, sideways,
upwards, down, inside out),
this kind.

(27)

In studied understatement, the poem extends the indictment to include us all. What turns our stomach, what turns our sense of involvement or responsibility inside out, is the recognition that no part of humanity is free of complicity in such guilt, especially when individuals like Captain Benzien either do not know, or will not say, what made them act as they did. The effectiveness of the poem is paradoxical in nature. To show why it is difficult to do justice to a sense of outrage that acknowledges general responsibility is to do what the poet also implies cannot be done adequately. The effectiveness of de Kok's undertaking requires a combination of empathy and resistance. Poetry accedes to the impulse to respond to violence, but not without recognizing that its moral imperatives must be addressed by the rhetoricity of language as form. An ethical compulsion must become aesthetically binding, as in the rhetoricity of the following type of question from 'Revenge of the imagination':

Which one, like Isaac,
his head on a rocky altar,
will we sacrifice in mind
to our dazed and shadowy
reverie of revenge and recovery?

(29)

The alliteration twins words that refer to notions we might think separated by a wide difference: revenge and recovery; the need for rough justice and the need to move on. The illusory difference between these opposed concepts, and the manner in which human agency soils both, are precisely underlined.

De Kok presents the ritual act of public inquiry as a form of communal self-appeasement. This ritual is based on the guilt of having allowed all this brutality to be repressed, ignored, or forgotten during the decades of apartheid. The question raised by her poems is not whether bringing up past atrocities for present inscription can be adequate witness to a forgetting from which there is no satisfactory retrieval, but the question of whether language can ever be adequate to the responsibility of bearing witness. A transcriber at the 'Truth Commission' asks, in a dramatic monologue:

> But how to transcribe silence from tape?
> Is weeping a pause or a word?
> What written sign for a strangled throat?
>
> (32)

Like radio, poetry is supposed to edit, connect, broadcast. The medium of radio points up the breakdown of the communicative function, because the turnover rate during the hearings is highest among reporters for radio: the job most frequently quit during the hearings was that of radio reporter. The act of broadcasting guilt is too painful to continue with for long:

> Listen, cut; comma, cut;
> stammer, cut;
> edit, pain; connect, pain; broadcast, pain;
> listen, cut; comma, cut.
> Bind grammar to horror...
>
> (33)

The poem slows down the act of mediation, forces attention to note the conjunction of the grammar of pain and the grammar of language. The narrative of exposure acknowledges the need for justice, punishment, truth, witness, and healing. However, in 'Today, again', the poet wonders if that will suffice for the task of reparation to begin:

> If we go on like this, everyone
> will know somebody this week dead,
> watch somebody die, kill somebody
> or film it, write about it
>
> (35)

Or read about it. The complicity stretches wide. The poem points to the need to halt, to turn, and to begin afresh.

Seitlhamo Motsapi's *earthstepper/the ocean is very shallow* (1995/2003) provides a radical alternative. Despite misgivings, de Kok falls back on the tradition of the European or Anglo-American lyric. In sharp contrast, Motsapi invents an exuberant and uniquely personal style that derives inspiration from the extrovert energies of African song. His idiom is equally hospitable to metaphor, slang, and cliché.

Experience is tackled at a level that expands the personal to represent the communal. The verse line is economical in rendering metonymic details as laden with symbolic intent. These features are exemplified at their most effective in 'earth', whose lower case format and minimal respect for punctuation and grammar is part of a larger rhetoric of resistance. The first and third stanzas lament the fate of those led on by the allure of gain into a contemporary wilderness:

> to say bread
> we tamed mountains
> assaulted distances
> noses stuck out & up
> for the shallow odour
> of silver
> [. . .]
> but now you see me
> all earthscent & skewed skunk
>   pulp in the rot to a fetter
> now you see me
> a bruising stagger
>   hammered to hell
>   & screwed to a grovel by capital
>
> (2003: 15)

The freshness of effect produced by such poems thrives on the improvisatory quality of phrases and metaphors swept along by an energetic rhythm. 'to say bread' compacts a narrative of want in which great toil had to be undergone before the utterance of the word could correspond to the availability of the food. 'noses stuck out and up' is comic about pretensions that became overextended, and 'the shallow odour | of silver' is cheerily blithe in the synaesthesia of its mixed metaphors. 'skewed skunk' is vigorously self-deprecatory, 'a bruising stagger' is a novel way of evoking the stagger produced by bruises. 'hammered to hell' is close to cliché, but the demotic effect gains novelty with 'screwed to a grovel'. Being exploited can hardly be phrased with more vitality. The style provides the clue to how the predicament it addresses is to be overturned. Where de Kok is defensive and expiatory, such writing is affirmative. Her sense of form leans towards containment, precision, the linguistic understatement of the emotively hyperbolical. Motsapi's spills over into profusion and excess, words exhilarating by their own flair, as in these lines from 'river robert', the final poem in a book that serves the function for contemporary South Africa that was served for American poetry in its time by Whitman's continually revised *Leaves of Grass*:

> i have one eye full of dreams & hintentions
> the other is full of broken mirrors
> & cracked churchbells
> [. . .]
> i have
> a memory full of paths & anointings
> a mouth full of ripe infant suns
> seven legs for the dancing river & the clement abyss
> & a hope that corrodes the convulsions
>
> (2003: 84)

PART II

THE DEVELOPMENT OF LOCAL TRADITIONS

3

South Asia and Southeast Asia

Overview

Asia has served as a magnet for invaders from Europe ever since Alexander the Great turned back reluctantly from what is now Pakistan. South and Southeast Asia presented Europeans with climates and demographic densities that did not encourage settlement, although they offered ample opportunities for trade and territorial control. The British were the most successful among European colonizers in Asia. This chapter surveys the growth of Asian poetry in English in a context where national and postcolonial agendas focus on keeping multi-racial and multicultural societies on the path to modernity, and English prevails as the language of internal unity and international globalization.

3.1 Macaulay's minutemen

> 'Bleddy Macaulay's minutemen! Don't you get it? Bunch of English-medium misfits, the lot of you.'
>
> Salman Rushdie, *The Moor's Last Sigh*

The history of Asian writing in English is an account of the struggle to prove that 'Macaulay's minutemen' were not misfits in their parts of the world. The British Empire in Asia was a gradual accretion spread over several centuries. The combined outcome of greed, perseverance, technological superiority, administrative acumen, and the strategic use of force enabled Britain to accumulate enormous wealth and power, while controlling large and diverse populations through a relatively small British presence in the region.

In 1600, British colonial ambitions followed early Portuguese and Spanish success in charting sea routes west and east of the African continent. The desire to emulate and rival these powers led to the founding of the East India Company. A royal charter of 1600 granted the Company monopoly over English trade in Asia. Several other European nations formed similar companies, which competed vigorously with one another over the next two centuries for Asian outposts, markets, and commodities. Their fortunes followed a loose pattern that began with exploration and trade during the seventeenth century, and grew to territorial ambitions during the eighteen century, until trade had metamorphosed into varying forms of indirect or direct European rule.

By the beginning of the nineteenth century, the British had outmanoeuvred their European rivals in the Indian subcontinent and the Malaya Peninsula. Their control over India was consolidated after an uprising was suppressed in 1857, and the Crown took over administration of territories previously controlled by the Company. Meanwhile, trade in the Far East led to the founding of Hong Kong in 1842 after the defeat of the Chinese in the First Opium War. The colony expanded further after a British victory in the Second Opium War in 1860, and a 99-year lease of the New Territories adjoining the island was signed in 1898.

British administrative policy thrived on the logic of 'divide and rule'. Charmayne D'Souza (b. 1955, India) remarks in 'Trains of Thought—II':

> The British knew
> how to bring a nation together—
> an elbow in the rib,
> a space divided.
>
> (1990: 63)

The legacy of that policy laid the foundations for the Asian division into nationhood after the end of Empire, which began in 1947, with the partition of British India into West Pakistan (now Pakistan), East Pakistan (Bangladesh since 1971), and India. Ceylon (now Sri Lanka) became independent in 1948. The division of British India was the cause of much grief on either side of the border. Many would echo the sentiments expressed by Sujata Bhatt (b. 1956, India/Germany) in 'Partition':

> 'How could they
>   have let a man
> who knew nothing
>   about geography
> divide a country?'
>
> (2000b: 34)

Similar divisions occurred in Southeast Asia, where the creation of the Malaysian Federation in 1957 was followed by the splitting away of Singapore from Malaysia in 1965. Hong Kong remained an outpost of Empire until it was finally returned to mainland China in 1997.

The consolidation of British colonial dominance was accomplished by a relatively tiny European presence in Asia, largely male. Colonialism was a double-edged phenomenon. On the one hand, Asian resources were exploited for the benefit of European nations; on the other hand, Asian societies were given variable degrees of access to the Western endowments that had made colonization possible: modes of knowledge, technology, economic practices, and European institutions of civil society. Colonial rule was accompanied by a mixture of planned and unplanned acculturation, some of it initiated by the British, some undertaken by Asians in pursuit of a modernity based on European models.

Europe's mastery over Asian societies extended from the military and the economic spheres to the intellectual project of creating a new body of knowledge about the 'Orient'. In Britain's Asian colonies, Orientalism went hand in hand with reconstructing the colonized along the lines recommended by Thomas Babington Macaulay in 'Indian Education: Minute of the 2nd of February, 1835':

> We must at present do our best to form a class who may be interpreters between us and the millions whom we govern; a class of persons, Indian in blood and colour, but English in taste, in opinions, in morals, and in intellect.
>
> (1952: 729–30)

Macaulay's recommendation—that the Company should ignore Asian languages, and invest in disseminating English in India—became policy. It produced effects that went well beyond the purposes for which they had been proposed. Admiration for and emulation of British literature was the first direct result, colonial writing in English was the second. Post-independent Asian societies retained English as the language of unification, modernity, and international relations.

This ensured that postcolonial writing would continue the legacy of Macaulay in directions that have since moved past mimicry to various forms of literary self-representation.

Of all the European empires in Asia, Britain was the most successful in propagating its language and literary traditions in the colonies. For instance, large parts of the island of Ceylon were controlled by the Portuguese and the Dutch for more than two hundred years, but their languages and literatures did not influence local writing in quite the way that English did once the British acquired control over a large portion of the island in 1815. The same is true for most parts of Asia that came under British rule, with the exception of Burma, where writing in English never quite took hold.

Karl Marx wrote in 'The Future Results of British Rule in India' (1853), 'England has to fulfil a double mission in India: one destructive, the other regenerating—the annihilation of old Asiatic society, and the laying down of the material foundations of Western society in Asia' (2001: 70). Marx referred to the effect of colonization on the economic base in India, but Asian intellectuals like Rammohun Roy (1772–1832) hoped for a more comprehensive transformation of society and culture. The novelist Amit Chaudhuri remarks, 'From the early 19th century, the growing Bengali intelligentsia in Calcutta was increasingly exercised by what "modernity" might mean and what the experience of modernity might represent, specifically, to a subject nation, and, universally, to a human being' (2004: online). In its more sedulous aspects, such aspirations became part of what a character in Rushdie calls 'Westoxication' (1995: 178). Writing in English is part of this 'Westoxication'. In South Asia, local poets aspired to English well before their societies had begun the struggle for political autonomy; in contrast, Southeast Asian poetic aspirations in English followed political independence.

3.2 The Indian subcontinent

> Of what concern to me is a vanished Empire?
> Or the conquest of my ancestors' timeless ennui?
>
> Jayanta Mahapatra, 'The Abandoned British Cemetery at Balasore'

English is everyone's language in India; and it is no one's language. Because it is the former, everyone can read the

> Roman alphabet and knows the meanings of words; because it is also the latter, they can completely miss the tone and emotional charge the words carry, as in poetry words must, always.
>
> A. K. Mehrotra, 'A Legend Springs', *Hindustan Times*, 9 October 2004

Indian poetry in English began in a spirit of imitation that took more than a century to shed. The first Indian poet to use English was the Eurasian Henry Derozio (1809–31), whose volume of *Poems* (1827) pre-dates Macaulay's *Minute* of 1835. Indian poetry of the nineteenth century was diligently imitative. In addition to the gifted but short-lived Toru Dutt (1856–77), whose work is fluent in adapting post-Romantic models of diction, style, and tone to indigenous materials, colonial post-Romanticism found three major Indian exponents. They had long careers, considerable literary success during their lifetime, and reputations partly based on spiritual and nationalist achievements outside the realm of poetry in English: Rabindranath Tagore (1861–1941), Aurobindo Ghose (1872–1950), and Sarojini Naidu (1879–1949). Tagore was admired by Yeats (and, more cautiously, by Ezra Pound), and won the Nobel Prize for Literature in 1913, but wrote poetry far more effectively in Bengali than English. They still find many admirers, within India, and among overseas readers, but a significantly large number of subsequent Indian poets writing in English have shown themselves reluctant to write like 'Matthew Arnold in a sari' (to borrow a phrase from the Australian critic S. C. Harrex). Keki Daruwalla (b. 1937), for example, protested: 'Unfortunately, the Indian poets [Toru Dutt, Sarojini Naidu etc.] . . . thought that if they switched from Hellenisms to their own myths, exchanging naiads and nymphs for *apsaras*, or Orpheus and Eurydice for Satyavan and Savitri, they had done their job' (1980: xvi).

A contemporary tone was introduced into Indian poetry in English by Nissim Ezekiel (1925–2004) and Dom Moraes (1938–2004). Each published a book of poems from London in 1952. These were the first two volumes of poetry in English published after independence by Indians. Their range was comparable to the work of the Movement poets in 1950s Britain. Moraes essayed a clipped style, Ezekiel a dry and ironic manner. Moraes was based overseas, Ezekiel preferred Bombay (now Mumbai), his chosen 'backward place'. Both moved from formal to relaxed styles. That did not stop the idea of Indians writing poetry in English from being caustically dismissed in the two decades following independence. The Bengali writer Buddhadeva Bose wrote in Stephen Spender and Donald Hall's *Concise Encyclopedia of English and American Poets and Poetry* (1963): 'As late as 1937, Yeats reminded Indian writers that "no man can think or write with music and vigour except in his mother tongue"... "Indo-Anglian" poetry is a blind alley, lined with curio shops, leading nowhere' (Walsh 1990: 127). Another form of scepticism about the viability of an Indian tradition of creative writing in English was voiced by the Marathi novelist Bhalchandra Nemade, in the form of a nativist argument:

> Culture consciousness precedes linguistic consciousness and the latter depends upon the former. By encouraging a foreign language system to be a fit medium for creative writing we bring our already low-value culture still lower. It is doubtful whether this writing will add any 'Indianness' to World writing in English.
>
> (1985: 35–6)

Most poets keen to use English either ignored such misgivings, or quickly defended their choice of language. Those who continued to worry about the issue stared silence in the face. In 1965, Lakdasa Wikkramasinha (Sri Lanka) feared that 'To write in English is a form of cultural treason' (Goonetilleke 1991: xiv). In 1982, R. Parthasarathy (b. 1941, India) confessed that he had been 'whoring after English gods'. In the 1990s, Wong Phui Nam (b. 1935, Malaysia) declared, 'The non-English writer who writes in English is... in a very deep sense a miscegenated being' (1993: 140).

Other Asian poets writing in English treated the question of choice as largely illusory, though they made it matter for some deft shadow-boxing. Yasmine Gooneratne (b. 1935, Sri Lanka/Australia) wrote of English in 'This Language, This woman': 'do not call her slut, and alien, | names born of envy and your own misuse | that whisper how desire in secret runs' (Thieme 1996: 765). Among Indians, Moraes, Ezekiel, Adil Jussawalla (b. 1940) and Gieve Patel (b. 1946) had no other viable language. Others like Arun Kolatkar (1932–2004) adopted a bilingual approach, reaching different or partially overlapping audiences through the contrasting resources of English and an Indian language. During the 1960s and 1970s, Indian poets worried self-consciously over their choice of language. Daruwalla was energetically self-deprecatory about the English Muse in India, calling her 'The Mistress':

> No one believes me when I say
> my mistress is half-caste.
> [...]
> her consonants bludgeon you;
> her argot is rococo, her latest 'slang'
> is available in classical dictionaries.
> She sounds like a dry sob
> stuck in the throat of darkness...
>
> (1982: 22)

Kamala Das (b. 1934) was the first Indian woman to write in English with candour about feminine sexuality. She declared in 'An Introduction':

> ...I am Indian, very brown, born in
> Malabar, I speak three languages, write in
> Two, dream in one. Don't write in English, they said,
> English is not your mother-tongue.
> [...]
> The language I speak
> Becomes mine, its distortions, its queernesses
> All mine, mine alone. It is half English, half
> Indian, funny perhaps, but it is honest,
> It is as human as I am human...
>
> (1986: 7)

On the Indian subcontinent, poets continue to use English in the shadow of local languages and literatures. The Indian constitution recognizes fifteen official languages, each with millions of local speakers. *The Oxford Anthology of Modern Indian Poetry* (1994) contains 125 poets in fifteen languages, of which only twenty-three write in English and of those, four are bilingual. Translations and bilingualism among poets has kept English interactive with the local linguistic environment. The English language has been transmogrified by local speech habits. 'Soap', one of Ezekiel's wickedly funny parodies from 'Very Indian Poems in Indian English', shows how linguistic ineptitude provides matter for satirical monologues:

> Some people are not having manners,
> this I am always observing,
> For example other day I find
> I am needing soap

for ordinary washing myself purposes.
So I'm going to one small shop
nearby in my lane and I'm asking
for well-known brand of soap.

(1989: 268)

Ezekiel targets Indian English as individuated largely through error. The failure to adhere to the norm of Standard English offers limited scope for anything but mild satire, lacking the more aggressive energy of West Indian Creoles. Nevertheless, a humane sympathy lightens the effect of Ezekiel's subversions, allowing authorial parody to be countered by his subject's self-evident sincerity.

While Ezekiel could be said to have indigenized English to the rhythms and flavour of Bombay, the poetry of Adil Jussawalla illustrates a different predicament. His poetry presents the colonized intellectual in a double bind: out of sorts with the West, and deprived of an uncomplicated relation to his ex-colonial matrix because of his acute Westernization. Bruce King describes this type of intellectual as preoccupied by 'an historical awareness of his own situation as a representative of a decaying class soon to be replaced by forces of which he cannot be part' (2001: 247–8). Jussawalla finds an emblematic image for dispossession in the *Missing Person* (1976). Homi Bhabha diagnoses this work as a harrowing of bourgeois identity, for whom 'Caliban | is still not IT' (1994: 45):

No Satan
warmed in the electric coils of his creatures
or Gunga Din
will make him come before you.
To see an invisible man
or a missing person,
trust no Eng. Lit. That
puffs him up, narrows his eyes,
scratches his fangs. Caliban
is still not IT.

(Mehrotra 1992: 134)

A different preoccupation is revealed in the poetry of Sujata Bhatt, who grew up in India, studied in the US, and lives in Bremen. Her writing moves between several societies, cultures, and languages. 'A Different History', from *Brunizem* (1988), asks rhetorically,

'Which language | has not been the oppressor's tongue? | Which language | truly meant to murder someone?' (1988: 37). 'The One Who Goes Away', from her third volume, *The Stinking Rose* (1995), begins with a dual recognition: 'I am the one | who always goes away', 'But I never left home...I carried it away | with me' (3–4). Her figurative home accommodates the Gujarati language into her English poems. The reader unfamiliar with Gujarati is likely to pick up little beyond the fact of the dual affiliation. The effect is polyglot and provocative, without being altogether persuasive, especially to Indian readers. More convincingly, the question of how a poet is made, and the notion that languages choose poets, become the focus of 'History is a Broken Narrative', from her fourth volume, *Augatora* (2000). The poet muses over the differences between getting and taking, and between making and changing:

> You take your language where you get it.
> Or do you
> get your language
> where you take it?
>
> (2000: 40)

The poem concludes:

> History is a broken narrative
> where you make your language
> when you change it.
>
> (2000: 43)

The ability to use English unselfconsciously has been the principal achievement of the poets of the Indian subcontinent, from the generation represented in A. K. Mehrotra's anthology (1992), to that represented in Ranjit Hoskote's *Reasons for Belonging: Fourteen Contemporary Indian Poets* (2002). Mehrotra brings a sophisticated minimalism to his craft, as in 'Disjecta Membra Poetae', where 'the gristle of poems' can come from a medley of associations ranging from the smell of ink, to the shape of Wyoming, or the colour Burma green:

> Words like
> *Slough*, off-rhymes,
> Translations,
> Dead metaphors,
>
> (1984: 53)

A later poem, 'Scenes from a Revolving Chair', describe the unceasing quest for adequacy of language as 'The long walk through elephant grass | In search of common speech' (1998: 20). Jayanta Mahapatra (b. 1928), who happens to be one of the few postcolonial Asian poets to have attempted an ambitious long poem, *Relationship* (1982), adds another dimension to the maturity of poetry in India, a gift for metaphor. 'Another Love Poem' declares:

In a country drugged with its image,
I only find my way in metaphor.

(1992: 63)

A long poem needs a narrative, a humble truth whose avoidance brought Modernist attempts at a long poem to grief, whether for T. S. Eliot's first draft of *The Waste Land* (1922), Ezra Pound's *Cantos* (1925–72), or William Carlos Williams's *Paterson* (1946–51). Vikram Seth (b. 1952), found a neat and unexpected, if mannered, solution to the problem in *The Golden Gate* (1986) by going back past the Modernists to a contemporary and ingenious adaptation of a Byronic manner to a verse novel in rhyming tetrameter sonnets. The achievement remains anomalous in Asia, although long postcolonial narratives in verse are successfully handled by poets elsewhere. Seth's fluency is too close to doggerel to bear repetition, but it does represent a movement out of the Modernist shadow, characterized by an easy-going style of cosmopolitan decolonization:

. . . she reads out her composition:
"*Young, handsome, yuppie, 26,*
Straight, forward, sociable, but lonely,
Cannot believe that he's the only
Well-rounded and well-meaning square
Lusting for love. If you, out there,
Are friendly, female, under 30,
Impulsive, fit, and fun, let's meet.
*Be rash. Bax*____Cuff, off that sheet!

(1986: 25)

The English language stitches together for Asians at one level what political events tear apart in other ways. Independence defined nations through boundaries often dictated by the divisive logic of ethnic and religious affiliations. The separation of Singapore from Malaysia in 1965 was preceded by violence. Alfian Sa'at (b. 1977) reminds contemporary readers of 'Six Riot Chants' that the split between Malaysia and Singapore was preceded by 'instigated riots between the Malays and the Chinese' (2002: 3). Another bitter harrowing of the postcolonial nation torn by religious fundamentalism—the Ayodhya riots (1992) of India, in which a mosque was destroyed by Hindus because it was alleged to have been built on grounds previously occupied by a Hindu shrine—is addressed through a series of allusions to the Hindu scriptures by Rukmini Bhaya Nair in *The Ayodhya Cantos* (1999). The bitter division between Muslims and Hindus that was sanctioned, however reluctantly, by Britain in 1947, is also remembered by the Pakistani poet Alamgir Hashmi (b. 1951) in a poem that reflects on the consequences of Partition, 'On hearing that the wall in Berlin':

> has come down in part, I want
> to acknowledge...
> Maybe it's too late for some.
> Even dying were easier than some divisions—
>
> (1997: 37)

In India, on 30 January 1948, less than six months after independence, a right-wing Hindu shot and killed M. K. Gandhi, the chief exponent of passive nonviolence and resistance to British rule, and also one of the chief architects of the Partition, which the Hindu right wing regarded as a betrayal of the political ideal of undivided nationhood. This is how Zulfikar Ghose (b. 1935, Pakistan/UK/USA) evokes the assassination of Gandhi in 'The Loss of India':

> a Moses and a Mohammed thinned
> to the bones of a self-denying innocence,
> mild as foam on the tortured crest of his
> people's violence, straight as a walking-stick
> on the savage contours of his country.
> When the bullets hit him, his body was cut
> into the bars of a jail he had never left,
> his stomach shriveled in another hunger fast.
>
> (1991: 5)

And this is how he makes a personal valediction to the India of his youth in 'This Landscape, These People', claiming that the forces unleashed in the new nation generated a centrifugal turbulence:

India halted: as suddenly as a dog,
  barking, hangs out his tongue, stifles his cry.
  An epic turned into a monologue
  of death. The rope lay stiff across the country;
  all fires were eaten, swallowed all the swords;
the horizons paled, then thickened, blackened with crows.

(1991: 10–11)

Shirley Lim (b. 1944, Malaysia/USA) describes Ghose as 'an orphan of the British Commonwealth, formed by an imperial world culture, and by the disintegrative violence that broke the empire into numerous untenable nation states' (1994b: 61). The poet becomes a culturally displaced migrant who revisits the fear that 'all is a scattering, all is a vanishing' (Ghose 1984: 5). Personal and familial pasts are quarried in order to redefine an ever-changing self, making Ghose representative of a postcolonial condition in which 'what one composes as a definitive statement | is only a memory of a memory' (1984: 3).

In Sri Lanka, independence was followed in 1956 by a form of aggressive-defensive nationalism that displaced English as the primary language of education. Ironically, this gave impetus to writing in English, whose traditions in Sri Lanka have since been dogged by three problems: the dominance of Sinhala as the language of the majority, the looming presence of India to the north, and the tendency of writers to migrate overseas from a land torn by ethnic strife. *An Anthology of Modern Writing from Sri Lanka* reckoned, as late as 1981, that 'In present day Sri Lanka, English is . . . spoken minimally by a fair per centage of the urban middle class, but not to the point where there is any great interest in literary works in English' (Obeyesekere 1981: 16).

Ten years later, another anthology, *The Penguin New Writing in Sri Lanka*, assessed the effect of nationalist sentiments on the role of English in Sri Lanka as follows: English 'was neglected for two decades and even reviled', yet paradoxically, this fate 'led to fruitful results in the field of creative writing' (Goonetilleke 1991: x). The last two decades of the twentieth century have been dominated in Sri Lanka by ethnic violence between the (largely Sinhalese) State and Tamil minority insurgents. The conflict has forced poets into a corner from which they have either protested (in vain), or left (turning their back on the island and its fate). Among those who protested, irony and foreboding prevailed. Reggie Siriwardena (1922–2004) adopted a stoic stance in 'Waiting for the Soldier' (1987):

> ... don't say
> I am escaping. In a world without sense
> one must look for meaning wherever one
> can find it—if only, perhaps, for a day
> or two. I know the Roman soldier—
> in one shape or another—is on the way.
>
> (Goonetilleke 1991: 106–7)

In 'The Poet', Jean Arasanayagam (of Burgher descent, and married to a Tamil) remarks sadly of contemporary Sri Lankan realities:

> Today it's the assassins who are the new messiahs
> Their voices herald salvation
> With a hail of bullets
>
> (1991: 42)

'Letters from Warzones Anywhere' reiterates the need for poetry to find a voice

> that demands
> Answers out of confusions on a journey
> Where the routes are changed, landmarks
> Altered or effaced, where a man sits down
> Ordered not to proceed, sits down and bleeds
> Slowly, from his bullet wound, to death.
>
> (2003: 30)

'The Nullur Quartet' tries to find such a language, in which penitents worshipping at the shrines of Skanda, where they address him in all 'his thousand names | Murugan, Kartikkeya | Arumugam' (106), cannot drown the cry of those who come with guns and grenades, 'in celebration | of the great festival of Death' (111):

> the shadow of long bodies shrunk in death
> the leeching sun has drunk their blood...
>
> (105)

The ruination of land and people is cause for stark lament:

> The empty hands that held nectar
> Like the cut halves of fruit
> Scraped clean by the teeth of famine.
>
> (117)

Michael Ondaatje (b. 1943, Sri Lanka/UK/Canada) is well known as a novelist. His career as poet began in 1967 with *The Dainty Monsters*. His fourteenth volume of poems—*Handwriting* (1998)—returns to the land of his birth in a personal 'archaeology' (4). He writes less as an orphan of the former Empire than as a cosmopolitan member of contemporary Canada, who looks for a relation of significance with the colonial island of his birth. The migratory self thus comes closer to its prehistory. The first section of the volume is pieced together from fragments of narrative about hiding and unearthing statues of the Buddha. In the remote past, these 'stone and bronze gods' (7) were buried by priests as acts of political expediency. The poet narrates their recovery as a form of allegory, an imaginative redressal of a time and place torn by racial violence. The hidden 'gestures of the Buddha' (7) offer hope in a scene marked by 'a black lake where water disappears', and 'the arc of the dagoba that echoes a mountain' (10).

The dagoba—a structure that houses the Buddha—is the structure of faith around which memory recovers an image of community: 'families below trees | around the heart of a fire' (18). Gemstones that were the eyes of a Buddha statue smuggled 'from temple to temple for five hundred years' (21) serve as metonymies of that faith. No recovery can afford to forget

> What we lost.
>
> The interior love poem
> the deeper levels of the self
> landscapes of daily life
>
> (24)

The list of what was lost includes the rule of courtesy, the art of the drum, the limits of betrayal, gestures between lovers, and many other acts that provided ancient Sri Lankan society with its rituals, like an Asian version of Hesiod's 'works and days' (25).

Ondaatje's poetic technique can be described as a method of establishing correspondences between inner and outer worlds. This method is widely recognized by poets from different cultures. A. K. Ramanujan called it the relation between *akam* and *puram* (Tamil words for inner and outer experience); Gerard Manley Hopkins (1844–89) used the term 'Inscape' to invoke a sense of the relation between uniqueness and pattern to objects of poetic contemplation; W. H. Auden called it '*paysage moralisé*' (the allegorical landscape); and Robert Frost described it as parallel concerns with outer and inner weather.

Ondaatje's second section, 'The Nine Sentiments', is a poetic meditation on 'Historical Illustrations on Rock and Book and Leaf' (31). Art and being are collated as 'the Sloka, the Pada, the secret Rasas | | the curved line of her shadow' (42). In the first section, the buried Buddha is unearthed; in the second, love is consecrated; in the third, the poet's persona seeks water from wells. We travel with the poet on his return flight to his first home, looking into past places and times, as if diving for water, 'Hypnotized by lyric' (48):

> The Last Sinhala word I lost
> was *vatura*.
> The word for water.
>
> (50)

The poet remembers his first ayah Rosalin. She becomes a figure for all that the migrant poet left behind before he found poetry. He muses: 'Who abandoned who I wonder now' (50). He offers a prose poem that meditates on the need for water, on how 'What I write will drift away. I will be able to understand the world only at arm's length.... It was water in an earlier life I could not take into my mouth when I was dying' (55–6).

Journeys—he invokes a belief—are inevitable for a child, since his first forty days are given over to 'dreams of previous lives' (60). A story is remembered in which a king asks his pregnant wife to keep in mind that when war breaks out, he and six others will make a journey. The wife falls asleep before his words are done. The poet admits, 'I no longer guess a future. | And do not know how we end | nor where' (63). The son in the story is now one of the seven who have crossed into enemy territory. He cannot remember how the journey ends. The poet reiterates, 'We do not know what happened' (66). His poem, meanwhile, voices a need to imagine what it cannot know. That is how 'desire became devotional' (70). *Handwriting* makes a poetic descent into a Buddhist purgatory:

> And though it is no longer there,
> the pillars once let you step
> to a higher room
> where there was worship lighter than air.
>
> (71)

In Ondaatje's short Odyssey for a postmodern age, acts of homecoming become acts of departure, what is recovered can be lost and recovered again, and we walk a twisted loop between longing and belonging.

Longing and belonging took a different turn in Pakistan, where writing in English met resistance from indigenous languages and the State. Traditionally, poets in Pakistan preferred Urdu and Persian to English. Muhammad Iqbal (1877–1938), for example, wrote with brilliance and passion in both. His long poem *Shikwa* (1911, Urdu for complaint) invokes Islam for having disseminated an idea of community that is specifically Muslim, and yet capable of sustaining ideals that can be described as universal. He is revered in Pakistan, but his lament on behalf of Islam voices the kind of religious zeal that continues to divide Pakistan and India today:

> Make abundant that rare commodity love, so that all may buy and sell,
> Convert to Islam India's millions who still in temples dwell.
> Long have we suffered, see how grief's blood flows drown the drain,
> From a heart pierced by the scalpel, hear this cry of pain.
>
> (1981: 54)

In contemporary Pakistan, English has to reckon with the prevalence of Punjabi, Sindhi, Baluchi, and Pashto, each with roots in orality, and the underlying influence of an older imperial language, Persian. Alamgir Hashmi notes that in Pakistan 'Prior to 1947 the quantity of creative writing in English by Muslims was minimal, though by no means negligible' (1996: 110). The Delhi-born bilingual Ahmed Ali (1908–94), better known for his novel *Twilight in Delhi* (1940), published a volume of poems called *The Purple Gold Mountain* (1960), which evokes the traumatic effects of Partition in a style influenced by the spare elegance of Chinese verse comparable to the translations of Arthur Waley (1889–1966, UK). Later poets, writing in the 1970s, were more willing to relate style to contemporary reality, chiefly after the example of Taufiq Rafat (1927–98). The poise of his verse is matched by compassion for those who suffer or meet defeat, as in 'The Kingfisher', which ends:

> But what about tomorrow? Will they hiss
> And boo from the sidelines
> As you find, pause, fold, and dip towards
> The horror of your first miss?
>
> (Omar *et al.* 1975: 18)

In 'Air Raid', Maki Kureshi (1927–95), the first woman to write poetry in English from Pakistan, alludes to one of several wars fought with India since independence:

> . . . if morning breaks with chrysanthemums
> we know how it will end.
> We must black-out the sun and hide.
> Let the guns, our spokesmen, shatter the birds;
> Let the bombs explode
> Our childish stories of compassion;
> Sit blind and plug our ears.
>
> (Omar *et al.* 1975: 32)

Pakistani poetry in English underwent a kind of renaissance in the 1990s, after almost two decades of relative indifference from publishers and disapproval of English as a non-Islamic language by the State. Pakistani poets published overseas, as in the case of Hashmi, and Kamal Daud's *A Remote Beginning* (1985). More recent work from Pakistan includes Waqas Ahmad Khwaja's *Miriam's Lament* (1992), Athar Tahir's *Just Beyond the Physical* (1991), and *Certain Season* (2000). In 1997, celebrating fifty years of independence, Oxford University Press in Karachi published a number of selections that have reinforced this change: apart from *Taufiq Rafat: A Selection* and Maki Kureshi's *The Far Thing*, new titles included Adrian A. Hussain's *Desert Album* and Salman Tarik Kureshi's *The Landscapes of the Mind.* In *Baramasa: Seasons of Rural Life* (2002), Ghulam Fariduddin Riaz celebrates the Punjab and its agricultural cycle. The rural truth affirmed by Thomas Hardy's 'In Time of the Breaking of Nations' is reiterated from the Punjab (the province of five rivers), whose history of survival counts many invaders and colonizers, where

> The Hun, the Mongol, the Greek,
> The Persian, the Afghan, the Scythian
> Have all triumphed briefly
> In our sun, have been washed
> Inside and out by the five waters.
>
> (13)

The most striking verse in English from Pakistan comes from Kamal Daud (1935–87), remarkable for its surreal imagery, and the economy of means with which he manages to be suggestive without being tied down to mundane detail. Quick, intense images are his forte: 'a ruptured pool | in which sunlight | licks its own salt-whiteness' (1997: 17, 'A Ruined Monastery'); 'Crows are eating carnations of blood' (21, 'Barbaric Flags, Flying'); 'Petalled laughter, the pure, rib-breaking | misery of other people's needs' (35, 'The Street of Nightingales'); 'So many died | that they had to be buried | standing up' (43, 'The Golden Oriole'). In 'But the lines remain', a young mountain woman is described as gathering dry twigs against an impending storm:

> One scorpion for each eyelid—
> a layer of dust
> under the tongue.
> Stay away from the window.
>
> (3)

Compressed images make the elliptical transitions arresting, as in 'An ancient Indian coin':

> Look, the Indus is choked with stars
> and the glaciers are beginning to melt.
> I try to calm myself
> But my tongue is smothered
> By its own thickness.
>
> (16)

'A Remote Beginning' asks, 'Where will I find | My true inheritance?', and answers the question with the startling reply, 'In the mad calligraphy of trees | or a clear plunge into | the pool of many betrayals?' (19).

Modern poetry in English from Bangladesh (formerly East Pakistan) had its origins in undivided India, with *Essays in Verse* (1937) by the diplomat and art-historian Shahid Suhrawady (1890–1965). Later writing in English from Bangladesh has been meagre and intermittent in comparison with the output in Bangla. Translations of Bangla verse into English, such as Pritish Nandy and Tambimuttu's *Poems from Bangla Desh* (1972), are variable in their interest. Razia Khan Amin and Halima Khatun published poems in English during the 1970s. The former is now better known for her work in Bangla. The English poems of Kaiser Haq remain the exception, from *Starting Lines* (1978) to *The Logopathic Reviewer's Song* (2002).

3.3 Southeast Asia

> The writers inhabited two cultures. Although the first generation were—with few exceptions—students of English literature, they had deep roots in their own cultural universals.
>
> Edwin Thumboo, 'Strands In The Labels—Innovation and Continuity in English Studies: A View from Singapore'

The strategically located ports of Singapore and Hong Kong differed from Britain's other Asian colonies in being sparsely populated at the onset of colonization. They grew rapidly in population and economic resources through trade. The system of indentured labour introduced by the British after the formal abolition of slavery in the 1830s shifted sizeable ethnic communities from the neighbouring regions, including India, to the Malay Peninsula and to islands in the Indian and Pacific oceans. For a long period of their histories, such mixed societies remained more preoccupied with trade and profit than cultural self-representation.

The fate of English in Malaysia is addressed in Chapter 9, through a case study devoted to Ee Tiang Hong. In Singapore after the split from Malaysia, state policy ensured that English acquired a strong local base. Its role as link language prevailed over the use of Mandarin, Malay, and Tamil. Earlier than Hong Kong, and unlike the Philippines, where writing in English is the consequence of American rather than British colonialism, Singapore developed an interest in using English for creative purposes during the late 1940s and early 1950s. Undergraduate publications inspired by a British-style university education were drawn concurrently to cultural nationalism and the adaptation of twentieth century poetic models—from Yeats to Auden—to local conditions.

Early poetry from Singapore also experimented briefly with amalgamating local expressions from Malay and Chinese into English: the result was called 'Engmalchin', that is, 'Eng(lish)-mal(ay)-chin(ese)'. 'Ahmad', from Wang Gungwu's *Pulse* (1950), the first volume of poetry in English to be published from Singapore, provides an example of this portmanteau effect:

> Only yesterday his brother said,
> 'Can get lagi satu wife lah!'
>
> (Brewster 1989: 4)

This experiment was soon abandoned, though it served as the ancestor for subsequent attempts to incorporate Singlish (Singapore English) into verse. As 'hawker-centre' demotic, Singlish is tolerated rather than supported by the State and its educational apparatus. When poets incorporate Singlish idioms or phrases into international English, the effect tends to sound satirical, self-deprecatory, or self-conscious. Many eschew it altogether. Given the success of Creoles and local versions of English elsewhere, this is a pity, and can be accounted for as a form of literary caution or diffidence.

Arthur Yap (b. 1943) is one of the few whose occasional use of Singlish shows willingness to shed this diffidence. For the most part, his style blurs the distinction between originality and eccentricity in an unusually rewarding fashion. The personal voice he developed during the 1970s and '80s uses a bookish version of Standard English, marked by elliptical irony and a dry manner that can modulate easily into a more casual syntax and diction. This is how 'on reading a current bestseller' opens:

> the naming of parts, never direct,
> is nevertheless carefully alluded to. the lovers,
> anatomised, have their parts, if not their roles,
> a paragraph's a huff,
> a page a pant.
> (who was it ran a mile under 4 minutes?)
>
> (2000: 49)

A handful of Yap's poems ventriloquize Singlish voices with economy and precision. His mimicry retains a broad human sympathy for its subjects, managing to keep representation distinct from satire. '2 mothers in a hdb playground' begins:

> ah beng is so smart,
> already he can watch tv & know the whole story.
> your kim cheong is also quite smart,
> what boy is he in the exam?
> this playground is not too bad, but I'm so always
> worried, car here, car there.
>
> (2000: 101)

Neighbourliness and competitive rivalry were rarely dramatized in Singapore with such tongue-in-cheek control:

we also got new furniture, bought from diethelm.
the sofa is so soft, I dare not sit. They all
sit like don't want to get up, so expensive.
nearly two thousand dollars, sure must be good.

(2000: 102)

Yap at his best excels at projecting a voice that is uniquely personal, but capable of absorbing Singlish into the dramatization of a wide range of local sensibilities and speech habits. In recent years, younger poets have shown willingness to move beyond the lyric mode to the dramatic monologue, as in *broken by the rain* (2003) by Felix Cheong (b. 1965).

Singapore poetry engages in an obsessive debate between the private and the public dimensions of social change, a secular version of an ongoing dialogue between poetry and the body politic. This debate can be illustrated briefly from poets of three generations. Their work reveals anxiety that the hard won achievements of their modern, efficient, and prosperous island might be chimerical, fragile, or vulnerable. Edwin Thumboo (b. 1933), whose career parallels the history of English poetry in Singapore, adopts the persona of a friend to the post-independence nation. His poems emphasize the need for individuals to build bonds with one another, and to participate in the collective will to community and nation. His writing is informed by an awareness of literary developments in other parts of the formerly colonized world, and the gap separating political independence from cultural maturity, in Singapore and Asia. His private and public voices come together in the search for new symbols adapted from old worlds for the new nation. Thus, in 'Ulysses by the Merlion', the Ulysses from the twenty-sixth canto of Dante's *Inferno* becomes one with Tennyson's Ulysses, a patron-figure invoked by migrant voyagers settling this tiny island, where they hope to put an end to displacement:

Peoples settled here,
Brought to this island
The bounty of these seas,
Built towers topless as Ilium's.

They make, they serve,
They buy, they sell.

Despite unequal ways,
Together they mutate,

Explore the edges of harmony,
Search for a centre . . .

(1993: 80–1)

Such myth-making has met with local, gendered, intertextual resistance. Thumboo's poem was published in 1979. In 1997, Lee Tzu Pheng (b. 1946) responded with 'The Merlion to Ulysses'. The Eurocentric male wanderer of Thumboo's poem is interrogated quizzically by Lee's Merlion—a local mythical beast, half lion, half sea monster—which she treats as an emblem for Singapore's pragmatic materialism:

what do your exploits avail you?
You think I belong
to that misbegotten crew
that urged your malingering?
I am none of that ilk!
I am the instant brainchild
of a practical people,
for whom the likes of you
spell decadence, instability and dreams.
Newly arrived you have already outstayed
your welcome.

(1997: 8–9)

Later poets have continued to meditate on the costs, paid for in daily living, of a prosperity and stability that is the envy of many postcolonial nations. Yap notes with wry ambivalence that, in a city committed to perpetual upgrading, 'nothing much will be missed | eyes not tradition tell you this' (2000: 16). Confronted by incessant change, he titles a poem 'there is no future in nostalgia', and follows the title with a verse line that reverses the syntax: '& certainly no nostalgia in the future' (2000: 59). Sardonicism elides protest, matter-of-factness restrains elegy. Other poets show greater willingness to be placated. Robert Yeo (b. 1940) acknowledges, in 'Raffles Shakes His Head', that writers are inclined to worry about a life in which we are used to 'Air-con for sea breeze' and 'Daily rituals to placate | Our new Goddess of Wealth' (146). As in the days when there was war in Vietnam, they move back from what the poem 'Gesture' calls 'further exercises in futility' (1999: 137). For a Singaporean, at any rate, 'Home, I Suppose' declares with disarming reluctance:

> ... it feels good to be
> Able to come back to
> A still rather chaste
> Absolutely safe
> Absurdly clean
> Incredibly green
> Familiar and cosy
> Home.
>
> (1999: 134)

Kirpal Singh (b. 1949) is more astringent in his account of the link between remembered friendships and the dream of community in the poem 'At Lake Balaton':

> You cautioned me against being frank
> Ours, you said, was not a society
> Tolerant of robust, opposing views
> We prefer, you advised,
> More public agreement, less public argument
>
> (2004: 186)

The notion that Singapore's modern success is paid for by certain kinds of amnesia is a theme taken up aggressively by Alfian Sa'at. 'Singapore You Are Not My Country' declares, 'Singapore you have a name on a map but no maps to your name' (1998: 41). A more recent work, 'X (The Counterfeit Poem)', makes a similar point through verbal collage:

> The poem speaks too plainly and it disturbs you.
> How about a few of these then: 'That which exists
> Between two words is not a vacuum but friction:
> This is the meaning of meaning'. Or 'Memory is not
> Threatened by forgetfulness, but by memory itself'.
>
> (2001: 82)

Roy Harvey Pearce began his account of *The Continuity of American Poetry* (1961) with the interesting paradox that 'the power of American poetry from the beginning has derived from the poet's inability, or refusal, at some depth of consciousness wholly to accept his culture's system of values' (1987: 5). Poets in Singapore seem tied, involuntarily, to a similar position in relation to the life of their country.

Among Britain's Asian colonies, Hong Kong was the slowest to muster interest in writing English poetry. Shirley Lim, who taught there briefly, describes the Hong Kong educational system as particularly 'utilitarian' (Bolton 2002: 266). English served as the language of colonial administration and international trade, but it never displaced the dominance of Cantonese among the Chinese majority. Interest in English poetry remained the narrow preserve of expatriates and bilingual academics, from Edmund Blunden in the 1950s to Lim and others like Peter Stambler (b. 1944, USA) half a century later. As often as not, the young writer using English in Hong Kong is a would-be immigrant to the West. Bilingual writing has done better with the Cantonese poems of Leung Ping-kwan (b. 1948) and Laurence Wong Kwok-pun (b. 1946).

Leung's *Foodscape* (1997) shows how the social practices and rituals that surround, or mediate between, food and its social consumption become ways of inscribing culinary exchanges into narratives of cultural identity. In 'Tea-coffee', sociality and hybridization are measured by tea ceremonies: 'Tea fragrant and strong, made from | Five different blends' (Bolton 2002: 202). The effects of migration are felt through the new vegetable names that slip into the language. The mercantilism that created Hong Kong is transmuted into the specificity of touch, taste, and smell. Rey Chow describes Wong's poetics as informed by 'an ethics of consumption': 'Rather than modalities of glamour, excess, extravagance, and waste—modalities normally associated with (Hong Kong's) materialism and consumerism—he teaches us ways of discovering treasures in the plain, the modest, and the prosaic' (Leung 2002: 14).

Louise Ho, who teaches in Hong Kong and lived for a period in Australia, concedes that 'Hong Kong writing in English has not yet reached a critical mass whereby it can claim nomenclature and locality' (Bolton 2002: 176). Another academic-poet, Agnes Lam, admits that a narrow definition of Hong Kong poetry currently produces only a handful of names (188–9). Recent volumes by Ho and Lam give signs of a new beginning. In 'New Year's Eve, 1989', Ho attempts to do what her literary heroes—Marvell, Dryden and Yeats—did for their time and place, 'record the events of the sword':

> But think, my friend, think: China never
> Promised a tea party, or cakes

For the masses. It is we,
Who, riding on the crest of a long hope,
Became euphoric, and forgot
The rock bottom of a totalitarian state.

(1997: 23)

This is bracing, and prosaic (in more than one sense, possessing what Ezra Pound once described as the virtues of good prose). Hong Kong changed its status as colony in 1997. Its absorption into a huge nation, with a very different history of political change and economic development, did not go through the postcolonial experience shared by other ex-colonies. Ho's 'Island' reflects on this uniqueness:

We are a floating island
[...]
We shall be
A city with a country
An international city becoming national

(1997: 61)

As witnessed by poetry, Hong Kong worries over its ambivalent postcolonial relation to mainland China. Neither economic success nor pragmatism allied to the pleasures of consumerism quite reassures the poets of Singapore and Hong Kong that the path to globalized modernity also leads to poetic voice and authority. Their goal is to make poetry secure against the need for such reassurance.

4
The Caribbean

Overview

The chief feature of Caribbean societies is their extreme heterogeneity, which is the product of several centuries of slavery and indentured labour organized into plantation colonies in order to generate profit for Europeans. The contemporary Caribbean is also notable for a restless energy that domesticates language to local rhythms and intonations, while propelling many of its writers into diasporic movement from the homes to which their ancestors were transplanted. Caribbean plurality partakes equally of the exuberant and the troubled. Its logic of self-discovery is driven by a powerful sense of collective displacement.

4.1 Colonization and hybridity

> In the vast Atlantic
> The sun's eye blazes over the edge of ocean
> And watches the islands in a great bow curving
> From Florida down to the South American coast.
>
> A. J. S. Seymour, 'For Christopher Columbus'

Derek Walcott describes the Caribbean archipelago, in 'Homage to Gregorias', as 'a broken root, | divided among tribes' (1986: 196). To Antonio Benítez-Rojo (1992), it is a 'repeating island' characterized by a fractal diversity that is never far from entropy or chaos. Grace Nichols visualizes the region as

these blue mountain islands
these fire flying islands
these Carib bean
Arawak an
islands
fertile
with brutality

(1983: 31)

From Canada, Afua Cooper's 'Christopher Columbus' responds with a similar sentiment to the memory of a public monument: 'I look at the statue | its shadow covers the sun | and all around me are the spirits of dead Arawaks' (Wallace 1990: 42). The Caribbean basin is more water than islands. The Francophone writer Édouard Glissant (b. 1928, Martinique) describes it as 'a sea that explodes the scattered lands into an arc' (1997: 33). In 1492, this arc became the arena for the first sustained encounter between Europe and the Americas, the momentous outcome of the mistaken idea that travelling westwards from Europe would circumnavigate the globe and lead to the East Indies. The Spanish discovery of the Americas became part of an Iberian expansion that saw Spain expel the Moors and Jews, and sent the Portuguese round the Cape of Good Hope in search of a sea-route to the Indian Ocean.

By 1521 the Spaniards had demolished the Aztec Empire of Mexico, at a time when, as Dennis Walder remarks, 'the Aztec capital Tenochtitlan (later Mexico City) was five times larger than Madrid' (1992: 15). Within three decades of the arrival of Columbus in the 'New World', the European appetite for gold and conquest, combined with an incredible capacity for brutality, decimated the indigenous peoples of the Caribbean: the Ciboney (Cuba and the Bahamas), the Arawak (the Greater Antilles), and the Caribs (the Lesser Antilles and the adjoining mainland). Eric Roach (1915–74, Trinidad) evokes that extermination in 'Carib and Arawak':

Bright was their blood and bitter
Upon Spanish steel.
On the armouries of Aragon,
On the blue lined blades of Seville.

(1992: 40)

Tzvetan Todorov estimates that the population of the Americas in 1500 was about 80 million: 'By the middle of the sixteenth century, out of these 80 million, there remain ten'. Within three decades, Mexico was reduced from 25 million to one million (1984: 133), making it the site of one of the worst genocides in history. Other historians give lower figures, but the essential point made by Walcott, in the poem 'Air', remains unchanged: 'they devoured | two minor yellow races, and half of a black' (1986: 113).

The 'New World' was subjugated through the force of European technologies, and a will to domination against which the indigenous peoples had few resources. The Europeans also brought with them a religion they propagated aggressively among those who survived conquest. Control of territory was followed by mining, agriculture, and trade. After 1634, the intensive cultivation of sugarcane by the Spanish in the Caribbean and by the Portuguese in Brazil led to an economy based on imported labour and a policy described by Kamau Brathwaite in *The Arrivants* as 'cutlass profit' (1973: 48). Slaves were shipped in steadily increasing numbers from various parts of West and Central Africa (stretching from the Senegal and Niger rivers in the north to Angola in the south). A very small portion reached North America; the majority was shared between the Caribbean and Brazil. The crops they toiled to produce and the mines they worked became major sources of wealth for Europe in the period from the sixteenth to the nineteenth centuries. In Eric Roach's 'Fugue for Federation' (1958), the transplanted slave accounts for why he was uprooted, with a retrospective knowledge paid for by his descendants:

> Frey Bartolomo
> Fetched me from the Congo
> Since the Arawak, soft and green
> As lilies, and the Carib wild
> As 'latcho' would not, could not
> Yoke, lift, dig, endure
> Nor suck sweet gold from ground
> In the tall and succulent cane.
>
> (1992: 130)

Grace Nichols dramatizes plantation culture through an unexpected but apt perspective in 'Sugar Cane', where the eye runs down the page to enact the upward movement of the cane:

> Slowly
> pain-

fully
sugar
cane
pushes
his
knotted
joints
upwards
[...]
comes
to learn
the
truth
about
himself
the crimes
committed
in his name

(1984: 58)

The Spanish and the Portuguese were followed into the Caribbean by the British, the French, and the Dutch. The British presence began with Barbados in 1627, and eventually spread to twenty-two islands, which became known as the British West Indies, chief among them Jamaica, Barbados, and Trinidad, along with British Guiana (now Guyana) and British Honduras (now Belize) on the South American mainland. From the seventeenth century, Portugal and Spain declined as colonial powers, and the Dutch concentrated on their possessions in the East Indies. The Spanish lost Jamaica to the British in 1655 and Trinidad in 1797, although they retained control over Cuba and Puerto Rico until the end of the nineteenth century. The British and the French retained control over their Caribbean colonies for longer periods.

English, French, and Spanish remain the primary languages of the region today. The influence of French and Spanish culture on their respective colonies differed in kind from the British influence. Laurence Breiner points out that 'from an early date the French and Spanish islands had established colonial cultures... Until very recently, the Anglophone territories had nothing to match the intellectual atmosphere of Port-au-Prince or Havana' (1998: 60). From the 1970s and '80s, North America provided alternatives to London or Paris as targets for migration. Merle Collins (b. 1950, Grenada/UK/USA) summarizes the point: 'In a post-Independence situation where neocolonial economies are very fragile, the strength of the U.S. economy remains a potent attraction' (1998: 121). In 'The Star-Apple Kingdom', Walcott is sharply apprehensive about 1970s neocolonialism:

> What was the Caribbean? A green pond mantling
> behind the Great House columns of Whitehall,
> behind the Greek facades of Washington,
> with bloated frogs squatting on lily ponds...
>
> (1986: 393)

Political independence came to the region in two waves: the first occurred in the early nineteenth century, bringing freedom to the colonies of France, Portugal, and Spain; the second occurred in the 1960s, bringing freedom to the British colonies. Haiti's violent and heroic path to freedom was commemorated as 'the only successful slave revolt in history' by C. L. R. James in *The Black Jacobins* (1938). The Francophone poet Aimé Césaire invoked its heroic struggle in *Notebook of a Return to the Native Land* (1939), alluding to the imprisonment and death in Paris of the revolutionary Toussaint L'Ouverture as 'a lonely man imprisoned in | whiteness' (1983: 47). Eric Roach invoked the figure as exemplary for the region in his elegy 'A Tear for Toussaint':

> Yet still with Toussaint's heart may islands hope
> And ships steer down the channel of his dream
> And climbers try his cliff path up the hill
> Between white courage and the black forbearance.
>
> (1992: 93)

The British ended the slave trade in 1807, and passed an Act of Abolition in 1833 (the French followed in 1848, the Spaniards in 1886). Roach speaks feelingly on behalf of the victims:

> The Slave Trade's buried
> But its eternal tares of scorn
> Breed in our barren soul,
> Batten on the black, despised blood.
>
> (1992: 130)

The journey from Africa to the Caribbean—the Middle Passage—went unchronicled in its time, at least from the point of view of the enslaved. The experience was chronicled largely from the side of the slavers. In 'Laventille', Walcott broods on that forgetting:

> The middle passage never guessed its end.
> This is the height of poverty
> for the desperate and black;
>
> climbing, we could look back
> with widening memory
> on the hot, corrugated-iron sea
> whose horrors we all
>
> shared.
>
> (1986: 86)

For Grace Nichols, in 'Eulogy', there is no reparation for what happened, only acts of remembrance:

> How can I eulogise
> their names?
> What dance of mourning
> can I make?
>
> (1983: 17)

The rhetorical question gets an imaginative answer in David Dabydeen's long poem 'Turner' (1994), which takes as its subject 'the shackling and drowning of Africans' in J. M. W. Turner's painting *Slave Ship* (1840, currently in the Museum of Fine Arts, Boston). Dabydeen (b. 1955) migrated to Britain from Guyana with his parents in 1969. His ancestors came to the Caribbean from India as indentured labourers, but his identification with the victims of the Atlantic slave trade stretches beyond any narrow question of personal ancestry. 'Turner' speaks on behalf of all those who made a forced and perilous journey westwards. It engages in an oppositional dialogue with two illustrious British representatives of the Romantic tradition in art. Turner's painting evokes a lurid splendour of sea, sky, and ship. It also includes a token of human tragedy in 'the submerged head of the African in the foreground' (1994: ix). This metonymic image equivocates between acknowledging and repressing the fate of sick slaves deliberately thrown overboard in order to claim their insurance value as goods lost at sea. John Ruskin celebrated Turner's painting as one of his noblest conceptions. He allowed esteem for sublimity to displace awareness of the tragic elements acknowledged by the painting. Dabydeen applies poetry to the task of fictive reparation: inventing names and histories for the drowned and forgotten souls minimally present in Turner's painting.

What Dabydeen approaches through painting and blank verse is tackled by Nourbese Philip through the practice of law and an enactment of the breakdown and reconstitution of language. Her long poem *Zong!* (forthcoming) reanimates the issues that came to court in London when the owners of a slave ship, the *Zong*, which set out with 470 slaves in 1781 from the west coast of Africa for Jamaica, claimed compensation for cargo lost at sea (that is, for slaves thrown overboard by the captain). Her poem adopts a variety of linguistic strategies at the levels of rhythm, syntax, and coherence to address that violence in retrospect, using the printed page to evoke the implications of what was drowned of humanity and justice in the case of 'Gregson v. Gilbert':

africa
is
the ground
is
the negroes

evidence is
sustenance is
support is
the law is
the ship is
the captain is
the crew is
perils is
the trial is
the rains is
the seas is
currents is
jamaica is
tobago is
the case is
murder is
justice is
the ground is
africa is

negroes

was

(Philip: *Zong!* #24)

No sooner did the British relinquish slavery than they found a new source of cheap labour in a system of indentured labour that enlisted recruits, chiefly from India, and in smaller numbers from China and elsewhere. Beginning in 1838, the poorest Indians from two regions, the Ganges plain in the North, and the southern city of Madras (now renamed Chennai), were encouraged, induced, and sometimes duped into migration on fixed-term contracts, a traffic that continued until 1917. Sasenarine Persaud (b. 1958, Guyana/Canada) evokes that experience in 'Spring, Toronto':

Rigged over the *Kaalaa Pani** (*Hindi: 'Black Water')
so the British Raj
could sweeten European teas

(2002: 28)

The system 'was characterized by fraud, deception, and kidnapping—the very practices widely associated with the transatlantic slave trade from which British entrepreneurs had profited for generations, and which Britain was now attempting, at great cost, to suppress' (Kale 1995: 75–6). In 'We have Survived', Arnold Itwaru (b. 1942, Guyana/Canada) evokes a powerful sense of 'a scatter of worlds and broken wishes' from the Indian Middle Crossing of 'Shiva's endless dance' (Dabydeen and Samaroo 1987: 292). So does Mahadai Das (b. 1954, Guyana), in 'They Came in Ships':

From across the seas, they came.
Britain, colonizing India, transporting her chains
From Chota Nagpur and the Ganges Plain.
[...]
They came in droves
like cattle
brown like cattle,
eyes limpid, like cattle.

(Dabydeen and Samaroo 1987: 288)

Most indentured 'coolies' did not return to their homeland; instead, they continued working in the colonies beyond the duration of their original contracts, often in circumstances no better than those of slaves, and for smaller wages. 'Despite grueling work, harsh conditions, racial prejudice, and political hostility', 'these communities survived to become a distinctive component of the cultural life not only of Guyana and Trinidad, where they are majorities, but of the whole Caribbean' (Balderston *et al.* 2000: 302). In 'Earth is Brown', Shana Yardan (b. 1942, Guyana) laments:

> For you cannot remember India.
> The passage of time
> has too long been trampled over
> to bear your wistful recollections,
> and you only know the name
> of the ship they brought you on
> because your daadi* told it to you. (*paternal grandmother)
>
> (Brown, S. 1984: 79)

The indentured labourer of Indian descent faced a double prejudice in the Caribbean. 'In the Heat', by Sasenarine Persaud, explains bitterly:

> I walk in the equatorial heat
> Of discriminations everyday
> I chew gum with blacks
> Who grind apartheid into
> Molar dust
> And practise it
>
> Here they are the white
>
> (1989: 33)

The estimated number of indentured labourers sent to the Caribbean from India alone—over 400,000 (Kale 1995: 73)—gives an indication of the size of the 'plural societies' created by indenture:

> Societies with sharp ethnic divisions and very little cohesion or sense of unity to transcend their divisions. In such a society the different elements of the population largely keep apart from one another and do not recognize a common identity... At the top was a small white elite... Below the whites and separate from them and from one another were layers of immigrant peoples.
>
> (Marshall 1996: 287)

4.2 Poetry and place

too trapped by grievous memory to escape history.

David Dabydeen, 'Turner'

The literary cultures of the Caribbean islands developed along relatively independent lines based on the linguistic communities created by the colonial languages. These lines ran parallel in three ways. The peoples of the region suffered an abiding sense of displacement, which Édouard Glissant describes as follows: 'The conquered or visited peoples are thus forced into a long and painful quest after an identity whose first task will be opposition to the denaturing process introduced by the conquerors' (1997: 17). In varying degrees, his description is applicable to all postcolonial societies. Second, the sense of displacement found expression in a compulsion to set off on real and symbolic journeys, in a constant and restless search for a home that might appease displacement. This motif is explored further in Chapter 9. Third, slavery 'deterritorialized' African languages, and set up a confrontation between 'the power of the written word and the impulses of orality' (1997: 5).

The Caribbean was colonized for a longer period than Asia or Africa, yet its literary beginnings were slower. The economy of the region was primarily organized for plantation labour. 'Meditation on Yellow', by Olive Senior, adds up a bill of complaints for the exploitation suffered by slaves and their descendants:

I've been slaving in the cane rows
for your sugar
I've been ripening coffee beans
for your morning break
I've been dallying on the docks
loading your bananas...

(1994: 14)

During the colonial period, literacy remained the privilege of a tiny minority, and the pursuit of leisure, reading, and the arts depended on thin soil for sustenance. That is why a fictional islander like Robinson Crusoe acquires a symbolic value for Walcott in 'Crusoe's Journal':

...from this house
that faces nothing but the sea, his journals
assume a household use;
we learn to shape from them, where nothing was
the language of a race...

(1986: 94)

A sense of collective self-confidence did not develop in West Indian poetry until after World War II. The verse in English from the long colonial period was largely written by British poets, and it followed the conventions of Britain. It retains the limited antiquarian interest of European pastoral models applied to new topographies without feeling the need to change the style to fit new materials, from the anonymous *Whole Proceedings of Captain Dennis's Expedition* (Jamaica, 1718) to M. J. Chapman's pro-slavery poem *Barbadoes* (1833), published—ironically—in the year slavery was abolished. In his lively essay 'On Not Being Milton: Nigger Talk in Britain Today', David Dabydeen describes the conventions of colonial poetry as 'the wrapping of stark experiences in a napkin of poetic diction' (1989: 122).

The earliest known poem in a European language by a black West Indian is Francis Williams's Latin 'Ode to Governor Haldane' (1759). Williams (1702–70) was the product of an experiment to establish that 'nurture' in England could transcend 'nature' in Jamaica, which placed him in a predicament not unlike that of the American slave poet Phillis Wheatley (1753–84). The earliest native verse about the life of plantation workers, the anonymous *Jamaica: a Poem in Three Parts* (1776), was published as the time for emancipation drew near. However, as noted by Louis James, it was 'not until William Hosack's *The Isle of Streams; or the Jamaican Hermit and other Poems* (1876)... that black people became acknowledged as the inhabitants of the landscape rather than as decoration' (1999: 13). The first local newspaper began publication from Jamaica, the largest of the British West Indies, in 1834, and the first literary magazine began publication from Jamaica in 1883.

The first signs of local poetic ambition appeared towards the end of the nineteenth century in Egbert Martin's *Poetical Works* (1883) and Tom Redcam's *Jamaica* (1889). Redcam (Thomas Henry MacDermot) showed commitment to the cause of black people, and was declared Jamaica's first poet laureate, posthumously, in 1933. Redcam's interest in local history was followed from Trinidad by Canon Nelson

Huggins's long poem *Hiroona* (1930), which celebrated the rebellion of the St Vincent Caribs against the British in 1795. Both poets are distinguished more by their politics than by their mastery over verse. The literary situation in Jamaica was to remain uninspiring up to the early decades of the twentieth century (except for Claude McKay, of whom more below). While the Poetry League of Jamaica (formed in 1923) was content with minor variations on a genteel form of transplanted pastoralism, the poetry of Una Marson (1905–65, Jamaica/UK) and A. J. Seymour (1914–89, Guyana) was the first step out of this mode. Other regional literary activity of note included J. E. C. McFarlane's anthology, *Voices from Summerland* (Jamaica 1929), and N. E. Cameron's more ambitious *Guyanese Poetry 1831–1931* (1931).

From 1942, the monthly journal *Bim* began publication from Barbados, largely under the editorship of Frank Collymore, who mentored many Caribbean writers and brought their work a regional audience through the journal. It was followed from Jamaica in 1943 by *Focus*, edited by Edna Manley, whose husband Norman Manley later became the first Prime Minister of Jamaica. In 1945, *Kyk-over-al* began publication from Guyana under the editorship of Seymour. These journals had small readerships, but they played a pioneering role in fostering interest in poetry among young writers.

From 1942 to 1959, the BBC broadcast a monthly radio magazine program called 'Caribbean Voices', prepared first by Marson and later by Henry Swanzy. David Dabydeen claims, 'it is doubtful whether it made any significant impact on promoting Caribbean writing among a British readership' (2000: 70). Regardless, the prestige conferred on writers from the colonies by a metropolitan institution like the BBC acted as a very effective stimulant for writers in the Caribbean and those who had migrated to Britain. From Guyana, Seymour launched a Miniature Poet Series (1951–55), which published 'several individual collections by poets in pamphlet or monograph form' (Brown, L. W. 1984: 80).

The West Indians had been loyal members of the British Empire during World War I. The end of World War II left many dissatisfied with home conditions. Labour openings in low-income service sectors in Britain contributed to a wave of emigration. This included authors such as Sam Selvon, George Lamming, V. S. Naipaul, and Andrew Salkey, who abandoned the isolation and meagre prospects of their home islands for the opportunities of the metropolis, where their fiction continued to quarry the culture of the societies they left behind. The period also saw the establishment of the University of the West Indies in Jamaica (1949). Other campuses were to follow in Trinidad, Barbados, and Guyana.

Caribbean fiction achieved widespread international recognition with works such as George Lamming's *In the Castle of My Skin* (1953), Wilson Harris's *Palace of the Peacock* (1960), and V. S. Naipaul's *A House for Mr. Biswas* (1961). Martin Carter suffered political imprisonment in Guyana and published *Poems of Resistance* (1954). 'I Come From The Nigger Yard' reveals a tone of anger and bitterness that does not find many counterparts in later Caribbean poetry:

> I come from the nigger yard of yesterday
> leaping from the oppressor's hate
> and the scorn of myself.
>
> (1999: 97)

Poets from the Caribbean made their reputations more slowly than did the novelists. Derek Walcott began writing in the late forties. His first major collection, *In a Green Night*, was published in 1962. In 1966, the Caribbean Artists movement was initiated in London by Kamau Brathwaite, Andrew Salkey, and others. After that, the link between West Indian writing and the West Indian presence in Britain became part of a single complex narrative. Brathwaite's first verse trilogy (*Rites of Passage, Masks, Islands*) was published from 1967 to 1969, at about the time that the US Black Power movement made its impact in the West Indies. Walcott and Brathwaite became the two major poetic voices of West Indian writing in verse, and we shall explore the salient features of their writing through the motif of the voyage in Chapter 9.

Caribbean writing is often preoccupied by the sense that it has to react to the involuntary displacement suffered by enslaved or indentured ancestors. Lelawattee Manoo-Rahming (Trinidad/the Bahamas) remembers her great-great grandmother in 'Ode to My Unknown Great-Great Grandmother' as 'the first | to belong nowhere | Born on the wide Kala Pani | between Calcutta and Port-of-Spain' (2000: 12). Such writing is drawn to a nostalgia for origins that is all the more powerful for being unavailing. The poets of the Negritude movement made an ideology out of this longing in the 1930s and 40s. They wrote on behalf of a Black Diaspora that could recuperate the feeling of severance from an ancestral homeland. They wished to redress an

African psyche brutalized by colonialism, and recover for the diasporic African the self-respect lost through slavery: 'The thrust of Negritude among Caribbean intellectuals was a response perhaps to the need, by relating to a common origin, to rediscover unity (equilibrium) beyond dispersion' (Glissant 1989: 5).

Their cause was plangent. Their remedy—the revalorization of unified African identity—proved controversial among black writers. Brathwaite's later work is sympathetic to their sentiment, but Fanon rejected nostalgia as 'the great black mirage', Walcott dismissed it as an inversion of the desire to be like the colonizer, 'a longing to become black' (Bongie 1998: 50), and Glissant's 'Aesthetics of rupture and connection' (1997: 151) rejects nostalgia as a false option. 'The Jaguar and the Theorist of Negritude', by Abdhur Rahman Slade Hopkinson (1934–93, Guyana/Canada), is acidic about the debate:

> In the middle of an important street
> An inventor of the black man's soul lies dead.
> His fingers clutch neither machete nor bomb,
> But an anguished book he wrote—published in England.
>
> (1992: 33–4)

The Caribbean suffered during the Great Depression of the 1930s, and economic difficulties led to labour unrest and the first stirrings of nationalism. The political map of the British territories in the Caribbean did not change until the formation of the West Indies Federation in 1958. The Federation split up soon afterwards, and a series of islands became independent over the next two decades, starting with Trinidad and Tobago in 1962. As in other former colonies, independence was an equivocal blessing. Louise Bennett (b. 1919, Jamaica/Canada) treats the new development with charming irony in 'Independance':

> Independance wid a vengeance!
> Independance raising Cain!
> Jamaica start growing a beard, ah hope
> We chin can stan de strain!
>
> (Burnett 1986: 35)

'Tell Me Again' by Paul Keens-Douglas (b. 1942, Jamaica) applies a milder technique to deflate the clichés that surround the old ways of the new nations of the region:

Tell me again
how oil don't spoil,
how we have plenty of dollars
but no sense,
an how money is no problem
but de problem is no money,
tell me again.

(Burnett 1986: 56–70)

Satire notwithstanding, very little of the poetry from the English-speaking Caribbean shows a direct engagement with politics of the kind that animated the early poems of Martin Carter. A generation later, Merle Collins, in her early work, sustains the tension between ideological commitment and an alert use of language and form, as in the poem 'Rock-Stone Dance', in which the 1979 American invasion of her home island of Grenada is represented with power and precision, adapting the rhythm and syntax of nursery rhyme to a very adult education:

I watched
[...]
the ships that came
to scorn my tears
to mock our dreams
to launch the planes
that dropped the bombs
that ripped the walls
that raped the land
that burnt the earth
that crushed the dreams
that we built

(1985: 85)

The challenge of achieving poetic identity in the Caribbean context focused on resolving the tension between literary and popular cultures, colonial models and local alternatives, indigenous practices and those derived from African or American sources, and the dialectical relation between the cultures of writing and voice. And what this relation affirms, repeatedly, is the need to remember a huge and hurtful forgetting. Collins's 'A Dream' begins: 'I remember the urgency | of the poem that I dreamt', and ends:

I remember the doubt
I remember the sadness
I remember the force

I remember the poem, you see
is just the words I forget

(Kay *et al.* 1996: 108)

Amidst the bitterness and anger, the Ghanaian trickster figure Anansi (also spelt Anancy) provides many Caribbean poets with a more sanguine resource. The figure represents a spider-emblem, which animates the spirit of protest and tongue-in-cheek mischief, 'calm and cunning as a madman' (Nichols 1983: 65). In *The Tempest*, Shakespeare invented the character of Caliban (an anagram for 'cannibal'), as an allusion to the people populating the Caribbean islands during Europe's first encounter with the 'New World'. The writers of the Caribbean often see themselves as the progeny of Caliban, using the colonizing Prospero's language to express a self that is beset by hatred and self-loathing: 'You taught me language, and my profit on't | Is, I know how to curse' (I. ii). In the context of the need to resist the colonizer's language, Jahan Ramazani observes, 'If Caliban allegorizes the anti-imperial resistance of the West Indian writer, Anancy more accurately suggests the playful and polymorphous, all-ironicizing folk-wit of a Creole poet like Bennett' (2001: 108).

4.3 **Poetry as performance: Caribbean orality**

'dialect cool | but not for school'

Paul Keens-Douglas, 'Tell Me Again'

In the Caribbean, as elsewhere, colonial print-culture eventually displaced orality. Oral forms of language preserved and transmitted history, legend, and myth. They served multiple functions, at once expressive, affective, communicative, didactic, and cognitive, giving shape to song, incantation, and ritual, and embodying the beliefs, values, and wisdom of a community. These mnemonic forms held the articulacy central to poetry close to the imaginative, speculative, and regulative reason of communal life by anchoring language in speech, and speech in the dramatic and performative aspects of interpersonal relations.

The Jamaican Michael Smith (1954–83) provides a candid account of his predilection for oral performance: 'a whole heap of we can't read and write, you know. And we seem to rally round the spoken word very nice' (Markham 1995: 277). In the Caribbean, colonialism brought different races and language-communities into contact with one another. These situations resulted in the development of pidgins. Jennifer Jenkins explains that 'A pidgin arises in the first place to fulfill restricted communication needs between people who do not share a common language' (2003: 10). Pidgins developed into Creoles when the descendants of slaves and indentured labourers lived and worked together over successive generations.

Creoles were in use in the Caribbean for a long time before they were used in poetry. Louise Bennett recollects, 'When I was a child, each day contained a poem of folk songs, folk stories, street cries, legends, proverbs, riddles' (Pearn 1985: iii). Popular materials and practices were transmitted from one generation to the next through songs, proverbs, riddles, and folk tales. During the colonial era, the oral traditions lacked respectability. Bennett recollects, 'They had no social status... In fact, they were to be deplored and despised as coming from the offspring of slaves who were illiterate, uncultured, and downright stupid' (iii).

When orature finally made its impact as performance and in print, it gave literary representation to a wide range of social types, while also enabling writers to achieve new forms of self-individuation. Through Creoles, orality was able to resist, infiltrate, subvert, and modify the norms of Standard English. It challenged the assumption that in creating works of art, the standard form of a European language was the only way to access either the local or the universal.

The Jamaican Claude McKay (1889–1940) was among the earliest to use Creoles as the staple of individual poems. His *Songs of Jamaica* and *Constab Ballads* were published in 1912, the year he left Jamaica for New York, where he became the leading figure of the Harlem Renaissance, and championed the cause of the black races in verse and fiction. His first two volumes use both Standard and dialect registers, although he later left out all work in dialect from his *Selected Poems.* McKay's two registers correspond in reverse to the stylistic split in the Afro-American poet Paul Dunbar (1872–1906), who wrote fluently in Standard English, then switched to stereotyped dialect.

Dunbar stuck to dialect once he realized that it made him popular, although he also felt that his adherence to a narrow register produced 'A jingle in a broken tongue' (Innes 1990: 17). In contrast, McKay settled on a persona based on literary English. His early use of dialect gave voice to a wide range of middle- and lower-class social types drawn from Jamaican society. The difference between the two registers can be illustrated briefly by comparing two passages, the first from 'My Native Land, My Home':

> Jamaica is de nigger's place,
> No mind whe' some declare;
> Although dem call we 'no-land race',
> I know we home is here.
>
> (Donnell and Welsh 1996: 64)

The second passage is taken from a sonnet published forty years later, titled 'Outcast':

> For the dim regions whence my fathers came
> My spirit, bondaged by the body, longs.
> [. . .]
> For I was born, far from my native clime,
> Under the white man's menace, out of time.
>
> (Donnell and Welsh 1996: 69)

Neither is successful, but the first is more vigorous, although its declaration of attachment to the Caribbean reads ironically, since the poet chose self-exile soon after writing it. Meanwhile, the lugubrious tone and literary affectation of his sonnet remains vulnerable to the kind of deflation administered by Louise Bennett's 'Back to Africa' to poetry that professes nostalgia for an ancestral Africa:

> What a debil of a bump-an-bore,
> Rig-jig an palam-pam
> Ef de whole worl start fi go back
> Whe dem great grampa come from!
>
> (Brown, S. 1984: 18)

At the social level, Creoles represented classes and individuals whose use of language was not accommodated in the norms of the genteel middle-class minority that benefited from colonial education. At the literary level, Creolization gave linguistic subcultures a place within a revised concept of literature. Brathwaite gave the phenomenon a name, 'nation language' (1984: 5), which, as Denise Narain points out, 'is not really pinpointing a distinctive language-use but *renaming* dialect as a way of *reclaiming* it from its low status categorization' (2002: 91). Poetry that learns to inhabit a Creole continuum with conviction dispels linguistic subservience, and creates new linguistic styles based on what Glissant calls a 'poetics of relation' (1996: 104–6).

Glissant's theoretical writing (*Caribbean Discourse*, 1981/1989, and *Poetics of Relation*, 1990/1996) distinguishes between 'voice-languages' (referring to the vertical authority of the European languages) and 'use-languages' (referring to the lateral solidarity between Creoles) in order to claim a unity that transcends linguistic diversity: 'There are communities of use-language that cross the barriers of voice-language. I feel closer to the writers of the English- or Spanish-speaking Caribbean (or, of course Creole-speaking) than to most writers of French' (1996: 214–15). He also calls for 'A conspiracy to conceal meaning' (1989: 125), arguing that the decolonizing function of Creoles requires freedom from the conventional norm of linguistic transparency. The idea of resistance thus leads him to the argument that a poetics of relation must also provide for the deliberate use of linguistic opacity. His fiction and verse practises what he preaches.

This call for resistance finds another analogue within European history. Brathwaite equates 'nation language' with Dante's preference for the Italian vernacular over the imperial Latin of thirteenth-century Europe (which is an echo of the claim made for McKay in the preface to *Songs of Jamaica* by Walter Jekyll in 1912). Each politicizes the linguistic register a poet might choose from the several resources at hand in his time and place. In *History of the Voice* (1984), Brathwaite provides an account of how Caribbean poetry was shaped by interactions between European languages and the oral cultures of the 'slaves and labourers, the servants who were brought in by the conquistadors' (5–6), and lived the 'forced poetics' of a 'prison language' (16). 'Nation language' brings 'the *submerged* area of that dialect which is . . . closely allied to the African aspect of the experience in the Caribbean' to the surface that is the poem (13). The influence of African orality on the cultures of the Caribbean becomes an even more complex resource when we consider the additional layering produced by the languages bought to the region from Asia.

In the Caribbean, creolization proved a more viable strategy than Negritude. Brathwaite's idea of Creole resistance focuses on breaking down the iambic rhythm, displacing it with the intonation and rhythms of the calypso. Here is Bongo Jerry in 'Sooner or Later':

So have-gots, have-nots,
trim-head, comb-locks, dread-knots,
find yourself, row your own boat,
'be ready for the day'
it's been a long time coming,
but a change is on the way.

(Brown, S. *et al.* 1989: 101)

In such writing, the poem is not the experience of an isolated individual reading a book; it is sounds shared as utterance with an audience who participates in the experience of poetry as community. 'I am no poet | no poet | I am just a voice | I echo de people's | thought | laughter | cry | sigh', declares Oku Onuora in 'No Poet' (Glaser and Pausch 1994: 5). Brathwaite distinguishes such linguistic self-assertion from the use of dialect by the self-exiled McKay. He argues that McKay was ambivalent about the linguistic evidence deposited in poetry by an ethnicity that he feared might hamper his aspiration to be read for his 'universality' (20). McKay was willing to forsake the natural rhythms of his birthplace since he aspired to a style that would be indistinguishable from its European models. For Brathwaite, McKay is betrayed by the speaking voice. In his performances and recordings, 'the' becomes 'de'. The involuntary habit can 'subtly erode' (22) the expectations created by his scrupulous adherence to the stress pattern of the iambic pentameter verse line.

In the 1920s, the Jamaican nationalist Marcus Garvey (1887–1940) called upon his fellow blacks to think of Africa as the home they might return to, with Ethiopia and its Emperor as the figurative or literal focus of that longing. His call appealed at a spiritual and popular level to an uprooted community whose daily life of miserable labour needed a focus for its hope of betterment. The community received a sign when Ras Tafari Makonnen was crowned Emperor Haile Selassie I of Ethiopia in 1930, the latest in a line of descent allegedly going back to the Biblical King Solomon. The Italian invasion of Abyssinia highlighted the plight of that African connection in the 1930s. In the ensuing decades, Rastafarianism became a way of life, and an intrinsic part of mid-twentieth-century Jamaican culture, acquiring an assortment of associations, from spirituality, dreadlocks, and marijuana, to a rejection of white or conventional values. In music, its influence found expression in reggae, whose rhythms began infiltrating poetry in the late 1950s, where they combined with other popular forms such as Trinidadian calypso, as in 'Bassman' by 'Mighty Shadow' (Trinidad):

Ah was planning to forget
calypso
And go and plant peas in
Tobago,
But I'm afraid,
Ah can't make the grade,
Cause every night I lie down
in my bed,
Ah hearing a bassman in meh
head.
Poom poom poom poom

(Brown, S. *et al.* 1989: 132)

Creole lent itself readily to the complaint, as in 'dis poem' by Mutabaruka (b. 1952, Jamaica):

dis poem
shall speak of the wretched sea
that washed ships to these shores
[...]
dis poem is vex about apartheid racism Nazism
the ku klux klan riots in brixton atlanta
jim jones
dis poem is revoltin against 1st world 2nd world
3rd world man made decision

(Donnell and Welsh 1996: 462)

Brathwaite sets the growth of a Caribbean tradition in English in the context of such assertions of popular culture. Its components include calypso from Trinidad, and jazz (both local and American). It came into its own in the 1960s and 1970s. To begin with, in a poet like John Figueroa (1921–99, Jamaica/UK), Standard English remains the '*Prosperian* element' (Brathwaite 1984: 38), as in 'Ignoring hurts', where it remains part of a debate about dialect without quite becoming an affirmation of 'nation language':

Watch dis pentameter ting, man.
Dat is white people play!
[. . .]
Like metronome, yu'd say,
But a black bwoy should play
Widout dem mechanical aids
Full of rydhm like all true spades.

(Figueroa, in Brathwaite 1984: 39)

A fuller expression of the potential of the 'riddimic aspect of Caribbean nation language' (34) arrives on the scene of writing and performance poetry with the Jamaican reggae/dub poets Oku Onuora, Michael Smith, and from Black Britain, Linton Kwesi Johnson. Mervyn Morris, in an interview with Pam Mordecai recollected hearing the term 'dub poetry' for the first time from Oku Onuora (then Orlando Wong) in 1979 (Glaser and Pausch 1994: 63). Morris cites several examples of the kind of relation between music and words of which dub poetry is an instance, including the Elizabethan songwriters, the Spanish poet Lorca, and Edith Sitwell in 1930s Britain.

Meanwhile, Johnson, in interviews dating from 1982 and 1986, recollected using the term 'dub poetry' in 1974 to describe DJs whose practice was to 'get a piece of instrumental music or a song with the lyrics taken out, and improvise spontaneous lyricism describing everyday happening and events' (Markham 1995: 256). He acknowledges learning a lot from the DJs, but distinguishes between the practice of poetry, even when performed (with or without accompanying music) and the art of the DJ. *Dread Beat An' Blood* was the title of his second book of poems and his first LP (1975/78). The first stanza of 'Di Great Insohreckshan' gives an idea of how rhythm and music contribute to his poetry:

it woz in April nineteen eighty-wan
doun inna di ghetto of Brixtan
dat di babylan dem cauz such a frickshan
dat it bring about a great insohreckshan
an it spread all owevah di naeshan
it woz a truly an histarical occayshan

(2002: 60)

Johnson's inspiration and themes have remained consistent throughout his career. Inspired by W. E. B. Dubois's *The Souls of*

Black Folks (1903), and determined to write about the circumstances of Black people living in Britain, he found that 'from the moment I began to write in the Jamaican language music entered the poetry. There was always a beat, or a bass line, going on at the back of my head with the words' (Markham 1995: 253). Fred D'Aguiar notes, in his Introduction to Johnson's *Selected Poems*, that the typical Johnson poem 'maintains a reggae rhythm and a regular iambic mostly tetrameter line-beat. More often than not his lines begin with a trochee and the poems sustain a rhyme scheme locked to a few rhyming sounds, same word sounds or word endings, like the ballad, the sestina or villanelle' (2002: xi).

From another direction, Don Drummond, the Jamaican jazz musician of the 1950s and '60s, is given credit by Brathwaite for bringing poetry in performance closer to '*ska*, the native sound at the yardway of the cultural revolution that would lead eventually to Bob Marley, reggae and The Harder They Come' (1984: 41). Here is a small example from 'Butta Pan Kulcha' by Mutabaruka (b. 1952, Jamaica):

mi walk de lane
inna sun and rain
mi nuh feel nuh pain
mi nuh ave nuh shame.

(Brown, S. *et al.* 1989: 116)

Other voices went on to consolidate and sustain the Caribbean connection with Harlem and New Orleans jazz, and with American poets like Langston Hughes (1902–67) and Imamu Baraka (b. 1934). Orality was reinforced by a number of popular musical forms in the Caribbean, which shaped the development of dub poetry during the 1970s. Gordon Rohlehr, the author of *Calypso and Society in pre-Independence Trinidad* (1990), offers a condensed and illuminating account of the significance of these cultural developments in *Voiceprint* (1989): 'The DJ became high priest in the cathedral of canned sound, fragmented discotheque image projections, broken lights, and youth seeking lost rituals amid the smoke of amnesia' (Brown, S. *et al.* 1989: 17). Christian Habekost identifies several features that play a prominent role in the performative aspect of dub poetry: rhythm, rhyming patterns, alliteration, repetition, onomatopoeia, and a highly individuated performance style that combines musicality with dramatic flair (1993: 91–8).

The Caribbean dialectic between writing and voice, literary and popular culture, thus finds one of its many contingent resolutions in favour of a mixed mode. Words come off the page and move to a beat learnt from music. This music crossed the Atlantic and took root in West Indian immigrants to Britain, or, in some cases, it travelled north to Canada. It continues to give contemporary performance poetry physical presence as sound, gesture, music, and movement. It gives anger and suffering an opportunity to be enacted as a ritual of popular culture. It gives ethnic and linguistic diversity its space in the sun and rain, links modernity to the past, and ameliorates the condition of those who feel uprooted in time and displaced in space. It mobilizes verbal energy and anguish into an expressive force for social change.

More recently, however, some of the poets liberated into Creole and dub have shown signs of a tendency that we might link to the stylistic dilemma faced at the beginning of the twentieth century by McKay. Denise Narain draws attention to the manner in which Jean Binta Breeze (b. 1957, Jamaica/UK), after becoming well known as one of the very few dub poets who is a woman, moved from a performative style to a quieter, personal idiom. In 1985, Breeze is quoted as saying: 'I had to get out of the confines of dub poetry... it was so restricting having to write poetry to a one drop reggae rhythm' (Narain 2002: 110). The fact that many contemporary poets who use, or have used, Creole in their poetry routinely speak Standard English indicates the gap always present throughout the tradition from McKay, Marson, and Bennett, to Lorna Goodison, Grace Nichols, David Dabydeen, Jean Binta Breeze, and others.

Creole first came into verse as social representation, mimicry, and ventriloquism. It became part of a counterculture as the voice of an unrecognized humanity. Once poets migrated and settled in Britain or North America, dialect provided a way of invoking or exorcising the past, but away from the Caribbean, it also became a diminishing component of the poetic repertoire for individuals seeking assimilation into mainstream traditions. Linton Kwesi Johnson, Benjamin Zephaniah, and a few others keep their Creole and their 'normal' idioms relatively close because it serves as their calling card. Other contemporary poets of Caribbean descent seem willing to set aside 'nation language', as in the case of David Dabydeen's 'Turner' (1994), or Lorna Goodison's *Turn Thanks* (1999). Denis Narain notes that

Dabydeen and Amryl Johnson (1944–2001, Trinidad/UK), when reading or performing their poems, self-consciously 'assume a different speaking voice from that of their "normal" speaking voice and sometimes the "fit" between voicing and language on the page is not a perfect match' (2002: 136). In 'Multiculture Abroad', Merle Collins indicates resistance to playing a minority role that subsidizes a tired cliché:

> They want me to perform a poem
> a poem like they say the Blacks perform
> with black English and tenor pans
> and bongo drums and musical stuff like that
>
> (Kay *et al.* 1996: 91)

The poet is disinclined to oblige. Such cases suggest that the Creole continuum served a particular historical function whose liminality changes as poets move towards idioms and tonalities more suited to their new homes and societies. Future literary historians might well see the period from the 1960s to the 1980s as the phase in the evolution of West Indian poetry when this resource was at its most prolific.

5
Black Africa

Overview

Contemporary African poetry remains implicated in the life of politics and the fate of nations with a fixity of concern not found in Asia or the Caribbean. The end of colonialism was followed in most African countries by decades of native misrule. For three generations, African poets have given voice to a wide range of experiences, always conscious that their use of English links them across regional boundaries, while they present the language with the challenge of dealing with the local in all its uniqueness, in circumstances ravaged by civil war, natural disasters, human greed, and political misrule.

5.1 From colony to nation in Africa

> to kill the soul in a people—this is a crime which transcends physical murder.
>
> E. D. Morel, *The Black Man's Burden*

African poets represent their continent in a habitually tragic light. During the struggle for political decolonization, the Angolan poet Augustinho Neto (1922–79) described it as 'The Grieved Lands' (Moore and Beier 1998: 6). More recently, Niyi Osundare (b. 1947, Nigeria) describes it as 'a dinosaur left panting in the wilderness' (2002: 6). In 'Admonition to the Black World', Chinweizu (b. 1943 Nigeria) prefaces a litany of Africa's woes with a chronicle of all the invasions suffered by the peoples of the continent in ancient, medieval, and modern times. The bereavement of African poetry can be contextualized in terms of the two large-scale encounters with Europe from which Africa has yet to recover fully: the Atlantic slave trade, and colonization.

From the latter part of the fifteenth century, the Portuguese and the Spanish, followed by the British, the Dutch, and the French, set up a thriving slave trade between the Atlantic coast of Africa and markets for slave labour in the Americas and the Caribbean. Herbert Klein estimates that this trade transported over 9 million Africans to the Americas between 1662 and 1867 (1999: 208–9); John Iliffe puts the figure for the entire period from 1450 to 1900 at over 11 million (1995: 131), as does Johannes Postma (2003: 35–6). Of these, over 5 million were exported by carriers from Portugal and Spain, and over 3 million by carriers from Britain. Over half of the total number was shipped in the eighteenth century. Ten to twenty per cent died in the crossing. By the middle of the nineteenth century, the population of Africa was about half of what it might have been without the slave trade. Britain, the nation that profited the most from the trade, abolished commerce in slaves from 1807, and slave-ownership from 1833. The other slave-trading nations followed thereafter.

Slaves liberated from North America were shipped back and settled in parts of West Africa, which later became the nations of Liberia and Sierra Leone. They produced the earliest writing in English and the first expressions of nationalism from Africa. Poets like Syl Cheney Coker (b. 1945) and Lemuel Johnson (b. 1941) from Sierra Leone show a preoccupation with their Creole ancestry that differs markedly from the more traditional approach of older poets such as Bai T. Moore (b. 1916, Liberia). Phillis Wheatley, a slave living in North America, provides one of the earliest examples of an aspiration for culture and poetry modelled on the master culture. 'On being brought from AFRICA to AMERICA' (1773) declares:

> Once I redemption neither sought nor knew.
> Some view our sable race with scornful eye,
> 'Their colour is a diabolic die'.
> Remember, *Christians*, *Negros*, black as *Cain*,
> May be refin'd, and join th' angelic train.
>
> (Wheatley 1988: 18)

Her sanguine attitude provides an extreme contrast to the self-loathing voiced repeatedly by Cheney-Coker in 'Hydropathy':

The plantation blood in my veins
My foul genealogy!
I laugh at this Creole ancestry
Which gave me my negralized head
All my polluted streams.

(1973: 3)

African ecological systems deterred large-scale European settlement, except in parts of South and East Africa. Dutch settlers came to the Cape in the eighteenth century, and fought for territorial control with the British settlers that followed. At a conference held in Berlin during 1884–5, the major Western nations worked out a plan for the colonization of Africa. Eighty per cent of the continent was then free of colonial rule. By the 1920s, most of the continent had been carved out between the British, the French, the Portuguese, and the Belgians. Germany lost its territories in South and East Africa after World War I.

The British and the French left the most lasting imprint upon their colonial subjects. Kwame Anthony Appiah distinguishes between the two: 'the French colonial policy was one of assimilation—of turning "savage" Africans into "evolved" black Frenchmen and women—while British colonial policy was a good deal less interested in making black Anglo-Saxons' (1992: 3–4). This difference is reflected in the Africa idealized by the Negritude movement, as in 'Prayer to the Masks', by the Francophone Senegalese poet Léopold Senghor (1906–2001):

They call us men of cotton, coffee, and oil
They call us men of death.
But we are men of dance, whose feet get stronger
  As we pound upon firm earth.

(1991: 14)

Poets writing in English were less prone to this kind of idealization.

The first colonies to become free in Africa were French, followed by the British colonies in West Africa, starting with Ghana in 1957, where Kwame Nkrumah's government was overthrown in 1966, and successive military coups prevailed, until the restoration of parliamentary democracy in 2001. Poets and intellectuals were forced into a pattern of exile and reluctant return that became common to many parts of Africa. In 'Exiles', from *Night of my Blood* (1971), Kofi Awonoor (b. 1935, Ghana) asks:

> Should they return home
> And face the fences the termites had eaten
> And see the dunghill that has mounted on their birthplace?
>
> (23)

Nigeria, the most populous region of Africa, gained independence in 1960, and became a republic in 1963. Its three culturally distinct communities—the Hausa, the Yoruba, and the Igbo—soon found themselves in a civil war (1967–70): 'What began as a pogrom against Igbo traders in northern Nigeria led first to Igbo secession and then to a civil war in which Yoruba people aligned with the North to "save the union" ' (Appiah 1992: 165). The peace that followed was overtaken by successive coups in 1975 and 1983. Parliamentary government was restored in 1999 after sixteen years of military rule. In 'Welcome Home', Nigeria's oldest active poet, Gabriel Okara (b. 1921), cautions against undue optimism:

> This, alas, is not the land you left behind!
> Things bedevilled, demonic, you'll now find
> Displayed for unquestioning public praise
> By disembodied mindless sycophantic voices.
>
> (2003: 38)

Independence came to East Africa in the early 1960s. Tanganyika became free in 1961, and merged with Zanzibar in 1963 to form Tanzania. Uganda became free in 1962, but succumbed to a series of military dictatorships that culminated in the ethnic strife and economic ruin that accompanied them under the dictatorship of Idi Amin (1971–9). Kenya was the scene of violent resistance from the Mau Mau during the 1950s, and achieved independence in 1963.

The regions of white control to the north of South Africa followed a similar pattern of political development. Long-subjugated black majorities gained independence from white minority rule after varying periods and degrees of conflict. Zambia (formerly Northern Rhodesia), Malawi (formerly Nyasaland), and Zimbabwe (previously Southern Rhodesia, from 1965 Rhodesia) broke free from the Federation forced upon them by Britain in the 1960s, the first two in relatively peaceful ways, Zimbabwe after fifteen years of violent conflict. After independence, all three retained English as the national language. This was a pragmatic choice common to all former British colonies in Africa and elsewhere. It retained continuity with colonial institutions of education and governance, provided access to the international community of organizations and nations, facilitated modernization, and neutralized linguistic affiliations based on tribal loyalties.

Under the leadership of Kenneth Kaunda, Zambia opposed apartheid in neighbouring South Africa, and maintained a liberal atmosphere for the arts, but could not prevent its modest economy from declining to the point where Kaunda's leadership ended in 1992. During the same period, Malawi, led by Hastings Banda, maintained ties with the apartheid government of South Africa, and enforced a domestic policy of authoritarian rule and censorship that lasted until 1993.

The formation of an East African culture in English was the result of a pattern of education common to all the British colonies in Africa. Ngugi wa Thiong'o describes it as the Horton-Asquith model. It was similar in intention and effect to the policy implemented in India after Macaulay's *Minute* of 1835. It created local minorities whose elite status at home was based on their acculturation into the colonial language, a one-way process with little of the interculturation found in Caribbean creolization. Fanon analysed the process in terms of the formation of 'a national bourgeoisie' which was prone to degenerate into a 'get-rich-quick middle class' that was 'not even the replica of Europe, but its caricature' (1961: 175).

According to Ngugi, the colonial language and culture created a local intelligentsia that was 'alienated and collaborative' (2000: online). English gave opportunities for overseas travel and education, and seduced a few into expatriation, but the majority were drawn to local politics, administration, teaching, and the media, all of which carried status and power in an indigenous population that was largely rural and unaffected by Western patterns of development. The effect of such mutations is given lively representation in two long poems from East Africa, *Song of Lawino* (1966) and *Song of Ocol* (1970), by Okot p'Biket (1931–82). Here is a sardonic example from the second:

> Do you appreciate the beauty
> Of my roses?
> Or would you rather turn
> My flower garden
> Into a maize shamba?
>
> (1984: 139)

Appiah provides an account of African postcoloniality in terms of the kind of intellectual dramatized by Okot:

> Postcoloniality is the condition of what we might ungenerously call a comprador intelligentsia: of a relatively small, Western-style, Western-trained, group of writers and thinkers who mediate the trade in cultural commodities of world capitalism at the periphery... Postcolonial intellectuals in Africa ... are almost entirely dependent for their support on two institutions: the African university... and the Euro-American publisher and reader.
>
> (1992: 149)

When this intellectual took charge of the new nation, the excitement and euphoria of freedom quickly turned to ashes. Self-rule was superseded by factionalism, ethnic conflict, unstable governance, military rule, economic decline, corruption in public office, and widespread abuse of human rights. Tanure Ojaide (b. 1948, Nigeria) sums it up, in 'We Are Many', as 'the incubus of power' (1986: 72). Appiah's word for African misrule is 'kleptocracy' (1992: 150). Corrupt and inept regimes forced writers into a poetics of commitment that shaped postcolonial writing throughout Africa. In 'For Chinua Achebe', Odia Ofeimun (b. 1950, Nigeria) declares:

> none can afford the lyrical sanity
> of the hermit when his clothes are on fire
>
> (Soyinka 1975: 294)

The ideal of 'pan-African' unity promoted by the Negritude movement in the 1930s and '40s did not succeed in uniting postcolonial African nations, because the idea of an African unity was far removed from the realities that separated one tribe or community from another. Appiah explains: 'the new states brought together peoples who spoke different languages, had different religious traditions and notions of property, and were politically... integrated in different—often radically different—degrees' (1992: 161–2). 'Africa' and 'African poetry' are partially tenuous entities: neither race, nor a colonial history, nor post-independence suffice to provide more than a semblance of unity to peoples and cultures as disparate as their ecosystems. Moreover, and as in Asia, many patterns of life continued from before to after colonialism, while other radically new patterns changed the overall quality of urban and rural life.

5.2 The cost of protest

> I miss being able to shrug and say,
> Not us, not us, the Romans are to blame.
>
> Chris Mann, 'Saying Goodbye to the Romans'

The notion of 'African poetry' is held together, insofar as it holds together, by two ironies: resistance to colonial rule expressed in the colonial language, and anger and grief at the failure of the nation to live up to a dream of polity derived from colonialism. White minority rule in South Africa and Rhodesia (as in Portuguese-controlled Angola and Mozambique or French-controlled Algeria) gave urgency and focus to writing. After independence, the urgency acquired a dejected tone. Hope faded, as self-rule became its own bitter parody across most of the new nations.

In South Africa, a white minority took charge of the State in 1948, and quickly legalized the segregation of the black and coloured population from settlers of European descent, in all occupations, including education and urban housing. This state of affairs lasted until the collapse of white minority rule in the early 1990s. Under these circumstances, 'postcolonial' acquires a complex resonance. The entire period from 1961 to the early 1990s was 'postcolonial' for the white minority, while black and coloured South Africans continued to live under a regime that was effectively 'colonial'. After 1994, the application of 'postcolonial' has tended to reverse roles in the relation between white minority and black majority, while a fragile nation embarks on the untested path of multi-racial democracy.

How did black Africans in British Africa come to be writing poetry in English? During the nineteenth century, British missionaries introduced black oral poets to individual authorship in the written format, and commissioned the translation of texts like the Bible and Bunyan into African languages. The earliest poems in English by black writers date from the 1890s. An untitled 1897 poem by A. K. Soga shows the typical colonial pattern of local material expressed in a stilted British idiom:

> Was it the sun, uprising in his pride
> That struck with glittering sheen Hulushe's dappled side...
>
> (Couzens 1984: 72)

The first distinctive native use of English came with *Mhudi* (*c.* 1917, pub. 1930) by Solomon Plaatje (1876–1932). The narrative shows Plaatje's skill in the assimilation of African praise poetry and prophecy into English. It also showed awareness of black writing from America as well as Modernist developments in London. Plaatje handled his awareness of developments outside Africa as part of a network which Elleke Boehmer describes in terms of 'cross-national interrelations' focused on 'proto-pan-nationalist' inclinations (2002: 9, 147).

The first volumes published by black South African poets applied themselves to the articulation of black consciousness: *A Blackman Speaks of Freedom!* (1940), by Peter Abrahams (b. 1919), and *Valley of a Thousand Hills* (1941), by H. I. E. Dhlomo (1903–56). Both were products of a missionary-school education. Their styles reflected the European models prevalent among their white contemporaries, although their themes addressed the need to remember and recover the African dimension of their cultural ancestry. Abrahams drew upon the example of black American poets such as Langston Hughes (1902–67), while Dhlomo relied upon indigenous traditions.

The latter tendency was to find fuller expression during the 1970s in the Zulu poems of Mazisi Kunene (b. 1930), which he translated into English as a self-exiled academic living in the USA. The relationship of the original to the translations represents a dual challenge. In the epic poem *Shaka the Great* (1979), Kunene articulates a communal sense of history, mythology, and an African world-view grounded in the life and deeds of a great Zulu king and warrior. The need for translation recognizes that the partially obliterated past can be recuperated for a contemporary black society only through the colonial language. English also helps disseminate a cultural representation of pre-colonial Africa to a global audience. The heroic past may lack adequate mediation to an inglorious present, but it can hope to revive a sense of ethnic pride in a contemporary society humiliated by apartheid.

Sipho Sepamla (b. 1932) adopted a complementary strategy. 'Words, Words, Words', from *The Soweto I Love* (1977), speaks of how the notion of 'tribal wars' gets replaced by 'faction fights', and 'tribes' by 'nations', in a chain of euphemistic neologisms that move from 'multinational' to 'homeland' to 'independence', as part of the irony that words 'spell out our lives':

for there's a kind of poetic licence
doing the rounds in these parts.

(1977: 40–1)

The poet foregrounds the irony that he has to allude to a Western text (*Hamlet*) in order to complain against Western influences.

Several poets who began their careers in the 1950s, such as Dennis Brutus (b. 1924), and Keorapetse Kgositsile (b. 1938), found themselves forced into exile, along with many of the writers actively associated with the journal *The Drum* (founded 1951). Political discrimination came to a boil in 1960 in the form of violence in the townships of Sharpeville, Nyanga, and Langa. The African National Congress and the Pan African Congress were banned.

Apartheid also banned books and imprisoned authors or forced them into exile. Brutus was among the earliest to suffer. He wrote with gritty perseverance of 'the wordless, endless wail | only the unfree know' (Ndebele 1994: 47). His student, Arthur Nortje (1942–73), lived a short life that became emblematic of the involuntary expatriate condition. Here is the 'Immigrant':

... preparing for flight

dismissing the blond aura of the past
at Durban or Johannesburg
no more chewing roots or brewing riots

(Pieterse 1971: 127)

In poem after poem, Nortje returns to the realization that 'it is solitude that mutilates', and 'lack of belonging was the root of hurt' (Barnett 1983: 86, 87). He committed suicide in England at the age of thirty-one.

Resistance to racial discrimination became the all-consuming theme of black poetry. The early 1970s brought a new generation to prominence, chief among them Oswald Mtshali (b. 1940), Mongane Serote (b. 1944), and Sepamla. The success of Mtshali's *Sounds of a Cowhide Drum* (1971) created a new populist audience for poetry. The white novelist Nadine Gordimer surmised that 'black writers have had to look for survival away from the explicit if not to the cryptic then to the implicit; and in their case they have turned instinctively to poetry' (1973: 52).

Poetry became an effective instrument of protest because it could circulate orally without the aid of the print medium, and its performance was less susceptible to censorship than narrative. Speaking against apartheid was part of a larger social ferment, which returned poetry to 'its original moorings—the shout, the cry, the ballad, the praise, the epic' (Mphahlele 1972: 115). Numerous periodicals such as *The Purple Renoster* (1956) and *Staffrider* (1978), and presses such as Ravan Press, Renoster Books, David Philip, and A. D. Donker kept literature alive during the apartheid period.

Black poets abandoned the genteel European manners of their white contemporaries and wrote of their condition in plain and sometimes rough language, using rhythms close to native speech and music. They wrote primarily for a black, local, urban audience. Their use of English had little interest in the kind of complaint made by their white contemporary Guy Butler, that Mtshali and Serote were unaware of the British poetic tradition (1994: 150). Black poets saw themselves as exploiting a new relation between the syntax of writing and the rhythms of native orature. E'ssia Mphahlele, who returned to South Africa in 1970 after twenty years of exile, recollected that 'We were writing about our own lives, replaying our own experiences to our own people.... People had been suffering, and people had been living in harsh conditions without a voice. Well, they found a voice then' (Chapman 1982: 42–3).

In 1976, Mtshali explained his approach to language: 'I write in English for my present state of reality or unreality and I write in Zulu to establish my identity which will be translated by posterity' (Heywood 1976: 124). The choice was not without its ambiguities. Alvarez-Pereyre remarks: 'English has... for these young poets the same attraction and repulsion as the white civilization that goes with it' (1984: 261). The same ambivalence can be found in the lively and rebellious Dambudzo Marechera (1952–87, Zimbabwe/UK): 'I find that the only way I can express myself in English is by abusing the English language in such a way that it says what I want it to say' (Wild 1988: 131). He posed himself the question, 'Did you ever thinking of writing in Shona?', and replied, 'I took to the English language like a duck takes to water. I was therefore a keen accomplice and student in my own mental colonisation... For a black writer the language is very racist: you have to have harrowing fights and hair-raising panga duels with it before you can make it do all you want it to do' (Veit-Wild 1992: 4).

Black South African poetry acquired a sharper note after 1976, when legislation enforcing Afrikaans as a medium of instruction in black schools led to violence in the Soweto township of Johannesburg. 'Vengeance', by Kunene, gives a sense of how things developed:

> Day after day we kindled the fire,
> Spreading the flame of our anger
> Round your cities,
> Round your children...
>
> (Shava 1989: 117)

Don Mattera (b. 1935) gives evidence of the new resolve in 'The Poet Must Die' (1983):

> Ban him.
> Send him to the Island
> Call the firing squad.
> But remember to wipe his blood
> From the wall.
> [...]
> If their lies are to survive
> The poet must die...
>
> (Moore and Beier 1998: 365)

The death of the Black Conscious Movement leader Stephen Biko while imprisoned under apartheid was the occasion for a remarkable linguistic *tour de force* titled 'In Detention' (1979), by Christopher van Wyk (b. 1957). The poem displays its commitment obliquely, with a grasp of the grotesque and absurd aspects of life and language that a Kafka or a Beckett might have envied. It uses repetition, imitation, and parody in order to subvert the official violence perpetrated by the state against life and reason. Three lines of official explanation are all that the poem uses:

> He fell from the ninth floor
> He hanged himself
> He slipped on a piece of soap while washing
>
> (Hirson 1997: 140)

The poem plays variations on these explanations, treating them as propositions whose phrases are interchangeable. The notion of meaningfulness is reduced to token grammaticality: if a sentence can make grammatical sense, however absurd, it will do (since all explanations are a fiction in this State anyway). Thus, 'He hanged himself while washing' is acceptable. So also, 'He slipped on the ninth floor while washing', and 'He fell from a piece of soap while slipping', and so on (140–1). The poem creates a tension between the horrific and the absurd, reinforcing the point made from exile by T. T. Moyana, that 'for the creative artist in South Africa, especially the black writer... life itself is too fantastic to be outstripped by the creative imagination' (Ndebele 1994: 42). Likewise, in 'The Sentence', Ojaide provides an account of guilt imputed without cause, and punishment enforced without law, morality, or justice: 'Friend, from the day you were born you were sentenced to life. | For me it was hard labour'; 'I was sentenced before crimes swarmed my head'; 'My crimes are sown to my humanity'; 'I am guilty of complicity in life' (1986: 9–10).

Poetry from black South Africa found its counterpart in the Zimbabwean struggle for independence. The first writers to move from native languages to English appeared in the 1960s. The poetry of the 1970s and early 1980s measured the cost paid in misery and violence during the struggle against white rule. Emmanuel Ngara notes that this poetry was written at the level of ordinary individual experience, rather than the nationalism of the ideologue or the politician, as in contemporary Lusophone writing from Angola and Mozambique. The majority of Zimbabweans wrote as victims or witnesses. Freedom Nyamubaya (b. 1960) was one of the few who wrote as a former combatant. 'A Mysterious Marriage', from *On the Road Again* (1986), converts the familiar motif of lovers swearing fidelity into a political allegory for the disappointment of hope:

> Once upon a time
> there was a boy and a girl
> forced to leave their home
> by armed robbers.
> The boy was Independence
> The girl was Freedom.
> [...]
> After the big war they went back home.
> Everybody prepared for the wedding
> [...]
> The whole village gathered waiting
> Freedom and Independence
> were more popular than Jesus

Independence came
But Freedom was not there.
[...]
Independence is now a senior bachelor
Some people still talk about him...

(1998: n.p.)

The new nation of Zimbabwe suffered a fate not to be blamed solely on white rule. Native administrators internalized the colonial system of exploitation. In 'Two Photographs', Charles Mungoshi (b. 1947) compares his past and present photos as a way of reading history from facial topography:

My face is beginning to settle uncomfortably
into the torn-up landscape of these times.

(Wild 1988: 87)

From Joyce's Dublin, Stephen Dedalus recommended silence, exile, and cunning to the writer disgusted with his people and place. In Malawi, the Banda regime offered writers an additional alternative: imprisonment. The earliest black poet to use English from the region, David Rubadiri (b. 1930), went into exile soon after Banda came to power and returned only at the end of Banda's rule, thirty years later. Several younger poets who wrote against the injustices of the new nation also chose self-exile: Felix Mnthali (b. 1933), Lupenga Mphande (b. 1947), and Frank Chipasula (b. 1949).

For Chipasula, anger is all. In 'Manifesto on Ars Poetica', he declares, 'I will put the symbols of murder hidden in high offices | In the centre of my crude lines of accusations', and 'I have nothing to give you, but my anger | And the filaments of hatred reach across the border' (Ojaide and Sallah 1999: 25). In 'Where I Was Born', Mphande's outlook is focused less on 'the tyrant who at a swish of his flywhisk | Mowed people into dust' (1998: 40–1) than on the plight of the ordinary African, who is most likely to be one among millions of 'The Refugees', and has but one purpose:

a flight from sweltering drought
    that wilts their crops, depletes their stock
a flight from ethnic rivalries
    that maims their children, kill their kins

> a flight from cross-fire heat of ideologies
> that sizzle their minds, numb their senses.
>
> (1994: 52)

Another experience chronicled frequently by African poets is imprisonment. Wole Soyinka's *A Shuttle in the Crypt* (1972) describes it, in the 'Preface', as a rite of passage that is both 'harrowing and consoling' (2001: 95). Soyinka was put in jail for his campaign against the Federal side during the Nigerian civil war. Isolation, torture, death was the common lot for political prisoners, while elsewhere, as 'Procession' notes bitterly:

> Far away, blood-stained in their
> Tens of thousands, hands that damned
> These wretches to the pit triumph . . .
>
> (2001: 142)

In 1930s Europe, the intellectual Walter Benjamin worried about how art might relate to the violence that was Nazism and Fascism. He responded to the anxiety by suggesting that art had to be politicized in order to resist the aestheticization of politics practiced by totalitarianism: '*All efforts to aestheticize politics culminate in one point. That one point is war*' (2003: 269). Benjamin's formulation has relevance to the African context because Banda's regime was fascist in its policies. Two Malawian poets—Jack Mapanje (b. 1944) and Steve Chimombo (b. 1945)—adopted a veiled manner of alluding to Banda's aestheticizations. In 'We Wondered About the Mellow Peaches', Mapanje questions the decadence of the regime:

> . . . bringing
> Flashy girls with mellow peaches and vermilion
> Strawberries into lascivious range-rovers?
>
> (2004: 46)

Chimombo was one of the few poets *not* to go into exile. 'A Death Song' rejects the option:

> Exile, pretended, genuine,
> or self-imposed is not the answer
> to the holocaust or the apocalypse.
>
> (Maja-Pearce 1990: 101)

Instead, he drew upon the mythology of his people and an emblematic use of animal symbolism to give his poems a cloak of obscurity that managed to avoid censure. In 'Four Ways of Dying', he invokes the Crab for its ability to 'Avoid', 'Meander', and to 'Squat', contrasting it favourably with the Chameleon, the Mole, and the Kalilombe (Maja-Pearce 1990: 89–90).

Mapanje's resistance to his government received sympathetic international attention. In 1986, he spoke against Malawian censorship at a Stockholm Conference. The Malawian authorities promptly blocked the local circulation of his poems. Mapanje narrates the police interrogation that took place in 1987 shortly before he was imprisoned without trial: 'It was madness, more Kafka than you could ever think of. He was actually asking his prisoner why he should be detained ... The man was so embarrassed he didn't know what to do' (Bunting 2000: online). Mapanje's early poems are notable for cryptic references that satirize political oppression in a technique that utilizes local forms of riddling. Occasionally, the anger comes through directly, as in the conclusion of 'Furious', from *The Chattering Wagtails of Mikuyu Prison* (1993):

> We have liquidated too many
> brave names out of the nation's memory;
> I will not rub out another nor inscribe
> my own, more ignoble, to consummate this
> moment of truth I have always feared!
>
> (Lindfors and Sander 1996: 178ii)

Since the end of Banda's rule, Mapanje and Chimombo have struggled to address a problem faced by all poets who are intent on righting injustice. Protest is not only a zealous but also a jealous mistress, who turns away all other solicitations from the Muse. When the conditions that brought anger into being disappear, the poet finds his style and idiom unprepared to tackle life in a society no longer tyrannized by dictators. Mpalive-Hangson Msiska observes of Chimombo's *A Referendum of Forest Creatures* (1993) that it 'shows the pitfall of an aesthetic that has not adapted itself adequately to changed political circumstances' (1995: 96). In Mapanje's case, *Skipping Without Ropes* (1998) shows him still preoccupied with issues arising out of his experience in jail. 'The Seashells of Bidlington

North Beach' continues to brood over the 'Memory of the African lakes they were forced to | Abandon' (2004: 204).

Whether living in England or Harare, Marechera was alert to the danger of becoming fixated on anger and protest. In the poem 'When Love's Perished', his awareness speaks for African poetry on the cusp of the postcolonial:

> The poem, sticky with centuries' sleep
> And anaemic from lack of iron discipline
> And pallid from years' diet of political slogans
> And wedged under the door between Europe and Africa,
> The poem in consternation, began to pick its stanza-lip.
>
> (1992: 169)

Most protest poetry from Africa speaks with consternation, but unmindful of picking its 'stanza-lip'. It lives within the limits of passionate sincerity. Poets from other times and places have expressed a need for poetry to resist from within the demands made upon art by external reality. In a prose essay on 'The Irrational Element in Poetry' (1957), Wallace Stevens distinguishes resistance from escape: 'Resistance to the pressure of the ominous and destructive circumstance consists of its conversion, so far as possible, into a different, an explicable, an amenable circumstance' (1997: 789). In 'Stone from Delphi', Seamus Heaney hopes and prays, in the context of the political realities that press upon Irish poets, '*that I may escape the miasma of spilled blood*' (1990: 171).

Protest becomes more effective when it finds means within language and form to match the force of outer reality. The point can be made briefly by comparing two poems. In 'Hope Fleeing', Chenjerai Hove (b. 1956) speaks of 'the debt owed by so few to so many' (Wild 1988: 43). This is direct but flat. A related sentiment is expressed by Marechera with the flair of metaphor: hunger feeds an anger which will 'smite with white-hot steel | The reinforced glass between my want | And your plenty'. The poem goes on to evoke 'The Coin of Moonshire' in a punning image that is diagnostic as well as prophetic:

> ... ever the circling
> Moon gleams, a bright distended coin above the dark decade
> Casting beams of greed through my shantyhut door.
>
> (1992: 74)

Regardless of the self-destructive nature of his tragic gift, and the fitful nature of his insights, the most striking parts of Marechera's work find fresh metaphors informed by his reading of European literature. Such poems reveal a capacity to grip reality with surreal fingers. In contrast, protest poetry settles down to the narrow register of exhortation. Marechera stands out for expressing misgivings about protest. He asserted the need for a private poetry different from the work of contemporaries such as Zimunya and Hove: 'There you find the struggle with the feeling, if one has suffered, that the statement of one's suffering must necessarily be poetic. Now that is not so. The extent to which one has suffered through political oppression is not necessarily the substance of a poem' (1992: 211).

In 1973, Nadine Gordimer asked of African writing, 'Are we approaching it as testimony of social change, or as literature?' (1973: 7). She answered her own question with the assertion that 'The majority of African writers at present belong to the first category', pointing to the following (unattributed) lines as evidence:

> To label my utterings poetry
> and myself a poet
> would be as self-deluding
> as the planners of parallel development.
>
> (1973: 53)

The black intellectual Lewis Nkosi (b. 1936) took a similar position when he complained as early as 1964 that much South African writing was 'journalistic fact parading outrageously as imaginative literature' (1965: 132). More recently, Benita Parry urges recognition that 'resistance literature' is not simply a matter of 'form ... perceived as the handmaiden of the new content' (1994: 17). In any oppressed society, apart from writers who 'wear their politics on their sleeves', there might also be more interesting 'oppositional discourses quickening liberation energies' which 'reside in spaces where there is no obvious correspondence between image and social message' (1994: 13).

European discussions of related issues have something of relevance to offer here. Theodor Adorno begins an essay on 'Commitment' (1974) with a reference to an essay by Jean-Paul Sartre titled *What is Literature?* (1967). Sartre doubted if Pablo Picasso's painting *Guernica* (a form of protest against the violence unleashed by General Franco's forces at the onset of the Spanish Civil War in the 1930s) 'won a single supporter for the Spanish cause' (an argument that would not apply to the role played by black poetry in South Africa). Sartre went on to point out that 'Nobody can suppose for a moment that it is possible to write a good novel in praise of anti-semitism'. To this Adorno adds the now famous remark, 'to write lyric poetry after Auschwitz is barbaric' (1992: 84–6).

Extreme forms of oppression and injustice raise the question: How should art respond to violence? The question masks an anxiety based on a form of binary thinking. To accept the binary is to believe that (a) poets create artefacts that transcend or transmute their circumstances in order to provide lasting aesthetic pleasure and insight, or (b) when faced by oppression and injustice, poets set aside the aim of creating objects of aesthetic contemplation in order to resist injustice and foster change. The binary mode assumes that the two aims are incompatible, requiring poets to choose between the allegedly timeless disinterestedness of art and the urgently local commitment of politics. The South African artist Sidney Kumalo (1935–88) offers a credo that subscribes to this binarism in 'Explaining My New Style':

> I do not walk in the forest
> Admiring flowers and trees:
> But among policemen who check my passport
> And my political background.
>
> (Wilhelm and Polley 1976: 75)

In the binary predicament, the formalist accuses the committed writer of being a propagandist, and the committed writer accuses the formalist of being trapped in an ivory tower. However, there is a way of dealing with the tension that does not require a split in linguistic functions, but expects art to reconcile aesthetic criteria with political commitments. If binarism is resisted, commitment to poetry and commitment to issues outside poetry sustain a tense but meaningful equilibrium. The success of this equilibrium is confirmed when the aesthetic appeal of a poem is inseparable from its historical or political significance. Such acts of equilibrium are rare, not just in postcolonial poetry but in most poetry that finds itself drawn to take sides on matters of great political and moral import. Yeats's poems on the Irish troubles exemplify that equilibrium (as does Andrew Marvell on the seventeenth-century conflict between Cromwell and Charles I).

5.3 The ambivalence of cultural nationalism

we have at last nationalized POVERTY...

Taban lo Liyong, 'Another Nigger Dead'

The use of English for creative purposes in Africa was the indirect and eventual result of the propagation of English during the colonial period by the two professions whose interests were linked to the spread of literacy among indigenous populations: missionaries and educationists. Colonialism Christianized, and it introduced Africans to English and Western modernity. Recourse to writing in English was encouraged by three factors. State-sponsored bureaus set up by colonial administrations to nurture publications in the indigenous languages turned local writers, during or after the end of Empire, towards the colonial language. Second, local media such as newspapers and periodicals (often attached to college or university campuses) offered writers the chance of wider access within Africa. Third, metropolitan publishers (chief among them, Heinemann) set up local offices and initiated new series that combined a local market in educational texts with an overseas readership. These developments were followed by the establishment of local publishing houses in the major African cities, and the active influence on canons and syllabi of awards in writing administered by local, pan-African, and international bodies, such as NOMA, and the Commonwealth Association.

Writers from Nigeria and Ghana, led by the example of Chinua Achebe's fiction, laid the foundations for a powerful new interaction between old ways of life and new methods of writing. An older generation produced a scattering of poets described by Kofi Awonoor as 'a community of detribalized African intellectuals, culturally British, yet politically, though modestly and urbanely, rebellious' (1975: 186). New developments reached their first period of productivity, both in the West and shortly thereafter in the East, during the 1960s. In the 1980s, Ken Goodwin described the poetry of East and Central Africa as going through a pattern common to the transition from colonial to postcolonial writing: from the imitation of Romantic and Victorian models to the imitation of Modern writing (1984: 213). The most interesting part of this process was the interaction between European influences and local forms. One of the outstanding exponents of this interaction was the Ugandan Okot p'Bitek (1931–82).

Nadine Gordimer identified five recurrent themes common to the fictional writing of colonial-to-postcolonial Africa. These transpose plausibly to poetry. Gordimer describes the first four as a progression, and the fifth as a continuous preoccupation: (1) Countryman-Comes-To-Town, (2) The Return of the Been-to, (3) The Ancestors versus the Missionary, (4) The Way it was Back Home, and (5) Let My People Go. Her analysis was based on the belief that while 'Black writers choose their plots, characters, and literary styles; their themes choose *them*' (1973: 11). In the case of Okot p'Bitek, it would appear that all five themes chose him.

Okot developed a unique method of dealing with local materials, whose influence continues to dominate East African poetry, even to the point of exasperation, as in a half-jocular poem addressed to him by Jared Angira: 'For heaven's sake lie down and sleep' (Smith 1989: 109). Okot provides one of the most sustained engagements between writing and postcoloniality in Africa. His work dramatizes a contestation over the issue of cultural nationalism from a perspective that mixes a shrewd grasp of what Western culture brought to the colonies with a troubled attachment to indigenous ways of life. His prose speaks of a simple imperative: 'Africa must re-examine herself critically. She must discover her true self, and rid herself of all "apemanship"' (1973: vii). He also believed that the Western idea of culture as 'something separate and distinguishable from the *way of the life of a people*, that can be put into books, and museums and art galleries . . . is entirely alien to African thought' (1986: 14). Kwasi Wiredu confirms the suspicion that 'If the truth be told, p'Bitek was the true pioneer of conceptual decolonization in African philosophy' (1996: 200).

Okot went to England in 1958, as part of the Ugandan football team, and stayed on to study education (Bristol), law (Aberystwyth), and cultural anthropology (Oxford). Okot's poetry partakes in equal measure of loyalty to traditional customs and recognition of what modernity brings as a mixed blessing to Africa. The two elements generate conflicting energies whose force can be described as dialogic or self-deconstructive. *Song of Lawino* was written in his mother tongue, Acoli, and then reworked into English. The popularity of the translated version makes it a striking example of a poem that highlights the values of an anti-colonial culture while using a colonial language. Its political references contributed to Okot's expulsion from Uganda, and a period of exile that lasted until the final year of his life. Okot's legacy continues to subsidize belief in the validity of local cultures. It also highlights an equivocal attitude towards the hybridization under way in African societies.

Song of Lawino is a long work comprising thirteen sections, spoken by a village woman, Lawino, who complains against her husband Ocol, partly for abandoning her (in preference to a woman who has adopted Western habits), and partly for having lost touch with the vitality of his native culture. She accuses her husband of pursuing a modernity that apes an alien culture. The future he envisages for their society fills her with foreboding:

> Where is the Peace of Uhuru?
> Where is the unity of Independence?
> Must it not begin at home?
>
> (1984: 107)

Song of Ocol (1970) is briefer. It was written directly in English. The first of its nine sections accounts for the man's rejection of his 'primitive' wife. The poem then addresses Africa as an 'idle giant | basking in the sun' (125), and enumerates Ocol's ambitions for self and society while disgorging a vehement—partly self-parodic—rejection of the African way of life. Both poems are energetic, if long-drawn out. Their second-person mode of utterance makes them sound like dramatic soliloquies, two masks articulating contrary views about a society apprehensive of radical change.

The poems imply a dual readership: an African audience that is more or less familiar with the tribal way of life alluded to by Lawino, and a larger, more scattered audience that learns about Africa by reading the poem. Many attribute the popularity of *Song of Lawino* to its 'authentic' representation of African experience. Jahan Ramazani argues persuasively that the notion of authenticity in Okot has to contend with 'heteroglossic poems' whose 'split vision' shows that when 'the native informant takes center stage', the result 'is profoundly intercultural' (2001: 145). Ramazani discourages a reading of either poem as purely nativist or anti-colonial. The Lawino persona gives signs of realizing that the local culture she cherishes is eroding; the Ocol persona recognizes that the implementation of Western ideas of progress in Africa is prone to distortion.

The two poems suggest that practices rooted in communal beliefs cannot be dealt with as if they were abstract elements of ethnographic analysis. Okot presents his readers with a woman who is embedded in, and a man who is uprooted from, a network of cultural assumptions. These are expressed with vigour and conviction. Okot fills each poem with a wealth of ethnographic detail, which loosens the subjective fiction of an individual consciousness. The poems place the anthropological training acquired by Okot in an ironic light, since Lawino finds 'normal' Western habits baffling, grotesque, and absurd, while Ocol savages tribal customs as outmoded and derelict. Where does Okot stand?

The poems turn the axiomatic relation of cultural anthropology inside out. The observed observes; the observer is observed. The notion of objective knowledge is displaced by the relativity of contending subjectivities. The fiction of neutrality cherished by the ethnologist is abandoned to reveal how the project of accumulating knowledge is complicit with the power acquired through control over acts of naming, as in 'primitive', 'progressive', 'civilized'. 'He says I am primitive', complains Lawino (35), contrasting her fidelity to the old ways with 'The progressive and civilized ones' who 'Put on blanket suits | And woolen socks from Europe' (45). The two poems contribute to a larger debate about the role of anthropological knowledge in colonialism. In *The Invention of Africa* (1988), V. Y. Mudimbe remarks of colonial missionaries and anthropologists in Africa: 'The first seeks to reduce the "primitives" to his faith and cultural presuppositions. For the second, "primitives" constitute an "object topic".... All of them share...the conviction that colonization is both a providential accident and a historical benefit' (1988: 66, 67).

The fictional voices of Lawino and Ocol fit few of the conventions that shape Western reading practices, although Okot was in the habit of citing Longfellow's 'Hiawatha' as one of his remote inspirations. Commentators have identified several features that are adapted from traditional Acoli and Lango songs of praise and abuse: the second-person mode of address, repetitions of key motifs, images, proverbs from local culture, and explicit allusions to specific songs. *Song of Lawino* implies a relation between poet, speaker, and community that is closer to the function of the '*nanga* players who are the main composers of music and poems in Acoliland' (p'Bitek 1974: 13) than to the individual authorship of Western writing. The rhyme of the original is abandoned in the English version, where the short and varying line-length creates a sense of rapid movement, which hovers between the oral and the transcribed.

The poems also exhibit features not found in local songs: length, a verse line more suited to recitation than song, an ambitious and wide-ranging discursiveness, and an acute awareness of the political context. Through the mask of Lawino, Okot revives the traditional role of the poet, who preserves and commemorates the values and customs of the tribe. Okot's method corresponds to the logic of a Xhosa proverb cited by the Ugandan poet and academic Okello Oculi: 'A person is a person through persons' (Shutte 1993: 56). Conversely, the mask of Ocol gives voice to the new challenges confronting the traditional way of life.

Song of Lawino and *Song of Ocol* relate to one another as thesis to antithesis, with no prospect of an easy synthesis. Together, they constitute one of the most powerful allegorical treatments of the conflict over colonial and postcolonial acculturation. The woman laments and scolds that her man has lost touch with the vitality of the traditional way of life. The man rejects those traditions as outdated. Okot's prose appears to be unambiguous about the harmful effects of colonialism on native cultures. The poetry is less certain whether to subscribe to the role of an uncomplicated cultural nationalist or to that of an aggressive nostalgist.

How can the first temptation be resisted? By reading *Song of Lawino* in such a way as to avoid an unqualified equation between the poet and the native woman's attack on African mimicry, or between the poet and the native woman's utopian view of the rapidly disappearing past. *Song of Ocol* is in danger of being read as if it were fully ironic, a reading that could hardly apply to bald declarations like the following:

> Tell the world
> In English or in French
> Talk about
> The African foundation
> On which we are
> Building the new nations
> Of Africa
>
> (1984: 150)

The alternative is to read each poem as a mixture of the ironic and the serious, without having to suppose that Okot dissembles a politics of desire as a form of ethnographic recuperation.

The nativist might like his Okot uncomplicated, on the assumption that Okot doubts if Western culture is ever likely to be apt for an African context. But it is more tempting to read Okot as doing several things at once. On the one hand, and within the same poem, the plurality that shadows the voice of Lawino allows recognition that change is inevitable and modernity enticing. On the other hand, the plurality of voices allows ridicule of alien customs, and bitterness at the abandonment of the old ways.

The nativist position is prone to a specific view about how a rooted culture might deal with the many forms of change forced upon it by colonial influences. It is likely that Okot believed in the idea of an African culture that might be uprooted by colonialism. It is equally plausible to read his poems as acts of naming, which force local audiences to recognize the discordant elements within the post-independent nation. Meanwhile, the idea of a rooted culture raises another question. Does Okot believe that the modernizing project under way in postcolonial societies should and could be stopped? His energy is deployed in naming, recognizing, and calling forth. However, he is not interested in stopping or reversing the changes already under way. The nativist belief may be described as a type of 'reactionary traditionalism'. Patrick Hogan argues that nativism is an unavailing ideology: 'the desire to preserve rooted culture is a mistaken desire; the ethical desire to preserve a rooted culture is a mistaken imperative' (2000: 313–14).

Okot's contemporary, the Sudanese-born and Ugandan-raised Taban lo Liyong (b. 1930) criticized Okot's *Song of Lawino* for its departures from the original, and issued his own translation of the Acoli, *Wer pa Lawino* (2001). During the 1960s and '70s, Taban developed into a poet whose world makes one feel, in Angela Smith's description, 'like an inhabitant of Eliot's Wasteland' (Smith 1989: 98). His prolific output is explicit about its sense of belatedness, and energetic in the expression of an assortment of frustrations, as in 'the throbbing of a pregnant cloud':

> Visitations on ground familiar
> Masturbations on a form I see

Impotence has seized my frame
Pages torn
From the book
Of the dead

(1971: 21)

The postcolonial African nation and its woes are addressed with a profuse sense of indignation and black humour, most notably in *Ballad of Under-Development* (1976). A poem from *Another Nigger Dead* (1972), 'the filed man laughed and said', illustrates what can be done with this method of tackling post-independence mismanagement:

the filed man laughed and said
    nationalization is the answer
a reporter jested what is the question
    the filed man laughed and said
neocolonialism is the problem

(Taban 1972: 8–9)

6
The settler countries

Overview

The earliest poets to use English outside Britain came from the settler regions of the British Empire. Regional traditions grew in self-confidence as the strings that attached settlements to Britain became attenuated. Poets and critics from North America, Australia, New Zealand, and white South Africa do not generally see their poetic traditions as part of the narrative of postcolonial poetry. Their view of the national literature recognizes a colonial period, but rarely uses 'postcolonial' to refer either to the period or the processes that show political self-rule translated by writers into cultural self-confidence. Yet the development of local traditions in the settler countries depended on struggling to overcome colonial dependency long after political autonomy was accomplished. Their path to literary self-confidence ran roughly parallel, but prior, to the processes of cultural decolonization in non-settler colonies. A comparative view of developments in the settler countries thus contributes significantly to a broad-based account of postcolonial poetry in English.

6.1 Writing region and nation

> I like thee Canada; I like thy woods
> [...]
> Thy Seasons too, when Nature can imprint her
> Steps on the green—but the deuce take thy Winter.
>
> George Longmore, 'Canada'

In the Preface, I suggested that the differences between the poetic traditions of Britain's former colonies are as significant as the commonality. This chapter assembles some evidence to indicate how this dual claim is applicable to the settler colonies. The next two paragraphs highlight the chief features that distinguish one settler culture from another, and the remainder of the section emphasizes the commonality linking this difference.

The United States fought a civil war to abolish slavery; it was the first British colony to become independent, and evolved a poetic tradition that became autonomous well before the other settler regions. Canada is unique in its development of two linguistic cultures, English and French, within a single nation. Australia has often been haunted by the fact that it originated in a penal colony. The development of Australia and New Zealand reproduced the external tension between dependent colony and colonial power in the internal marginalization of their Aboriginal and Maori inhabitants respectively. In South Africa, the displacement of indigenous tribal societies was followed by struggle for territory between Dutch and British settlers, and then by apartheid, which lasted from 1948 to the early 1990s. In 'As an African', when Benjamin Zephaniah declared, 'I did not celebrate 200 years of Australia, | I overstand its history is black' (1992: 28), his replacement of 'understand' by 'overstand' applied to more than just Australia.

In the United States, Australia, and New Zealand, settler cultures became effectively monolingual and Anglophone; in Canada, French and Anglophone elements developed with relative autonomy. In South Africa, English became a language of uneasy compromise among embattled ethnicities, since 'in a country where the status of the formerly disadvantaged African languages is a delicate cultural and political issue, the power of English can be oppressive' (Silva 2001: 85). In a lively poem titled 'Three Reasons for a Mixed, Umrabulo, Round-the-Corner Poetry', Jeremy Cronin (b. 1949, South Africa) contrasts his predicament with the cultural freedom enjoyed by contemporaries in the West, who can draw upon allusions ranging from Homer to Yeats without fear of losing their readers, whereas

> I live in a country with eleven official languages,
> Mass illiteracy, and a shaky memory.
>
> Here it is safe to assume
> Nothing at all. **Niks.**
>
> (1997: 1)

Despite these differences, the development of poetry in the settler regions reveals several common features, of which I identify seven below. First, the consequence of settlement for native inhabitants and their poetic cultures: throughout the period of early settlement, each region witnessed the displacement of vernacular tongues by the languages of Europe. Orality was either marginalized, or assimilated into Western modes of writing when early settlers and missionaries introduced indigenous tribal societies to writing, authorship, and translation.

This one-way traffic began the process by which the Western canon and its values were introduced into the indigenous languages of North America, South Africa, Australia, and New Zealand. This, in time, led to the same kinds of displacement in all colonial societies: native inhabitants lost touch with their own indigenous languages and cultures once Europe had interposed its languages, literatures, and religious practices into the colonies. The devaluation of orality produced the effect, as noted by the authors of *Key Concepts in Post-Colonial Studies*, of 'helping to convey the impression that the oral was not as socially or aesthetically valuable as the literary' (Ashcroft *et al.* 1998: 166).

Second, settler poetry had its origins in circumstances full of hardship, and a sense of mixed excitement and alienation amidst new physical environments. Early settlers wrote in response to the exigencies of survival. Their writing took the form of reports, chronicles, journals, diaries, and letters. This was followed by songs, ballads, lyrics, and narratives in prose and verse. Settlers faced an ecological reality that was strange, and estranging. Judith Wright (1915–2000, Australia) notes that the settler predicament meant 'first, and persistently, the reality of exile; second, though perhaps we now tend to forget this, the reality of newness and freedom', adding that settler life consisted chiefly of 'hard work, loneliness and dreadful isolation' (1965: xi, xii). 'English Canada', remarks Margaret Atwood, 'was settled by displaced persons who brought their language and their preconceptions with them' (1980: xxx). From New Zealand, Allen Curnow suggests in 1945, 'It must come of the struggle of those early generations to sustain their feeling of identity with England, in a country so forbiddingly different, that we have so habitually upheld the pretended against the actual' (1987: 47). In 1960 he adds, 'nineteenth-century colonists achieved their migration bodily, but not in spirit', and admits that New Zealand 'is a stranger country than either strangers, or its own inhabitants, have been accustomed to suppose' (1987: 136, 134).

In South Africa, the first poet to write in English was the Scotsman Thomas Pringle (1784–1834), but the region had to wait until the formation of a semi-autonomous Union in 1910 before poets began to think of themselves as anything more than transplanted variants of European culture. André Brink claimed in 1976 that 'it was not until the publication of Guy Butler's *Stranger to Europe* in 1952 that the distinguishing "Africanness" of our experience became accepted by a broader spectrum of poets' (Gray 1984: 9). J. M. Coetzee underlines the preoccupation to which Butler returns frequently: 'an unsettling realization of his alienness in Africa' (1988: 169). He argues that poets of European descent, writing in South Africa, could not escape the feeling that 'This landscape remains alien, impenetrable, until a language is found in which to win it, speak it, represent it' (1988: 7).

In 1961, Judith Wright insisted: 'Australia is still, for us, not a country but a state—states—of mind. We do not yet speak from within her, but from outside' (Barnes 1969: 331). When Atwood gave voice, in 1970, to the disembarking of Susannah Moodie at Quebec in *The Journals of Susanna Moodie*, her Susanna declares, 'I am a word | in a foreign language' (1970: 11). From Canada, in 1972, while paying homage to the poet Al Purdy (1918–2000), Dennis Lee (b. 1939) conceded, 'we have been in North America but not whole-heartedly in it; and as we have lived those contradictions—consistently, though in confusion—our primal necessity has been to survive' (Kertzer 1998: 97).

Settler poetry ranges across the entire gamut from a sense of the alienating in nature to nostalgia for 'home', from anxiety and depression to curiosity and wonder at the unfamiliar in nature. Such reactions soon led to a determined effort by poets to assimilate nature to culture, to tackle the unsettling as well as the exhilarating dimension of their new environments. From Australia, A. A. Phillips noted that the relation between the old and the new often proved clumsy, 'as intimate and uneasy as that between an adolescent and his parent' (Barnes 1969: 297). Kenneth Slessor (1901–71, Australia) remarked of his nineteenth-century predecessor Charles Harpur (1813–68), 'his mode of thinking and his habits of expression are entirely under the English spell' (1990: 104). The derivative aspect of the colonial legacy could be shed only when poets realized that 'the independence, vitality and the *newness* required of genuine poetry imply the rejection of inherited words and ideas' (1990: 100).

Third, settler verse had its origins in forms of literary derivativeness that took a long time to shed. Averagely, it reads like 'mellifluous Jabberwocky' (Jackson 1991: 343), whose involuntary quaintness continues to provoke from later poets every possible reaction from embarrassment to apology. Such writing illustrates two aspects of an incomplete translation. People were translated (in the sense of being carried over) to new regions; but their new environment, which confronted them like an unfamiliar language, did not translate readily into categories of thought, feeling, and language shaped by former environments. John Kinsella (b. 1963, Australia) notes that languages, like people, became 'uprooted and translated', 'nomadic in origin', 'set adrift from the sight/sound sensorium of the concrete experiences of the English people' (1998: 65). In 'Sonnet of Brotherhood', R. A. Mason (1905–71, New Zealand) commemorated the early settlers of New Zealand as 'beleaguered victims' betrayed by fate:

> here in this far-pitched perilous hostile place
> this solitary hard-assaulted spot
> fixed at the friendless outer edge of space.
>
> (Bornholdt *et al.* 1997: 464)

Newness of environment often meant the discovery of a new tonality. In New Zealand, it took several generations for irony to displace a situation that presented itself to the New Zealander 'in terms of nostalgia or high adventure' (Curnow 1987: 50). Newness also meant the urgency with which certain questions were asked by poets of themselves. How was a poet to create a distinct local identity? How should a poet mediate between the local and the universal? What was the relation of the local language to the British tradition? The poets in whose writing these questions acquired focus and intensity during the first decades of the twentieth century exerted the greatest influence on subsequent writing.

Fourth, doubts and misgivings often found expression in the cultural anxiety that local traditions had failed to produce major figures, and the fear that the 'new' (nation, culture, tradition) was a fragile fiction. In 1945, Curnow wrote, 'Strictly speaking, New

Zealand doesn't exist yet, though some possible New Zealands glimmer in some poems and on some canvases. It remains to be created—should I say invented—by writers, musicians, artists, architects, publishers; even a politician might help—how many generations does that take?' He argued that the rediscovery of a colony as one's country required a 'reversal of the colonist's nostalgia for "Home"', adding in 1960 that there were many New Zealand poems 'which openly acknowledge such problems' (1987: 77, 59, 136).

Poems with titles like 'Canada' and 'Australia' abound in their respective regions (e.g. A. D. Hope, 'Australia'; Earle Birney, 'up her can nada', and 'Can. Lit.'). Such poems are rare in American poetry after Whitman. Robin Hyde's 'Journey from New Zealand' (1938) lends itself to being treated as a type of 'the regulation nationalist/contemplative poem (narrow-eyed, hard-edged, bloodstained) almost to the point of parody' (Leggott 1995: 274). Curnow's 'House and Land' (1941) juxtaposes recognition that 'The spirit of exile... Is strong in the people still' with

Awareness of what great gloom
Stands in a land of settlers
With never a soul at home.

(Bornholdt *et al.* 1997: 399)

Fifth, the attempt to localize poetic identity through a relation to landscape was met with resistance. The fact that most Australians live in cities while many painters and poets still continue to address 'Australianity' through landscape led to the recognition voiced by Bernard Smith that a 'preoccupation with landscape has been largely responsible for the creation and maintenance of a false consciousness of what it is to be Australian' (Hodge and Mishra 1990: 143). From Canada, Hugh Kenner remarked caustically in 1954, 'The surest way to the hearts of a Canadian is to inform them that their souls are to be identified with rocks, rapids, wilderness, and virgin (but exploitable) forest' (Glickman 2000: 132). Also from Canada, Northrop Frye declared in the 1960s that the country suffered from 'imaginative dystrophy' and 'a strangled articulateness... less perplexed by the question "Who am I?" than by some such riddle as "Where is here?"' (1971: iii, 220). In 1965, he claimed—to the irritation of several local writers—that 'Canada has produced no author who is a classic in the sense of possessing a vision greater than that of his best readers', adding that the literary imagination of such a community was bound to develop 'a garrison mentality'. As late as 1971, he maintained that Canada 'is practically the only country left in the world which is a pure colony, colonial in psychology as well as in mercantile economics' (1971: 213, 225, iii). In 1973, Dennis Lee confessed, 'If you are Canadian, home is a place that is not home to you' (Glickman 2000: 135).

F. R. Scott (1899–1985) gave this anxiety vivid expression in 'Mackenzie River':

A river so Canadian
    it turns its back
on America
[...]
In land so bleak and bare
    a single plume of smoke
is a scroll of history.

(1966: 32–3)

W. H. New comments: 'The nationalism of the Arctic metaphor, the resistance to American intervention in Canadian affairs, the indeterminate uncertainties of the northern landscape: these are familiar political and literary paradigms' (1997: 120). Scott's 'Laurentian Shield' (1954) enacts what it anticipates, the dissolution of a postcolonial frame of mind:

...This land stares at the sun in a huge silence
Endlessly repeating something we cannot hear.
Inarticulate, arctic,
Not written on by history, empty as paper....

But a deeper note is sounding, heard in the mines
The scattered camps and the mills, a language of life,
And what will be written in the full culture of occupation
Will come presently, tomorrow ...

(Smith 1960: 182–3)

W. H. New interprets Scott's attitude to 'the shield' as a form of romantic defensiveness, which shows that the poet *constructs* the image of wilderness that he purports to *describe* (1997: 131, 172). In sharp contrast, 'Laurentian Man' (1959) by Wilfred Watson (b. 1911, UK/Canada), ironicizes the anxious narcissism underlying the romantic preoccupation that tied poets to region to nation to typology in order to provide a deconstructed image of God creating '*homo Canadiensis*':

> Before him, obvious as a senseless crime, the first Canadian stood gaping
> At him, that magnificent blank complacency,
> That awful monotony of face, that face to face
> Blankness of mind, all cattle grass and trees, all wood and beef—
> *Comsummatum est*, God punned.
> [...]
> I'm not completely sold on brilliancy.
> I made the Greek too subtle and too sharp.
> The French too polished. The English too poetically glib of tongue.
> The Irish too fanciful, always fighting fairies.
>
> (New 1997: 173)

Sixth, the transition from colony to nation gave a crucial role for poetry. D. M. R. Bentley points out that notions like 'Young England, Young Ireland, and Young Canada are all offshoots of a Romantic nationalism' which can be linked to 'such German theorists of nationality as Johann Gottfried Herder and Friedrich von Schlegel, who argued that literature, especially poetry, is an essential ingredient of national consciousness and cohesion' (2004: 40). In the context of Africa, Frantz Fanon described a pattern of growth for intellectuals in a time of decolonization that finds an interesting analogue in the otherwise dissimilar circumstances of poets and intellectuals in the settler countries, as described by the Australian poet A. D. Hope (1907–2000). Fanon's essay 'On National Culture' (1959) describes a three-stage process. The intellectual 'gives proof that he has assimilated the culture of the occupying power'; then finds himself 'disturbed' about his ambivalent relation towards native as well as European cultures; and finally, 'after having tried to lose himself in the people and with the people', 'turns himself into an awakener of the people' (1963: 222–3).

From Australia, Hope gives a similar account of the development from colonial to 'autonomous existence'. In the first stage, writers are 'transplanted from the homeland to the new colony and their work is simply a part of the literary tradition of the homeland'. In the second, 'writers, for the most part born in the new land but educated in the literary tradition of the mother country, set out consciously to create a literature of their own'. Hope described this as 'a self-conscious attempt to follow literary fashions abroad at second remove, or a self-conscious attempt to turn one's back on the parent tradition and to create a new one rooted in native soil'. In the third stage, we find 'writers capable of influencing and leading the whole literary tradition, not only in the new country, but wherever the language is spoken' (1974: 74).

In Canada, 'interest in a national identity was subsumed in a persistent tension regarding the relationship between . . . French-speaking citizens and the Anglophone affiliation' (Corse 1997: 19). Earle Birney's 'Can. Lit.' expresses a sense of collective self-deprecation:

> We French, we English, never lost our civil war,
> endure it still, a bloodless, civil bore;
> no wounded lying about, no Whitman wanted.
> It's only by our lack of ghost we're haunted.
>
> (Kertzer 1998: 37)

Kertzer comments: 'Canada casts no heroic shadows because our bland, practical citizens lack the historical traumas and the responsive imagination to expose the dreams on which the nation was built'.

The ideology of cultural nationalism subscribes to the belief that writing fosters collective identity when it is intensely of, and responsive to, a specific environment, and the needs and aspirations of its inhabitants. The cruder kinds of cultural nationalism are easy to dismiss, but a persistent form of the desire to achieve communal identity by celebrating the human in unique space–time conjunctions continues to inspire poets from all the settler regions. Curnow was one of its more enlightened supporters: 'Reality must be local and special at the point where we pick up the traces'; 'the signature of a region . . . can attest value in the work' (1987: 133, 162). Cultural nationalism commits poetry to the conscious pursuit of a unique local identity. As a strategy, it comes at a price. It ties poets to their regions in a manner that risks provincialism, insularity, and tedious description-for-the-sake-of-description.

Seventh, poets discovered an alternative strategy that focuses on language instead of nation. It identifies mimicry as a narrowly literary rather than a broadly cultural problem. It requires poets to liberate themselves from dependency by renovating their diction, style, and forms. Atwood recollects that her generation met these alternatives as a choice between a 'cosmopolitan' and 'native' approach to writing

(2002: 22). This division was championed most determinedly in Canada by A. J. M. Smith (1902–80), and it provoked resistance from contemporaries as well as later generations (Glickman 2000: 128).

The rejection of nation as a useful category for poetry can be linked to the criticism made by Yvor Winters, and noted in Chapter 1, that Whitman's poetry commits the fallacy of 'national mimeticism' (1947: 441). In other words, it is not self-evident that being representative of one's nation necessarily leads to writing that is significant as poetry. Kenneth Slessor, for instance, was sceptical about the 'Australianity' of his nineteenth-century forebears Henry Lawson (1867–1922) and A. B. Paterson (1864–1941): 'not even the most intense nationalism is capable in itself of turning verse into poetry.... External landscapes and allusions to national ideas are not required by poetry' (1990: 113, 115). Related sentiments are dramatized by F. R. Scott in 'The Canadian Authors Meet' (1945):

> O Canada, O Canada, Oh can
> A day go by without new authors springing
> To paint the native maple, and to plan
> More ways to set the selfsame welkin ringing?
>
> (Smith 1960: 188)

6.2 Breaking with the past

> Australian flowers I prize nor scorn;
> Let those who in this land were born
> Admire them, praise them, pluck and wear
> On swarthy brow, in jet-black hair:
> I never gathered them, nor knew
> Where I a child to manhood grew;—
> What have I then with them to do?
>
> Richard Howitt, 'To the Daisy, on Finding One Unexpectedly in Australia, 30 July 1840'

American poetry managed to avoid the appellation of 'postcolonial' in the life and career of Whitman. When A. J. M. Smith promoted Modernist writing as a model for Canadian poets, his will to modernity submitted itself to tutelage at the level of style and poetic strategy in order to achieve freedom from cultural nationalism. His case illustrates a larger point. The myth of new beginnings is a compelling fiction that drives poets to fresh starts, but most types of poetic originality begin in some form of derivativeness. In American poetry, the sensuous melancholy of 'Sunday Morning' (1915), by Wallace Stevens (1879–1955), shows the best that could be done by a natural affinity for the styles of Keats and Tennyson:

> Passions of rain, or moods in falling snow;
> Grievings in loneliness, or unsubdued
> Elations when the forest blooms; gusty
> Emotions on wet roads on autumn nights;
> All pleasures and all pains, remembering
> The bough of summer and the winter branch.
>
> (1997: 53–4)

American poetry provides other examples of the relation between derivativeness and new beginnings. The doctrines of Imagism formulated and illustrated by T. E. Hulme (1883–1917) in pre-World War I London found its lasting expression indirectly, in William Carlos Williams. That the stylistic affiliations of Stevens or Williams are not described as 'postcolonial' shows how the critical discourse surrounding American poetry elides the vocabulary of derivativeness, although such elisions do not mean that the term might not apply. As noted in Chapter 1, the stylistic dimension of American poetic careers in the early part of the twentieth century shows a broad pattern of poetic renovation that is similar to the development of stylistic modernity in the major poets from the other settler traditions.

In Canada, a group that became known as the Confederation poets (Bliss Carman, Duncan Campbell Scott, Archibald Lampman, and Charles G. D. Roberts) continued to publish fluent but languid post-Romantic verse well into the twentieth century. Northrop Frye protested in the early 1930s at the 'phoney genius' of such verse. Sandra Djwa draws attention to a Roberts poem, 'Pan and the Rose', which declares unblushingly, 'Came Pan to the garden on a golden morning | The dew of the thickets adrip on his thighs' (Lee and Denham 1994: 132). The following generation of Canadian poets (E. J. Pratt, A. J. M. Smith, F. R. Scott, and Raymond Knister) began to weed out decayed post-Victorianism from their styles during the 1920s and early 1930s, drawing upon varying combinations of local inspiration, individual talent, and the example of modernist writing. The Canadian apprenticeship to American and international models did not impress everyone at home: the poet Robert Kroetsch (b. 1927) claimed, half-jokingly, that Canadian literature 'evolved directly from Victorian into Postmodern . . . the country that invented Marshall McLuhan and Northrop Frye did so by not ever being Modern' (Glickman 2000: 127).

In Australia, poetry took more than a century to drop British models. The interim produced its share of what Les Murray (b. 1938) describes as 'poems so choked with outworn poetic tropes and phrases that nothing alive struggles to the surface' (1997: 303). Two trends prevailed in matters of style and form. The first was a literary attempt to engage the realities of the Australian environment while continuing to rely upon Augustan, post-Romantic, or Victorian models. The second trend, prodigal of ballads and periodical verse, adapted popular forms to easy-going narratives with local colour that acquired large local readerships, and were followed in the 1890s by more than a decade of turgid nationalism in verse.

In a retrospective essay of 1954, Slessor explains that the kind of poetry he wanted to write had little use for the 'bush' tradition of nineteenth-century Australian verse (Charles Harpur, Henry Kendall, A. G. Gordon, Henry Lawson, A. B. Paterson), and later nationalist poetry (Victor Daley, Bernard O'Dowd). Slessor felt that 'it is not until . . . Hugh MacCrae's *Satyrs and Sunlight* . . . in 1909, that poetry can be considered to have begun any consistent growth in Australia'; he felt that Australian versifiers of the late nineteenth century were no different from their American counterparts in the inability 'to free themselves from those inherited obsessions and ascendancies' (1990: 107–8). By 'inherited obsessions and ascendancies' he meant British models of style and form.

Judith Wright made a stronger claim on behalf of Christopher Brennan (1870–1932), whose work she saw as 'Australia's first real contribution to international literature' (Wright 1965: 80). A sonnet from 'Secreta Silvarum' begins:

> Fire in the heavens, and fire along the hills,
> and fire made solid in the flinty stone,
> thick-mass'd or scatter'd pebble, fire that fills
> the breathless hour that lives in fire alone.
>
> (1984: 49)

Neither Brennan's Europeanized sensibility nor the low-key lyricism of John Shaw Neilson (1872–1942) quite managed the renovation of language needed by later poets. McAuley said of Brennan: 'We are at present in a phase of literary fashion opposite to his: the predominating preference recently has been for an ordinary-language poetry, with very reduced pretensions to be doctrinal or prophetic, and tending to retreat into the private and the subjective' (1975: 39).

Modernization of diction and style, a preference for concrete images, a suspicion of abstractions, and a distrust of vague emotionalism became the established norms for Australian poets in the 1920s, with Slessor among the earliest to exemplify what became a general tendency in the 1930s and 1940s. These poets turned their back on habits of feeling and utterance described with some asperity by FitzGerald: 'I am glad to say I have not heard for years that horrible word "ineffable", which seemed intended to express so much in the early twenties. That is what a great deal of alleged poetry here was like prior to Norman Lindsay's indirect influence: ineffable' (1987: 29–30).

Poets like Slessor found their interests reinforced by contemporary developments in the West, though the majority of Australian poets have been cautious about following the more radical aspects of Modernist practice. Hope, for instance, professed combatively, 'I was never seduced, as so many of my poetic generation were, by the modish but essentially trivial fame of T. S. Eliot and Ezra Pound' (1979: 11). McAuley said more ambiguously of Yeats that he 'was the chief supplier of models and moulds for Australian poetry in the 1940s and 1950s, but his influence on my work was not great' (1988: 112). These poets illustrate what David Carter describes as the conservative element in the Australian intellectual: 'the decadence of Europe, modern culture in America, from jazz to cinema . . . were seen as alien to an Australia defined as young, vigorous, cheerful and manly, with a culture as wholesome as its climate' (2000: 265).

Contemporary Australian poets acknowledge that the local preference for plain and direct speech, especially when formalized in traditional metre, receives nourishment from the popular vernacular traditions of the nineteenth century. Les Murray, for instance, supports the claim that 'Australian poetry attained a relaxed modernity long before the rise of literary modernism' (1997: 292, 297–8). The values and attitudes that have come to characterize Australian perceptions of its own culture include sympathy for the underdog, impatience with cant, resistance to authoritarianism, and a preference for the commonsensical over the pretentious. These have made it easier for poets of English, Irish, and Scottish descent to balance their deference to European models, and their belated assimilation of the American freedoms of a post-Robert Lowell era (as in Kirkby, 1982) with the homespun lineage of their local forebears.

As with Canada and Australia, New Zealand poetry took almost a century to come into its own. Blanche Baughan's 'The Old Place' (1903) and 'A Bush Section' (1908) gave early evidence of what could be accomplished with a plain style packed with detail and free of affectation. The next step in the treatment of local materials in a contemporary idiom came in the late 1920s and early 1930s, with Ursula Bethell (1874–1945) and R. A. K. Mason (1905–71). The names of Katherine Mansfield, Eileen Duggan, and D'Arcy Creswell were added to this list when the first tough-minded assertion of a local canon was made by Curnow in two influential anthologies, *A Book of New Zealand Verse 1923–1945*, and *The Penguin Book of New Zealand Verse* (1960). Curnow defined a set of convictions that shaped a canon and defined the terms for future debate. C. K. Stead (b. 1932) describes the debate as an argument between Curnow's belief 'that a truly indigenous literature would be regional and nationalist' and the view of younger poets that 'mature New Zealand writing ought to be international, taking its local roots for granted' (1989: 136, 123).

The generation comprising Curnow, Charles Brasch (who edited the influential quarterly *Landfall* from 1947), and Dennis Glover fostered a poetry marked by sardonic self-questionings of 'our manic-depressive tendency—our big-small dementia' (Curnow 1987: 193–4). Curnow claimed that New Zealanders shared the 'tensions and inconsistencies, between sprout-thinking and tree-thinking' with all other nations of a 'province/metropolis provenance'. His own writing adhered to the belief that the universals of human experience can be approached in poetry only through attachment to the here and now of wherever a poet happens to live, and not through the internationalism of the 'literary hitch-hiker' and the 'tourist in the Bibliosphere' (1987: 203). Stead was impressed by Curnow's argument that 'unease in the environment' was 'proof of honesty, or clear-sightedness, a recognition "of reality" '; for Stead, as for Curnow, 'when New Zealand poetry stopped romanticizing the place, it became more truthful' (1989: 137).

Reaction against the prescriptive aspect of Curnow's regionalism set in early: 'In the 1960s... A new wave of young New Zealand poets discovered... the Modernist tradition' (Stead 1981: 147). Bill Manhire (b. 1946) confirmed in 1987: 'American poetry was read by a whole range of New Zealand writers in the late 1960s and early 1970s... for those of my generation it had an absolutely transforming effect.' Stead placed the dilemma between the regional and the modernist impulses in the context of an argument by Allen Tate (1899–1979), a poet and critic from the American South. Tate warned that release from regionalism into the internationalism offered by English as a global language might seduce poets into a new provincialism intended to 'compensate for the limitations of the little community by envisaging the big community', although the latter might not be 'necessarily bigger spiritually or culturally than the little community' (Stead 1981: 191). This account did not go unchallenged. Patrick Evans remarks sharply: 'a modernism that could hold late Curnow and Baxter and a certain amount of post-modernist practice as well as the "young New Zealand poets"... would have to be a very broad sort of modernism indeed' (1990: 233). Nevertheless, it can be argued that after the 1970s, poetry in New Zealand moved to a more relaxed repertoire of styles and tonal registers, capable of dissolving the tension between the local and the universal.

In South Africa, the break with the past took the form of a struggle between Boer and British culture that lasted over a century. The Boers lost their territory, their linguistic dominance (1828), and slave-ownership (1833) to British pressure. In the long poem *Englishmen*, Christopher Hope (b. 1944), commemorates the travails of the retreating Afrikaners:

> —The Boers thought North forever
> Until the tsetse
> Bit them back. They failed on a wall of flies,
> Retired, stayed put or turned East
> In anger, and fevered, died or disappeared.
> [...]
> They are not going anywhere. How outstrip
> Empire when all the world's imperial?
>
> (1985: 17)

The period from 1902 to the end of World War II saw an uneasy Anglo-Boer alliance between a British minority and the Boer majority. In Anglophone poetry, this period created a fragile sense of a tradition, which is exemplified by poets such as Guy Butler (b. 1918). The Boer Nationalists came to power in 1948. In 1961, they declared the region a Republic and left the British Commonwealth, breaking their last colonial link to Europe. They also enacted legislation to establish apartheid as a systematic form of racial segregation in South Africa (and in Rhodesia).

Themes of exile and alienation remain endemic to South African writing. During the 1920s and 1930s, several young poets left the country: Roy Campbell (1901–57), William Plomer (1903–73), Charles Madge (1912–96), F. T. Prince (1912–2003), and David Wright (1920–94). They chose the path of education in Britain as a one-way exit pass from the uneasy land of their birth. Plomer was among the first to introduce a modern tone into South African verse, incisive, sombre, and determinedly nomadic, as in 'A Transvaal Morning':

> The stranger started up to face
> The sulphur sky of Africa, an infinite
> False peace, the trees in that dry place
> Like painted bones, their stillness like a threat.
>
> (Butler and Mann 1979: 86)

His friend Roy Campbell, whose right-wing sympathies sent him to Spain and Portugal in 1926, bid farewell to his birthplace in the satirical long poem *The Wayzgoose* (1928):

> In fair banana land we lay our scene—
> South Africa, renowned both far and wide
> For politics and little else beside:
> Where, having torn the land with shot and shell,
> Our sturdy pioneers as farmers dwell,
> And, 'twixt the hours of strenuous sleep, relax
> To shear the fleeces or to fleece the blacks...
>
> (Butler and Mann 1979: 71–2)

Apartheid infected white South African poetry with a guilt that found expression in Afrikaans as well as English. Some of the most haunting effects can be found in the Afrikaans poet Ingrid Jonker (1933–65). In 'The Child Who Was Shot Dead By Soldiers in Nyanga', the fact of the brutal and needless killing of the helpless and the innocent is protested in a paradoxical series of assertions that abandon the conventional trappings of grief because these deaths are not like other deaths:

> The child is not dead
> not at Langa not at Nyanga
> not at Orlando not at Sharpeville
> not at the police station in Philippi
> where he lies with a bullet in his head
>
> (Hirson 1997: 18)

Apartheid also led to the kinds of political oppression that forced poets into exile and self-exile. Breyten Breytenbach (b. 1939) experienced imprisonment during 1975–82. His writing in Afrikaans and English combines political commitment with the aesthetics of a cosmopolitan sensibility. Peter Sacks (b. 1950), who moved to the US in the 1970s, looks back on what the Boer experience meant in 'Anthem':

> Burgers, Boers, Voortrekkers
> from a foreign crown,
> unfairly broken by an old empire
> until we came into our own.
> [. . .]
> Past reason or remorse
> we chew the toughened hope
> of our survival—red meat
> twisted to a hard black rope.
>
> (2002: online)

In a fascinating account of the relation between responsibility and complicity under apartheid, Mark Sanders draws attention to Breytenbach's prose work 'A View from the Outside', which declares, 'We are a bastard people with a bastard language. Our nature is one of bastardy. It is good and beautiful thus' (2002: 144–5). Sanders notes that 'bastardy' offers itself 'as an alternative to the violence of the purist identity formation', exposing the disavowal at the heart of Afrikaner nationalism (147–9). Breytenbach turned from Afrikaans to English. The case has a parallel in the Kenyan writer Ngugi, who recoiled from English to Gikuyu after his arrest without trial in the late 1970s. Breytenbach's poems in either language give poignant expression to the displacement that becomes the permanent mark of exile. Here is the first stanza of 'breyten prays for himself', translated by Denis Hirson:

> There is no need for Pain Lord
> We could live well without it
> A flower has no teeth
>
> (1978: 9)

A more agitated example in English from *Lady One* (2002), titled 'mene mene tekel', describes the writing of the exile as 'always in a foreign tongue | in nowhere land':

> some exiles
> after a flamboyant trajectory of cocktails
> die in a fetal crouch
> with uncombed head in the oven
> or fucked in a plastic placenta
> and the posthumous note a white silence
>
> (2002: 27)

Settler poets who chose to stay struggled to find 'a natural or Adamic language' that might shed the cultural baggage of English, which 'carries echoes of a very different natural world—a world of downs and fells, oaks and daffodils, robins and badgers' (Coetzee 1988: 8). The ambivalent relation of the South African poet to his language and landscape is read by Coetzee as part of the failure of the white community to find a balance between language and a natural environment full of silence and emptiness. He argues that writers of European descent find the South Africa landscape less hospitable to European ideas of the sublime than poets and painters in North America. He adds that South African poetry succeeds, as in the case of Sydney Clouts (1926–82), only when it finds ways to enact an experience of immersion in nature which sidesteps the visual and conceptual mastery implicit in the European genres of topographical verse and landscape painting.

Apartheid drove many writers away from Afrikaans, although a few coloured poets in the Cape region, such as Adam Small (b. 1936), continued using a local patois derived from Afrikaans. The rejection of the language of apartheid by the majority of bilingual authors saw to it that English became the language of choice for black writers, and for white writers who felt alienated from the politics of their race in

South Africa. South African poetry thus contains within it several very different kinds of writing, which only occasionally show signs of 'cross-pollination' (Attwell 2004: 506). During the 1960s, a generation of Afrikaan writers ('Sestigers': writers of the sixties), turned away from the conventions of Boer culture. As in Northern Ireland, the relation of writing to politics forced white South Africans to confront a choice between commitment to the political causes thrust upon them, and resistance to the co-option of poetry in the service of politics. Some tried to continue writing oblivious of apartheid. Their poetry lost conviction in its desire to deliver 'English back, in assured terms, as a lesson in civility to the linguistic babel that is South Africa' (Chapman 1996: 225).

The poet and translator Stephen Watson links the problems of using English in South Africa to the problems of liberalism as an ideology of the 'mediator and conciliator' (1990: 27). He argued that liberalism did not prevent its alleged 'neutrality' and 'objectivity' from being reduced to 'an instrument of estrangement, apathy and impotence' (1990: 28). In 'The Whiteman Blues', Lionel Abrahams (b. 1928) dramatizes the awkward unease forced by conscience upon white poets:

We can afford to say we know
the blacks are really given hell,
Big Boss is harsh and stupid and must go:
We say it—and it helps like one Aspro.
We still feel jumpy, mixed up, not quite well.

(Gray 1984: 11)

During the 1970s, several Afrikaner writers defied apartheid directly, willing to face exile, thus expressing solidarity with their black compatriots, regardless of how the blacks saw this solidarity. Others relied upon irony, as in Peter Wilhelm's 'A Very Short Story' (1976):

The President of the People's Republic of South Africa was taking a leisurely stroll in the Gardens, accompanied by his favourite dwarf, Tinyman. It had been a difficult, but rewarding day in Parliament.

'So, Sir,' Tinyman said, 'now your word is truth.'

The President frowned and paused. 'No,' he said, 'now my word is law.'

The dwarf looked up wonderingly at his master. 'You're always so precise,' he said.

(Wilhelm and Polley 1976: 72–3)

The nature of the break with the past in South Africa had an analogue in the case of Southern Rhodesia, which had a sizeable white settler community, and was annexed by Britain from the South Africa Company in 1923. In 1961, as apartheid tightened its grip in South Africa, Britain attempted to consolidate its hold on the territories it controlled to the north of South Africa by bringing them together into a Federation. The attempt failed: the territories that had very few white settlers (Nyasaland and Northern Rhodesia) split from the Federation and from British control in 1964 to become Malawi and Zambia respectively. In 1965, the white minority government ruling Southern Rhodesia broke free from Britain, declaring the region an independent country, Rhodesia. This break was challenged by Britain and by international opinion. Internally, it led the black population to militant resistance and guerrilla war against white rule. The violence intensified from 1972, eventually leading to independence. Rhodesia was renamed Zimbabwe in 1980.

Flora Veit-Wild and Anthony Chennells report of Rhodesian poetry before 1980: 'Of the over eighty volumes of verse published in Rhodesia the vast majority are of little interest' (2004: 451). The poems of John Eppel (b. 1947) illustrate the mixed sense of belonging and unbelonging with which white 'Rhodesianism' (2001: 32) suffers its sense of involvement in the violence of civil war. Reading Aristotle on fear and pity acquires a new edge when contemplated 'Lying on my back—horizontal rain | Of tracer bullets just above my nose' (31). 'On Browsing Through Some British Poems' drives home the realization that 'I know we do not belong', 'I know that we are merely visitors in Africa' (37).

The break with the past experienced by white rule in Rhodesia was re-enacted on a larger scale when apartheid finally collapsed in South Africa after the release of Nelson Mandela from prison in 1990. Poetry had long since anticipated the end of white dominance. In 'The Flight of the White South Africans' (1974), Christopher Hope alludes to a Xhosa priestess who prophesied in 1856 that the white invaders would be driven to sea, and concludes on a note of contemporary foreboding:

> ... We go to the wall
> But Mowgli, Biggles and Alice are not there:
> Nongquase, heaven unhoods its bloodshot eye

Above a displaced people; our demise
Is near, and we'll be gutted where we fall.

(Brink and Coetzee 1986: 117)

When the long-awaited transfer of power came in 1994, exile reversed colours. For white writers in post-apartheid South Africa, as remarked by Michael Chapman, 'the burden has been to write themselves out of a dead, white, racist and patriarchal past, and to re-inscribe themselves in a society that does not yet exist' (1996: 415). In 1983, Jeremy Cronin reiterated a sense of how this might be done, in 'To Learn How To Speak':

With the voices of the land,
To parse the speech in its rivers,
To catch, in the inarticulate grunt,
Stammer, call, cry, babble, tongue's knot
A sense of the stoneness of these stones
From which all words are cut.

(Hirson 1996: 163)

Listening to the older 'voices of the land' has been a persistent motif in South African poetry. It was attempted in the 1960s by Jack Cope. Likewise, Stephen Watson's *Return of the Moon: Versions from the /Xam* (1991/1995) transposes the nineteenth century 'Song of the Broken String' to poignant effect: 'Because | the string is broken, the country feels | as if it lay | empty before me, our country seems |as if it lay | both empty before me, | and dead before me' (1991: 59).

Poetry has reacted to the new South Africa with caution. Denis Hirson (b. 1951) lost his father to prison for nine years. After his release, the family went into exile in 1973. Hirson's prose poem, 'The Long-Distance South African' (1995), shows how a sense of remembered pain and guarded optimism merges the private realm of the exiled South African living in Paris with the public realm of a new era in the politics of the homeland. In an interview in the journal *New Coin* (1996), Hirson explains that events unfolding in 1990 played a part in 'allowing myself some 20 years later to actually experience the full release of emotion which I couldn't express in 1973' (1996: online). The son's experience of what it meant to have the father return from prison colours the exiled South African's sense of what it means for Nelson Mandela to return to public life: 'It's been twenty seven years of bootsteps and breaking stones. Out of time with all the elation, he is still alone.' In controlled understatement, the poet prepares to meet a long-awaited future with a sense of muted and cautious excitement, overshadowed by the recognition that all exiles inhabit a limbo: 'We belong to no single place, ours is the history of those who cross over' (de Kock and Tromp 1996: 11). Postcoloniality is here identifiable as the long-suspended moment of 'cross over'. Developments in post-apartheid society and literatures suggest that it is likely to be a long-drawn-out and difficult crossing.

Tatamkhulu Afrika (1920–2002) was born in Egypt of an Arab father and a Turkish mother. He was brought to South Africa in 1923, later he served in World War II, worked in Namibia, and was banned in South Africa for resistance to apartheid. His 1994 poem, 'Tamed' (de Kock and Tromp 1996: 18–20), dramatizes an emblematic occasion. A political leader addresses a gathering. No specific name or occasion is mentioned. The air is 'ambivalent as a new wine'. The assembled crowd includes two louts, of whom one stands 'imploded and intent', his face lit 'with something of the sublimity | he must believe you bring'. The voice of the poem asks if the leader is still he that 'sought the dream in even stone and iron'. The poem moves on to chronicle 'the small fumble of the tongue', the compliant closing move 'on to a new square in an old game'. The leader finishes with a blessing, the audience rises in rapture to 'the kitsch', and the speaker of the poem is left 'hanging my head lest | you see me weep'. The tone conveys dejection rather than reproach, the style retains a dignified poise despite the sadness.

Similar tones of wariness after trauma can be found in younger poets. Karen Press (b. 1956, South Africa) gives surreal expression to the sense of persistent trauma that haunts post-apartheid South Africa. 'Tiresias in the City of Heroes' remembers:

> In Pretoria your fingernails became joint chief of staff.
> In Pretoria your teeth ran the central bank.
> In Pretoria your hair was the president.
> That's what I remember.
>
> In Jo'burg your heart was tortured and died.
> In Cape Town your skin joined the enemy's police.
> In the veld and the mountains your memory buried its children.
> That's what I remember.
>
> (2000: 66)

A younger poet, Adam Schwartzman (b. 1973), who returned to South Africa in 1999 after several years in exile, expresses subdued expectations in 'Celeste':

> Once there was an empire here, somewhere there still is,
> but I can't see it.
> I'm just a white man
>
> today.
>
> (2003: 28)

Another poem, 'Osogbo', shows that the 'white man' is willing to submit himself to the stone gods of the forest:

> Suddenly a river came round the bend,   hissing like electricity cables,
> [...]
> I put my forehead on the foot of the god and the cool forest jumped into me,
> [...]
> *You be no man*   came the forest in me,
> *You now be no man,*
> and the river flipped a curl up the bank and tapped my ankle
> *Now you be no man-o!*
>
> (2003: 33)

6.3 Becoming modern

> And the Englishman, dogged and grim,
> Looks the world in the face as he goes,
> And he holds a proud lip, for he sails his own ship,
> And he cares not for rivals nor foes:—
> But lowest and last, with his areas vast,
> And horizon so servile and tame,
> Sits the poor beggar Colonial
> Who feeds on the crumbs of her fame.
>
> William Wilfred Campbell, 'The Lazarus of Empire'

Cultural nationalism redressed and continues to redress cultural dependency, but at the risk of provincialism, insularity, and factionalism. During the first three decades of the twentieth century, a handful of poets from each of the settler countries discovered more or less concurrently that issues of language could be addressed independent of national identity. They found that the capacity of verse to carry conviction depended on two aspects of a single factor: a language corresponding to the spoken idiom, and a verse style that related to tradition only after first negotiating a stable relation to local speech habits. The lesson they re-learnt was at least as old as the Preface to *The Lyrical Ballads* (1798) by Wordsworth and Coleridge.

Popular poetry had always been adept, even during colonial times, at integrating ordinary speech into poetic idiom. Alexander McLachlan (1818–96) provides an early example of this lively subculture in 'We Live in a Rickety House':

> We live in a rickety house,
>   In a dirty dismal street,
> Where the naked hide from day,
>   And thieves and drunkards meet.
>
> (Smith 1960: 12)

Margaret Atwood identifies such vigour as a feature 'that has been and is still very much present: the tug towards the narrative and the anecdotal, the tall tale, the kitchen-table yarn, which is also a pull in the direction of historical and local incident, vernacular speech' (1982: xxxiii). Linguistic modernization negotiated the relation between the local and the universal from the strength of a contemporary idiom, which Dennis Lee describes as a form of 'indigenous articulacy':

> The very language of the metropolitan imagination has had to be unlearned, even as it was being learned from. And a long struggle of independence has been necessary for writers of the hinterlands to imagine their own time and place as what it is, to become articulate as native speakers at all.
>
> (1986: 390)

Turning to New Zealand, we note that in *The Penguin Book of New Zealand Verse* (1988), Ian Wedde distinguished between 'hieratic' and 'demotic'. 'Hieratic' is 'language that is received, self-referential, encoded elect, with a "high" social threshold emphasizing cultural and historical continuity'; 'demotic' is 'language with a spoken base, adaptable and exploratory codes, and a "lower" and more inclusive social threshold emphasizing cultural mobility and immediacy' (Jackson 1991: 723). Modernity of language was an attitude and a strategy that related to cultural nationalism in two ways. On the one hand, it mitigated the provincial tendency inherent to nationalism by its use of a language relatively free of British models and associations. On the other hand, it worked against nationalism. In the latter case, it was allied to a form of transplanted humanism, which provided an international vocabulary of symbols and values to subsidize the humanist belief that the poetic pursuit of 'truth' and 'beauty' could aspire to express universals of human experience without being confined to the narrower aspects of the regional, the local, and the national.

In the context of postcolonial societies, the denotation of humanism as referring to the European Renaissance ideal of making human beings the proper objects of human study, in imitation of the achievements of classical Rome and Greece, brings up a different connotation. Fanon (and others, like Chinua Achebe) argued that intellectuals from the colonized world are susceptible to assimilating European ideals, just as European intellectuals are prone to disseminating them, whether consciously or unconsciously, as universals of human experience. This has the effect of consolidating a European monopoly on defining the human, while alienating the colonized from their selves and cultures. Humanism is thus complicit with the force of European colonialism, and capable of dehumanizing colonized subjects, who, once they fall into the habit of equating the human with the European, tend to associate any departure from this (European) norm of the human as confirmation of their own natural inferiority.

Contemporary poets from the settler nations sustain an ambivalent attachment to Europe, whose civilization and values continue to offer the solicitation of humanist values, which are often mistaken as, or assumed to represent, universals of human experience. Contemporary humanism subsidizes fictions of identity in which writers can elide postcoloniality by invoking the alleged universals of European culture; when the humanist appeal is resisted, writing falls back on the celebration of the regional, the local, and the national. However, when poetry distinguishes humanist from human, it can access the universal through the local, and cease to be postcolonial, without having to shed allusions, ideas, or beliefs merely because they are derived from a colonial culture. Patrick Hogan identifies four components of universalism: the view that all cultures share common properties, belief in shared humanity as the foundation for empathy, ethical principles that can be applied to specific cultures, and (more controversially) the assumption that cultures are not tied to particular lineages (2000: 307–15).

One of the best examples of poetry based on European humanism is provided by F. T. Prince's 'Soldiers Bathing' (1942), which mediates the violence of contemporary warfare through Renaissance representations of war. The poem shows how the specificity of European cultural icons can aspire to an intimation of what it means to be human, regardless of race or culture:

> I see
> The idea of Michelangelo's cartoon
> Of soldiers battling, breaking off before they were half done
> At some sortie of the enemy, an episode
> Of the Pisan wars with Florence.
> [. . .]
> Another Florentine, Pollaiuolo,
> Painted a naked battle: warriors, straddled, hacked the foe,
> Dug their bare toes into the ground and slew
> The brother-naked man who lay between their feet and drew
> His lips back from his teeth in a grimace.
>
> They were Italians who knew war's sorrow and disgrace
> And showed the thing suspended, stripped: a theme
> Born out of the experience of war's horrible extreme
> Beneath a sky where even the air flows
> With *lacrimae Christi.*
>
> (1993: 55–60)

Such poetry could be said to attempt a universal notion of humanity, mediated by Christian humanism. Another example of how the universal might be accessed through the local is provided by an elegy on the death of a son by Ruth Miller (1919–65, South Africa), from 'Cycle':

> . . . But to eat bread like pain,
> To eat pain like bread,
> To wake in the morning in sunlight
> Warm in the sun on the floor
> And know with the only real knowledge
> Complete, undivided, undoubted,
> That your voice will not open the door
> Your hand will not latch on the sunlight

Your footsteps not ring through the dark.
Ah, Greek with the visage of horror
How can you bear it, the stopping?

(Butler and Mann 1979: 147–8)

The editors of *A Land Apart: A South African Reader* (1986) express doubts about 'whether there is any generally acceptable standard of absolute literary excellence by which writers of various ambitions, working in diverse genres, addressing themselves to different audiences, in a time of acute ideological tension and political polarization, can be judged' (Brink and Coetzee 1986: 8). Poetry such as that cited above sharpens the question of whether the idea of a universal humanism is achievable independent of a specific location in history and geography, or whether it remains an affective value that is always culture-specific.

PART III

CASE STUDIES: VOICE AND TECHNIQUE

7

Minoritarian sensibilities

Overview

Poetry that speaks of and for the experience of islanders, aboriginal inhabitants, and recently migrated ethnic minorities in settler countries shares two features: it shows how the struggle for equality of rights and opportunities at once both motivates and delimits writing; it also shows how 'postcolonial' both applies to, and needs qualification in respect to, certain communities and their predicaments. In a broad sense, all postcolonial writing addresses predicaments of accumulated cultural and literary disadvantage. Islanders add a specific nuance to this broad commonality. Either they feel dominated by a mainland culture that happens to be in close proximity, or they are distant from any kind of mainland culture, in which case poets end up feeling isolated from any kind of tradition they can call their own. Aboriginal inhabitants find themselves marginalized within the region where their race has been displaced by later settlers and colonists. Finally, those who migrated to settler regions well after the establishment of societies and cultures of European derivation, find themselves writing from the position of an ethnic minority struggling to find representation and recognition in a cultural environment that discriminates directly or indirectly against them. In each case, poetry addresses a form of contemporary colonization that persists in the wake of Empire.

7.1 Oceania

> There was no Fall, no sun-tanned Noble Savages existing in South Sea paradises, no Golden Age.
>
> Albert Wendt, *Towards a New Oceania*

The Pacific islands known as Polynesia, Melanasia, and Micronesia had their first encounters with Europeans when the Spanish and the Portuguese explored the vast region, followed rapidly by other European explorers, traders, and colonists. In a pattern common to other colonized regions, commercial interests paved the way for the entry of Christianity, muskets, and European languages into the Pacific islands. The eventual consequence of this process can be sampled from a poem by Albert Wendt (b. 1939, Samoa), in which a question from a female missionary, 'Are you a Christian, sir?' gets the response, 'Nominally, yes. But, by right, a pagan', and the postscript, 'pagans | can never resist the mana of muskets' (1976: 3).

Over two hundred years of colonialism gave the native inhabitants a taste of European culture, while they became the object of curiosity, study, exploitation, and conquest by generations of explorers, traders, missionaries, anthropologists, and colonists. Vaine Rasmussen (b. 1961, Cook Island) muses on the residual loss-in-gain of this history in 'A Book and a Pen':

> When I grow old
> They gave me a pe'e* (*chant)
> A legend, a song
> And a language to master.
> A dying culture I had lost
> In my search . . .
>
> (Wendt 1995: 52)

The import of indentured labour from neighbouring regions saw to it that the population of many Pacific islands became thoroughly hybridized. Some of the ethnic divisions associated with hybridity flared up periodically before and after independence. Satendra Nandan (b. 1939, Fiji/Australia) had to leave his birthplace in 1987 when a military coup displaced the government he was part of. His poems evoke the life of his ancestors, who were brought to Fiji from India as 'girmit' workers (girmit: agreement), with mixed emotions. The poem 'Lines across Black Waters' narrates their journey as an act of imaginative recuperation. It has many analogues in Caribbean poetry.

They sailed the ocean
Stitched like blank pages in a book.
[...]
From a little village to the dark lines
Twelve thousand miles, sixty thousand lives.
On that unforgettable *pathar panchali**— (*Bengali: road song)
Rewa, Nausori, Wainbokasi and Nandi*: (*Fiji place names)
Generations have trod, have trod, have trod;
And all is seared with trade; bleared, smeared with toil...

(1997: 9–10)

Literary writing in the colonial languages (chiefly English) by native inhabitants of the Pacific islands began in the 1960s. What came into print was part of a general upsurge of interest in the prospect of freedom and modernization for the Pacific. Some part of this enthusiasm waned after independence turned out to be an anti-climax. Many who made a start in the 1970s turned to professional careers outside writing. Albert Wendt was one of those who persisted. His poetry imagines—virtually reinvents—an ancestral worldview that takes account of both sides of his mixed parentage. His first volume of poetry enshrines remembering in its title sequence, 'Inside us the Dead'. His Polynesian ancestors are like pods that are likely to burst 'in tomorrow's sun', or like plankton fossils dragging tidal waters 'into yesterday's lagoon' (1976: 7). His German great-grandfather is commemorated tartly as 'an atheist adventurer wormed | with the clap, dispersing snakes | into every missionary eden' (10–11). The self is the shadow cast by the assemblage of familial presences, but the poet shows that he has the resilience necessary to affirm a sense of rootedness that is distinctively Polynesian.

Wendt's remembering is an antidote to the anxiety of succumbing to neo-colonial influences, as in 'Master Future', where Mr Past has a stroke, and dies; Mr Future doffs his cap and prays over the dead in an American accent (1976: 15). The entire period from colonialism to Independence is summarized succinctly in a 1965 poem, 'Colonialism: Independence', which ends:

The palagi* Governor, he teach
me the white face of his God (*European)
and Government.
I learn that.

> Then the palagi Governor, he reward
> me with a musket,
> and, when he refused
> for to leave my house,
> I shot to him
> and he is dead.
>
> (20)

The sense of being displaced or possessed by foreign powers haunts all of Wendt's poems. Their resolute anger is similar to the mood of Ngugi's writings (from Kenya) of the same period. The mood acquires a self-divisive edge because, as noted by Paul Sharrad, Wendt is 'kidnapped' by Western education (2003: 83). When a 'Flying-Fox' is to be caught, skinned, gutted, roasted, and eaten, the poet can only liken the anticipated pleasure to 'chewing Batman, | Count Dracula' (1976: 26). Like Walcott, Wendt struggles with a riddling ambivalence about his mixed racial and cultural affiliations. The New Zealand that provides the avenue for education, also figures more darkly for its introduction to racialized identities. In 'He Never Once Lost His Way', which is set in Wellington, walking the night streets, he is frequently stopped and questioned by 'Cops in black cars', since 'Your dark skin reminds the cops | of midnight's terrors—you may | be on your way to rape their | virginal wives and daughters' (29). The poem 'To My Son on the Tenth Anniversary of our Country's Independence' speaks of 'the vision of our dead prophets | in a decade of betrayal', and laments that 'the slow bleed | of expensive compromise | discolours conscience'. The dream of the postcolonial nation marching toward modernity drowns in 'the insatiable cocktail glass' (38) of the politician and the dealer in futures. 'What You Do Now, Brother' declares, 'this tropical paradise it all a vampire's lie' (49).

7.2 'Indigenes' and settler minorities

> Racial designations, such as 'Indian' or 'Negro', are the outcome of the subjugation of populations in the course of European mercantile expansionism. The term Indian stands for the conquered populations of the New World, in disregard of any cultural or physical differences among native Americans.
>
> Eric R. Wolf, *Europe and the People Without History*

Two sets of poets, who write in English from minority positions, continue to suffer several forms of cultural disadvantage that the end of colonialism did not ameliorate: aborigines, and recent migrants to settler countries (especially when not of English or European descent). They find themselves drawn to a poetics of resistance in relation to a dominant majority. Their protest has a sense of the belated about it, since it occurs after the success of decolonization and nationalism in the former European colonies. Their circumstances remain colonial, even though the societies on whose margins they live ceased being colonial. Their poetry thus puts the efficacy of 'postcolonial' in question, requiring its connotations to accommodate contemporary societies divided by ethnic prejudice.

The 'native', the 'aboriginal', the 'Indian', or the 'indigene' (Terry Goldie's term) is a compound construct. It simplifies interactions between races into stereotypes. Indigenes are romanticized either in relation to their connectedness to land, myth, dreamtime, songlines, orality, or in order to subsidize idealizations and preoccupations of European provenance. The myth of the noble savage makes them a pretext for European fears and desires. The Australian group, the Jindyworobacks, illustrated one of the more benign forms taken by such projections. From the 1930s to the early 1950s, this group of white writers tried to mediate between Western and aboriginal modes of experience, an intention welcomed sympathetically in the next generation by Les Murray (Elliott 1976: 285–8). Their idealizations contrast with the more common settler habit, which finds it easy to demonize indigenes, reject their beliefs and practices, and make them objects of fear, loathing, disgust, and contempt, resenting their prior claim to the land, and despising them for the guilt they project onto settlers for having taken their land by force.

Whenever the tension between fascination and repulsion is internalized by indigenes, they suffer what Fanon called 'Manichean delirium' (1967: 44–5, 183; 1963: 41–2). Indigenes experienced the encounter with settler culture as loss (of freedom and ancestral lands), attenuation (of language and orality), and decline (of cultural practices that survive largely through the reification of archives, museums, and tourism). The indigene also suffered from the gradual assimilation of indigenous linguistic energies to settler modes of expression, in which writing tied orality to the conventions of print culture. Indigenes have had to struggle long and hard before even a tiny proportion gained admission to a literary canon controlled by the interests and prejudices of the dominant ethnic community. Like indigenes, writers from ethnic minorities have struggled against marginalization by making a badge of their minoritarian status, as in anthologies from the fringe that identify and promote minority writing, but at the cost of reinforcing the divisions in society that force minorities into the ghetto of subcultures.

In the context of aboriginal writing from Australia, 'postcolonial' is a 'confused misnomer' (Webb 1996: 105). To the descendants of the continent's oldest inhabitants, 'postcolonial' serves as the mark of a deferral, a gesture in the direction of a bitterly chimerical future, and a sign of the systematic misrecognition perpetrated by exploiting racial difference. The pioneering aboriginal poet Jack Davis (b. 1917) speaks to white fellow Australians on behalf of his people in 'Remembering':

> They can forgive you
> for the land you have stolen
> [...]
> But what they cannot forget is
> you have slowed their heartbeat
> and cast brute shadows
> over the face of their sun
>
> (1992: 60)

A note of pride mixed with protest is registered in the next generation by Mudrooroo Narogin (b. 1938, Colin Johnson until 1988) in 'Mudrooroo':

> Seeking Mudrooroo in the sap of a tree,
> Two hundred years of bloodshed water his culture,
> He stands proud, his feet rooted in the earth.
>
> (1991: 15)

Mudrooroo's prose reinforces the point: 'Traditional Aboriginal culture is a complexity which does not separate out a literature from ceremony or society', and 'Aboriginal writing has developed towards a spirituality interested in using and exploring the inner reality of Aboriginality in Australia' (1990: 192).

Kath Walker was the first aboriginal woman to turn to poetry in English. *We Are Going* (1964), like the rest of her work, has two goals:

to remind white Australians of the injustices suffered by the aborigines, and to encourage aborigines to remember their ancestral traditions with pride and self-respect. These are laudable aims of social protest and reform. However, writing committed to such goals faces the problem also encountered by protest poetry from Africa (and elsewhere): sincere statements and worthy sentiments do not suffice to ensure that the writing will be effective as poetry. Here, for instance, is part of 'Integration—Yes!':

> We who were Australians long before
> You who came yesterday,
> Eagerly we must learn to change,
> Learn new needs we never wanted,
> New compulsions never needed,
> The price of survival.
>
> (1992: 43)

Walker is much more effective when dealing with the challenge of evoking the mindscape of her community. 'The Curlew Cried' provides a rare instance of a poet not native to the British tradition who handles rhyme and stanzaic form with ease and poise:

> Three nights they heard the curlew cry.
> It is the warning known of old
> That tells them one tonight shall die.
>
> Brother and friend, he comes and goes
> Out of the Shadow Land to them,
> The loneliest voice that earth knows.
>
> (1992: 22)

Other aboriginal writers like Kevin Gilbert (b. 1933) use a form of English that is closer to aboriginal speech habits, which as Elleke Boehmer points out, infiltrate 'the scribal and poetic conventions of white culture' (1995: 230).

In New Zealand, *pākehā* (white) culture began displacing the oral traditions of the Maori during the nineteenth century. At the same time, the colonists translated Maori systems of phonology, grammar, ritual functions, and historical narratives into European systems of writing. European assumptions about the accumulation and dissemination of knowledge prevailed over the ritual oral transmission that had been traditional to Maori culture. After colonization, orality declined or adapted itself to the colonizer's traditions of writing, while the number of speakers using Maori as a first language declined. The case illustrates a larger pattern:

> Maori as a language is on the brink, and it is English which has put it there.... Languages are killed by other languages.... The litany of lost or losing languages is long and begins within the imperial nations themselves: Irish in Ireland, Gaelic in Scotland, Breton in France, then Aboriginal languages in Australia, and Native American languages of North and South America.
>
> (Bell 1991: 67–8)

The notion of multiculturalism has been invoked in the settler countries as a way of mitigating such loss. The efficacy of the term is limited. When Ian Wedde and Harvey McQueen included translations of Maori oral works in *The Penguin Book of New Zealand Verse* (1985) as part of the nation's literature, they were accused by C. K. Stead of perpetuating a 'very large white lie', because representing 'Maori poetry as part of a lively New Zealand literary scene is simply dishonest' (1989: 142, 144). Outside the activity of translation, the use of English by writers of Maori descent began to take root as a relatively recent and limited development. 'Not by Wind Ravaged', from the first book of poems in English by a Maori, Hone Tuwhare's *No Ordinary Sun* (1964), takes stock of his displacement while attempting the task of expressing a Maori sensibility in the language of the colonizer's culture:

> O voiceless land, let me echo your desolation.
> The mana of my house has fled,
> the marae is but a paddock of thistle,
> I come to you with a bitterness
> that only your dull folds can soothe...
>
> (1993: 25)

A more personalized use of English can be found in the work of Keri Hulme (b. 1947), a writer of Scottish and Maori descent, whose right to speak as a Maori has met with scepticism from some quarters in New Zealand. Her writing resolves the tension latent to a divisive genealogy in an affirmative spirit, as in the poem 'Against the small evil voices', which rejects the modern city 'where each hutch is nearly | insulated by the white noise of TV against | the nextdoor screams' (1992: 29). Like Albert Wendt, she is better known for her prose. Her poems reveal an attractive quiddity, evoking an Oceania that is more water than land, a world inhabited by fish, friends, words, and solitariness:

you smile at my rocks
but I murmur opals; you
say ancestors and I breathe,
Bones—

(2004: 1)

The Maori element animates an affirmative faith in 'He Hoha': 'I am my earth's child' (1992: 41). 'Winesong 23' shows how a song-like quality can be modulated by the incremental growth of a refrain into a stanza, as the poem plays variations on the question of how it might name the self:

I have a name I use at tideline
and another for swimming in the sea
and one for when I'm landbound
and several for flying free.

Pass the bottle lady,
observe the level of the wine.

As the poem progresses, the antiphonal refrain grows slowly:

Pass the bottle, lady,
observe the level of the wine—
time flows slowly, lady.

(1992: 60)

Such writing builds its integrity around solitude and love of natural process and phenomena. It can declare that 'gods are alive | are awake, and they walk the earth | of our hearts' (1992: 35), without forgetting the fact that 'sweet life' (1992: 31) is shared by human beings with everything organic, from cancers, tapeworms, bread moulds, and string beans to great white sharks.

The scene of minority writing in Canada presents a multicultural world in which the efficacy of multiculturalism remains an open question, as the performance poet Lillian Allen (b. 1951, Jamaica/Canada) reminds us in 'Liberation':

yes I have the same right
to live for myself as you do
to find my way as you do

to make mistakes as you do
yes I have the same right

(1993: 56–7)

That a poet should need to perform this demand shows the degree to which the principle of exclusion still obtains in Canadian society, leaving room for protest from several ethnic minorities.

Migrants from China came into the country in sizeable numbers from the mid nineteenth century, followed in the twentieth century by migrants from India and the Caribbean. These minorities took to writing relatively recently. Jim Wong-Chu (b. 1949, Hong Kong) dramatizes the voice of an old immigrant reassuring a newcomer in tones that mix anxiety with eagerness to assimilate in his poem 'And Then Something Went': 'I too was mired in another language | and I gladly surrendered it | for english' (Lee and Wong-Chu 1991: 17). In Lucy Ng's sequence, 'The Sullen Shapes of Poems', the migrant revisits the home province, and everything appears nice on the surface, but the poem cannot shed its unease about the split between those who stayed and the one that left:

The
newlyweds had vacated their room for you the day
before. You nodded and passed out American
cigarettes, chocolate candies for the children,
the edges of your smile hurting.

This little pig went to the market, this little
pig stayed home, this little pig...

(Lee and Wong-Chu 1991: 167)

Sean Gunn, a fourth-generation Chinese Canadian, experiments with a series of ironic variations on the typology of ethnic encounters in settler countries:

hey you
chinaman
what are you doing playing these here parts
I am *bok guey** come (*white devil, slang for white man)
in search of my long lost
brother the reason I shave my head
is so that I can say
etcetera etcetera etcetera
click click...

(Lee and Wong-Chu 1991: 29–30)

Canadian poets of Caribbean and African descent access a broad tonal register ranging across the entire spectrum from Creole to Standard English. African rhythms and the momentum of an oral tradition are utilized by Dionne Brand (b. 1953, Trinidad) in 'Canto II', which sustains an odd kind of tension between invoking an ancestor and ironicizing the Canadian context:

where are my bells?
my rattles
my condiments
my things
[. . .]
will you bathe me in oils,
will you tie me in white cloth?
call me by my praise name
sing me Oshun song . . .

(Wallace 1990: 23)

The scope for ambitious structures larger than the lyric, and based on the principle of the dramatic soliloquy, is developed through several novels in verse by Claire Harris (b. 1937, Trinidad). In *She* (2000), Harris invents a poet who suffers from a multiple-personality disorder, whose development is chronicled by a series of prose and verse letters written to her sister. The format enables Harris to deploy several linguistic and emotional registers. Fragmentation of identity and self-loathing are rejected in an assertion of 'variousness' that links selfhood to metaphor:

jes banal
to tink us aberashun
what dere
to heal
in we variousness?
we who ent
flourish
ent metaphor
dis is jes'
to say we is no fragment so
we is we own
undah long
division
undah multiplicashun

(22–3)

The other side of that confidence presents a different picture:

> yuh ent know mem'ry like dem ditch flower
> gorn seedy   root it out   it doan dead
> drip poison   it grown back maad   is weed
> is hydra head   She look
> in mirror who know wha She-so-see?
>
> (65)

Canadian poets like Harris, Brand, and Nourbese Philip, and others such as Laksmi Gill and Joy Kagawa draw upon cultural resources that are not easily reconciled: a Canadian present and a communal past that was shaped outside North America. Their work is gradually transforming the lopsided majoritarian shape of the literary canon that has prevailed in Canada since the end of Empire, transforming Empire into 'variousness'.

Minority poets assimilate awkwardly into the country in which they settle. Ania Walwicz (b. 1951) moved from Poland to Australia when she was twelve. Her prose poem 'Poland' represents the migrant as a young person. The key factor here is the age at which migration occurred. For the child, the birthplace is not a memory but an idea invented by adults and kept alive by photographs. The child is incapable of reproaching herself, since there is little to remember, and hence very little to forget. Nevertheless, the need to imagine a place of origin exercises its own compulsion. This is how 'Poland' begins:

> I forget everything. Now. More and more. It gets dim. And further away. It's as if I made it up. As though I was never there at all. Not real. Child stories. Told over and over. Wear thin. This doesn't belong to me anymore. This is now gone and it left me a long time ago. It doesn't stay with me. This is the past. This is child. This is too small for me. I grow out of this. I leave it. I lose my photos. I lost my photos.
>
> (1982: 37)

The voice of the poem records the struggle of a person twice dispossessed: of home and memory. The language enacts the effort required to learn a new skill: memory. Remembering the past is like learning a foreign language, translating thoughts into new sounds and hieroglyphs. Language itself is a foreign experience, an estrangement from feelings and ideas that has not found the forms in which to express them. The poem localizes the idea of home as a country of the mind, a fictional space masquerading as a real place. 'Poland' treats the past as the utopia (literally 'no-place') from which migration took place.

Another prose poem, 'Australia', describes the country migrated to as a dystopia. The poem disburdens itself of a biting list of complaints. It accuses the new homeland of closed habits of thought and feeling, provincial attitudes, and narrow prejudices. The migrant, dejected at the ruins of her dream, faces the irony of a double-crossing. To have moved from one empty space (the home that memory cannot recollect) to another space that is hostile merely exchanges one kind of homelessness for another:

> You big ugly. You too empty. You desert with your nothing nothing nothing. You scorched suntanned. Old too quickly. Acres of suburbs watching the telly. You bore me. Freckle silly children. You nothing much. With your big sea. Beach beach beach. I've seen enough already. You dumb dirty city with bar stools. You're ugly...
>
> (Hampton and Llewellyn 1986: 230–1).

A third prose poem, 'Wogs', dramatizes the racial hostility with which the migrant has to contend in Australia. The dramatization of xenophobia shows how postcolonial societies have yet to work out the latent tensions of a colonial legacy: the conversion of fear into hatred; the conversion of mutual adjustability into intolerance. The poem exposes the irony that a society built on the displacement of its predecessor cannot readily bring itself to share its living spaces with later migrants:

> you don't know what they think they got their own ways they stick together you don't know what they're up to you never know with them you just don't know with them no we didn't ask them to come here they come and they come there is enough people here already now they crowd us wogs they give me winter colds they take my jobs...
>
> (Gunew 1987: 133)

'Wogs' mimics the tone of resentment with which the migrant is met. The apparent monotony of the poet's technique—syncopated repetitions, plain diction, and simplified syntax—portray a range of discordant voices whose opposition articulates the central problems of the migrant experience. The language appears gauche: its apparent incompetence is the vehicle for a simple but powerful irony.

A migrant's limited command over vocabulary and syntax might seem to lack the power to express issues of complexity and depth. Paradoxically, the broken language adopted by the poem for its ventriloquism is apt to the challenge, expressing with concision what a more idiomatic style might have conveyed less vividly. A powerful linguistic energy is released by the poet working within the limits of an apparent linguistic impoverishment.

7.3 Black Britain and the Caribbean diaspora

> Put bluntly... the pressure is to become a mulatto and house-nigger (Ariel) rather than stay a field-nigger (Caliban).
>
> I cannot however feel or write poetry like a white man, much less serve him. And to become mulattos, black people literally have to be fucked (and fucked up) first. Which brings us back to the pornography of Empire.
>
> **David Dabydeen, 'On Not Being Milton: Nigger Talk in England Today'**

> Benjamin Zephaniah OBE—no way Mr Blair, no way Mrs Queen. I am profoundly anti-empire.
>
> **Benjamin Zephaniah, 'Me? I thought, OBE me? Up yours, I thought'**

In Lorna Goodison's poem 'Change If You Must, Just Change Slow' (National Poetry Day poem, 2002), Jamaica is referred to as 'country we leave from to go and make life'. The descendants of slaves forcibly transplanted to a place that left them unhappy keep making a special claim on the impulse to migrate. Very few had the doggedness of Eric Roach, who stayed behind, resisting the impulse he recognized as tempting, in 'Love Overgrows' (1957), where

> We take banana boats
> Tourist, stowaway,
> Our luck in hand, calypsoes in the heart:
> We turn Columbus's blunder back
> From sun to snow, to bitter cities;
> We explore the hostile and exploding zones.
>
> (1992: 127)

In 1974, Roach committed suicide by swallowing insecticide and then swimming into the sea off the coast of Trinidad, from the spot where Columbus was believed to have landed, almost five hundred years earlier. There was a long prehistory to that act of suicide. A 1952 poem, 'Letter to George Lamming', declares:

> I hold my narrow island in my hand
> While you have thrown yours to the sea
> And jumped for England ....
>
> (1992: 81)

More than any other Caribbean poet before or since, Roach voices a sense of belonging that is tied to despair. His 'we' is enslaved in cane, trapped in an inheritance of lust, where the brown-coloured scorn the black, and 'skins not white as white | Deny the black old matriarch in the cupboard' (82). 'We' are 'a displaced people lost on islands', he writes, architects without tradition, builders without foundations. In *Rights of Passage* (1967), Brathwaite enumerated the standard questions for those whose choice differed from Roach: 'Where to?'; 'Why do they go?' (1973: 51–2).

Speaking for those who *did* migrate, David Dabydeen is blunt in the Introduction to *Slave Song*:

> 'England' is our Utopia, an ironic reversal, for Raleigh was looking away from the 'squalor' of his homeland to the imagined purity of ours whereas we are now reacting against our 'sordid' environment and looking to 'England' as Heaven... Our desire for 'white-ness' is as spiritual as it is banal. On one level it is a craving for mind and soul—the 'savage' wants civilization of the renaissance kind; on a baser level what he wants is 'civilization' of cars and fridges—a mere material greed.
>
> (1984: 9)

After SS *Empire Windrush* unloaded several hundred West Indians onto English soil in 1948, writers from the Caribbean made England (rather than Africa) their preferred destination for the next three decades, although, as Susheila Nasta points out, 'The UK was already well established then, prior to *Windrush*, as an important literary crossroads for the larger-scale migrations that were to follow on' (2004: 570). Canada and the USA provided other popular alternatives, leaving the Caribbean region unique among postcolonial societies in being depopulated of a sizeable proportion of its writers. The questions they kept asking themselves have remained the same over half a century. In Amryl Johnson's words, 'where are you going?', 'how will you get there?', 'what will you find there?' (1985: 54). The logic of such imperatives acquires bite in Benjamin Zephaniah's 'A Modern Slave Song', which ends:

> Remember where I come from, cause I do.
> I won't feget.
> Remember yu got me, cause I'll get yu.
> I'll make yu sweat.
>
> (1992: 52)

Speaking for the 1970s, Brathwaite defined exile as 'the need—or the imagined need—to emigrate to metropolitan centres in order to exist as writers' (42). His fears proved accurate, as novelists and poets moved in increasing numbers from the Caribbean to England, or wrote as children born to immigrants who had just made it to what was treated, not without irony, as 'the Mother Country', and 'mother of all metropolises' (Markham 1995: 117, 118).

Older Caribbean writers left their home islands for the metropolitan centre, looking for a more receptive literary culture. They found Britain grudging in its acceptance of their reverse colonization, uneasy to acknowledge the cumulative and belated price it now paid for Empire. Regardless, there were many incentives for leaving the Caribbean: Vidia Naipaul remembered Trinidad as 'unimportant, uncreative, cynical'; Brathwaite described his rootlessness as a reaction to 'the stifling atmosphere of middle-class materialism and philistinism' at home (Markham 1995: 118); and Sam Selvon resisted the apathy of Caribbean society by seeking out 'the challenge of mainstream culture' (Dabydeen 2000: 66–7) in Canada.

Those not drawn to writing left in search of jobs that would provide alternatives to the limitations of their island economies, a problem to which Britain provided a kind of answer by absorbing workers from the Caribbean into various kinds of work 'in hospitals, factories and railway and bus depots' (Dabydeen 2000: 64). Those who left the Caribbean were generally glad they did, regardless of the problems they encountered in England. The poetry of Linton Kwesi Johnson, for instance, found its permanent political subject matter in those problems: 'the general conditions that black people were living under and what we were experiencing in British society' (Markham 1995: 259). Fred D'Aguiar notes in his Introduction to Johnson's work that the black and coloured minorities in Britain are still relegated to the status of 'those who are in it but thought to be not of it' (Johnson 2002: xiii).

The Caribbean migrant writer moving to England has often had a hard time of it in his new homeland, writing 'Poems that scrape bowl and bone | In English basements far from home' (Dabydeen 1988: 13). The role assigned to Caribbean migrants is invoked bitterly by D'Aguiar in 'Throwaway People':

> The problem that won't go away
> people.
> [...]
> The things have got to epidemic proportions
> people
>
> The we have no use for you
> people
>
> (1993: 10)

In more positive terms, the migrant writer drew upon memories of childhood, or on ancestral and communal memories, as a source of abiding inspiration in his new homeland. This resource was tapped by those born in the Caribbean, and also by a writer like Fred D'Aguiar.

D'Aguiar was born to Guyanese parents in England in 1960. At the age of two, he was sent back to Guyana to acquire—as he says in a video interview with Caryl Phillips—'a proper upbringing' (D'Aguiar 1999: online). At twelve, he returned to England, did well as a writer, and in 1992 moved to the USA. His book-length narrative poems (*Bill of Rights*, 1998, and *Bloodlines*, 2000) quarry the Caribbean for material. *Bill of Rights* deals with a mass suicide that occurred in Jonestown, Guyana, in 1978, and *Bloodlines* narrates the story of a black slave and her white lover. His case illustrates how a writer may live outside the culture and region of his ancestry, but its history, language, and ghosts can sustain the writing from distances in time and space.

Nevertheless, no amount of nostalgia can tempt the immigrant back to the Caribbean, as Merle Collins confesses in 'Seduction':

> Going home becomes harder, she told me
> cold winter is homely. The fire replaces
> the sun. And yet there's a longing
>
> for those places that gave me a longing
> for leaving. But what keeps me wandering
> still? She wonders. New roots, new shoots
> and home moving further away.
>
> (Kay *et al.* 1996: 85)

This dual feature provides a reason for looking at poets of Caribbean descent who are settled in Britain or North America within a survey of Caribbean writing, while also recognizing that their lives and work are now a part of the cultures and ethnic politics of the societies to which they have migrated, where their existence remains interstitial, held suspended in a ghostly space of the imagination. The basic challenge faced by the Caribbean immigrant aspiring to become part of British culture is neatly summarized in a grandmother's adage that D'Aguiar works into one of his poems: 'You think you are a bird and your station is the sky? | Lick the thread and feed it through the needle's eye' (1993: 8). 'Coolie Son', from David Dabydeen's *Coolie Odyssey* (1988), evokes the world of the first-generation migrant through a letter in which the young son reports:

> Englan nice, snow and dem ting,
> A land dey say fit for a king
> [...]
> And I eating enough for all a-we
> And reading book bad-bad.
> [...]
> Soon, I go turn lawya or dacta,
> But, just now, passage money run out
> So I tek lil wuk—
> I is a Deputy Sanitary Inspecta,
> Big-big office, boy!
>
> (1988: 17)

Evan Jones (b. 1928, Jamaica) captures the ambivalent experience of migration from a more insouciant perspective in 'The lament of the banana man':

> My yoke is easy, my burden is light,
> I know a place I can go, any night.
> Dis place Englan'! I'm not complainin',
> If it col', it col'. If it rainin', it rainin'.
> I don' min' if it's mostly night,
> Dere's always inside, or de sodium light.
> I don' min' white people starin' at me
> Dey don' want me here? Don't is deir country?
> You won't catch me bawlin' any homesick tears
> If I don't see Jamaica for a t'ousand years!
>
> (Figueroa 1982: 86–7)

At a more intimate level of interaction between the black and white races, a poem like Dabydeen's 'The Seduction' dramatizes an encounter in which the immigrant of colour is unable to consummate the sexual relation, reminding us that 'The British Empire . . . was as much a pornographic as an economic project' (1989: 121). This migrant persona finds that he carries more anxious baggage to the meeting than the white girl expects or accepts. The weight of his history contributes to a failure of nerve that is psychic rather than physical:

> She said her name was really Jane
> That she was sweet as sugarcane
> Unblighted by colonial reign
> That all he wanted was some pain
> To wrap himself in mythic chain
> And labour in his self-disdain.
> [. . .]
> Britannia it is not she cries!
> Miranda also she denies!
> Nor map nor piracy nor prize
> Nor El Dorado in disguise
> With pity gazed into his eyes
> And saw he could not improvise
>
> (1988: 30–1)

Dabydeen's Caliban cannot get rid of his internalized guilt or a sense of transgression at the prospect of despoiling Miranda.

Throughout the latter half of the twentieth century, the relation between Caribbean writers and Britain has remained a curious mixture of need and resentment. It also allows for the kind of question Merle Collins muses over in 'Whose Story?':

> Walking through the streets of this Britain
> which you seek to save from the painful fate
> of black invasion, I wonder
> if mine had been the invading nation
> would history just have shrugged
> written the story upside down
> left a different people clothed
> in this distant arrogance?
>
> (Kay *et al.* 1996: 94)

In the 1970s and '80s, Linton Kwesi Johnson gave expression to considerable anger and frustration at the relation between black and white communities in Britain, as in 'Inglan is a Bitch', which ends:

> Inglan is a bitch
> dere's no escaping it
> Inglan is a bitch fi true
> is whe wi a goh dhu bout it?
>
> (2002: 41)

A more generous recognition of what Britain can represent for its black minority can be sampled from Benjamin Zephaniah's work of the 1990s, who ends his preface to *Too Black, Too Strong* (2001) with the affirmation: 'it is because I love the place that I fight for my rights here. If it were simply a case of hating the place and all that it stood for, then I would have left when I first got expelled from school' (14).

Poets like Johnson and Zephaniah bridge the gap between popular culture and art, just as they move easily and frequently over the plank that links art to politics. They also ground the appeal of their poetry in the oral affirmation of a Creole identity whose auditory qualities are supplemented by the use of rhyme, repetition, and emphatic rhythms. Johnson's persona is fierce and narrow in tone and range. His use of music and his predilection for a heavily patterned rhythm often brings his performance style close to monotony, and sometimes succumbs to it.

Zephaniah is more freewheeling in his tonal register, less reliant on music or the politics of race for his inspiration. Unlike Johnson, he takes up causes on a wide front that includes much else besides issues affecting the black community in Britain. He is also prone to mix resistance or critique with an affirmative stance that absorbs class, gender, and race into an appeal to the notion of a universal human reason and compassion in the audiences that attend his performances, as well as those who listen to them on CD or audio, or read them as printed words on the page. He is adept at deploying candour, warmth, and charm without losing any of his satirical edge. After half a century in Britain, 'The Angry Black Poet' suggests gently that the tired typology of Black frustration might afford a little love and laughter:

> Next on stage
> We have the angry black poet,
> [. . .]

Don't get me wrong
He means it,
He means it so much
He is unable to feel,
He's so serious
If he is found smiling
He stops to get serious before he enters stage left...

(1996: 29)

8

Techniques of self-representation

Overview

The consolidation of local traditions in the former colonies has depended on the capacity of poets to take on the challenges of self-representation in a cultural climate relatively free of cultural cringe. The struggle to achieve that freedom is here illustrated in three case studies. The first shows African poets from the 1960s and '70s learning to use indigenous myths in a context informed by modernist writing. The second traces the growth of confidence in contemporary writing by women, chiefly from the Caribbean. The third examines the scope for creative overlap between a postcolonial predicament and a post-modern sensibility, as exemplified by the bilingual work of a poet from South Asia. The extended treatment given his work is meant to show how the literal and metaphorical activity of translation is at work in the spread of modernist and postmodernist practices to postcolonial poetry.

8.1 Modernism and hybridity: black Africa

> 'Our country is an abiku country. Like the spirit-child, it keeps coming and going. One day it will decide to remain.'
>
> Ben Okri, *The Famished Road*

A large proportion of African poetry in English from the period before independence shows a preference for an idiom closer to speech than to literary diction and syntax. As elsewhere in the ex-colonies, poets generally preferred free verse to the metres and stanzas of traditional British poetry. African poets excelled at patterning the verse-line through repetition, parallelism, and other syntactic devices based on local traditions of oral composition. This writing remains contemporary in feel and colloquial in tone without being implicated in the assumptions and practices of European modernism. The earliest poets to excel in this mode include Gabriel Okara (b. 1921, Nigeria), Kofi Awonoor (b. 1935, Ghana), Lenrie Peters (b. 1932, Gambia), David Rubadiri (b. 1930, Malawi), and Jared Angira (b. 1947, Kenya).

Peters, for instance, showed a predilection during the 1960s for contained forms and feelings that balance external influence with internal cohesion. An untitled poem such as the following reconciles a subdued formal allusion to a Western convention (the elegy) with a local form (the African dirge), producing an effect of unsentimental precision:

Isatou died
When she was only five
[. . .]
Her mother wept
Half grateful
To be so early bereft
[. . .]
The father looked at her
Through marble eyes and said;
'Who spilt the perfume
Mixed with morning dew?'

(1971: 21)

Jared Angira's 'Masked' uses a pattern of syntax and rhythm reminiscent of the style of T. S. Eliot's 'Journey of the Magi' and Ezra Pound's 'Hugh Selwyn Mauberley':

Some broke their legs
Some broke their arms
Some went tipsy with nectar
and lost their way homewards.

(1996: 3)

In such poetry, allusions to Western writing are unobtrusive. A more direct interaction between local beliefs and modernist practices can be illustrated through examples from three Nigerians—Christopher Okigbo (1932–67), Wole Soyinka (b. 1934), and J. P. Clark (b. 1935)—who grew up as contemporaries, knew each other, and developed very distinctive personal poetic styles. During the 1960s, each wrote a poem on the myth of the Abiku, a Yoruba word for 'born to die' (Irele 2001: 186). Soyinka explains the Abiku as involving a 'Wanderer child... who dies and returns again and again to plague the mother' (2001: 30). Igbo culture has a counterpart to the Abiku, the Ogbanje: 'A child is referred to as *ogbanje* when his behaviour is ambiguous, when he is difficult to deal with and above all when there are indications of a dual personality' (Acholonu 1988: 103).

The Abiku myth translates the sociological realm of child psychology, infant mortality, childlessness, and repeated childbirth into a personification that embodies these phenomena as mystery and prophecy, fate and destiny, curse and gift. The myth makes the visitation a recurrence that is feared and propitiated. It links the world of the present to the two other worlds that constitute the Yoruba continuum of existence, the world of the ancestor and the world of the unborn. The most accessible treatment of this myth is found in Clark's 'Abiku', which keeps close to the traditional belief-system. Niyi Osundare notes that Clark's poem is spoken from the point of view of supplicants who adopt 'a concessionary tone that invites the Abiku to stay' (1988: 100):

> Do stay out on the baobab tree,
> Follow where you please your kindred spirits
> [...]
> No longer then bestride the threshold
> But step in and stay
> For good.
>
> (Clarke 1981: 3)

The poem does not challenge either the Abiku or the system of belief from which it comes. Clark uses the genre of the dramatic monologue as a witness to the old ways, 'the poet's meditation upon a singular form of tragic predicament' (Irele 2001: 186).

Soyinka's 'Abiku' is just as firmly embedded in the African belief-system, but he presents the poem from the viewpoint of the Abiku, not the mother or the family. His Abiku sounds confident, playful, and cruel. It has mastered death and can afford to be dismissive of the divinations and charms that will fail to avert the blight it brings.

> Night and Abiku suck the oil
> From lamps. Mothers! I'll be the

Suppliant snake coiled on the doorstep
Yours the killing joy.

(2001: 31)

Soyinka is fascinated with the morbid and the macabre aspect of the myth. His syntax wears a self-conscious cloak of difficulty. The speaking voice relishes its play-acting. The hunter loves being hunted, exuberant that he will prevail. This Abiku does not mind that he is feared without being revered. The poem shifts affiliations between the human and the supernatural, providing room to alternate between despair and exultation, awe and pessimism. It dramatizes tensions that it does not wish to resolve.

Soyinka's poem engages with modernism from a distance, and with a difference. Osundare remarks, 'The enigma of Abiku is that he is a grand fusion of time past, time present and time future' (1988: 99). This could be said to produce an odd inversion of the drift of a modernist poem such as T. S. Eliot's 'Burnt Norton', which focuses on the idea that existence might be redeemed from time by brooding on the epiphanic moments of the past, which partake of a timelessness that might rescue human experience from mutability. Soyinka's poem could be said to voice an anti-epiphany, in which the recurrence of death and rebirth in the Abiku is the only relief from mutability. There is a further nuance to Soyinka's poem. It takes a solemn view of the poetic function, linking the child to the writer. In an essay written in 1992, 'The Writer: Child at the Frontier', Soyinka identifies the frontier as a metaphor for the liminal, that which the writer has to cross repeatedly in order to come into being (Quayson 1997: 73).

Okigbo's approach to poetry precludes the elements of fantasy and satire that are always at hand for Soyinka. He nurses an exalted attitude to the poetic function, and his treatment of the Abiku motif combines the intensely personal with the communal. The myth informs the allegory of the sequence 'Heavensgate', which Okigbo described as 'a fable of man's perennial quest for fulfilment' (1986: xxvi). In 1962, he told an interviewer that the sequence was influenced by the music of the French impressionists. Like them he wished to evoke an impression of 'a watery, shadowy nebulous world, with semitones of dream and the nuances of the rainbow' (1972: 138). In 1965, he declared to another interviewer that 'my maternal grandfather was the head of a particular type of religion which is intimately connected with my village and since I am a reincarnation of my maternal grandfather, I carried this on' (1972: 145).

The continually reborn child enters 'Watermaid', the third poem of 'Heavensgate', as a prodigal, a persona who nurses a sense of vocation in secret, until vouchsafed a fleeting vision of a goddess whose brief epiphanic presence vindicates the prodigal's commitment to his sense of personal destiny:

> eyes open on the sea,
> eyes open, of the prodigal;
> upward to heaven shoot
> where stars will fall from . . .
> BRIGHT
> with the armpit-dazzle of a lioness,
> she answers . . .
> So brief her presence—
> match-flare in wind's breath—
> [. . .]
> So I who count in my island the moments . . .
> my lost queen with angels' ash in the wind
>
> (1986: 26–8)

The poem illustrates several characteristics of Okigbo's style: a rapt tone; aspirations at once mystical, prophetic, and hermetic; and a style that is self-conscious and introverted. The poetry manages to sound intimate yet grand, and there is an element of bravura in its solemnity. The 'Heavensgate' sequence tries to synthesize a vision from an eclectic mixture of allusions to European music, literature, and African ritual. This is accomplished with considerable flair and panache, but it is easy to see why later poets reacted to Okigbo—the 'patron saint of modern Nigerian poetry'—with ambivalence: 'I was more overwhelmed by the music of his poetry than its meaning' (Osundare 2002: 111).

In Okigbo's early work, the reality of what he read seemed to matter more than the reality of what he experienced; in his later work, the African experience came closer to the surface, though it was still refracted by his reading. Okigbo was neither slavish nor imitative in what he took from Europe. He shared with the Modernists a willingness to experiment in ways that made severe demands on his readers, and a willingness to ventriloquize for posterity. Okigbo's work engaged with modernism in ways that go beyond details of eclecticism, allusiveness, and elliptical writing. It showed that assimilating wider influences could resist localism and avoid being contained within restrictive notions such as 'Nigerian', 'black', 'African' (and 'national', 'colonial' and 'postcolonial'). His work aspired to a universalism that could hold at arm's length the obligations imposed on, or felt by, poets that their work should stick to their place and time for inspiration and reference.

As noted in Chapters 1 and 6, Yvor Winters dismissed this type of imposition as the fallacy of national mimeticism. Okigbo shared the implication of that rejection: 'ultimately all literature is one' (1972: 142). His work raises a familiar question. Does one trust the universals of experience exported by Europe (or the West), or does one bracket them as culturally specific predilections? Regardless of the answer, Okigbo's methods did not find favour with later poets. In 'Poetry is', Osundare declares his preference for writing that is:

> not the esoteric whisper
> of an excluding tongue
> not a claptrap
> for a wondering audience
> not a learned quiz
> entombed in Grecoroman lore
>
> (1983: 3)

Meanwhile, the Abiku myth beckoned to another Nigerian poet. In 'Political Abiku', Ben Okri (b. 1959, Nigeria/UK) foregrounds an application latent but subdued in Soyinka and Okigbo, and prominent in Okri's novel *The Famished Road* (1991), where, as noted by John Thieme, the liminal space of the *abiku* expands to a national allegory of the 'country as a spirit-child nation' (2003: 1). Soyinka's poem implies a natural affinity between writer and Abiku in respect to difficult crossings, and Okigbo asserts a ritual role for himself as a kind of Abiku. Okri shifts the perspective from child to mother. His poem equates the child's coming with the pain of repeated childbearing. Birth becomes a tear in the fabric of her normal being.

> We heard her weep
> In our evening's settled
> Dust of betrayals.

> [. . .]
> 'Never again, Abiku-seed,
> Never to my body return'.
>
> (1992: 71–2)

Birth is feared as a form of recurrent abortion. Okri's poem is closer to the attitude of the Clark poem, but with a new political, post-colonial overtone. The people of Africa are like a mother, a potentiality that bears fruit only in waste, corruption, and suffering. Okri uses the metaphor of miscegenation to invoke a new nationhood blighted as calamity, as in the black humour of Salman Rushdie's *Midnight's Children* (1980):

> Our fingers bless
> The seepages of state.
>
> (1992: 74)

8.2 Gender and poetry: the Caribbean

> We push so much under the carpet—
> the carpet's now a landscape.
>
> Eunice de Souza, 'Landscape'

Colonialism resembles patriarchy and racism. Gender, like race, is a constructed category, used often in patriarchal societies as an instrument of containment and victimization. In Asia, Africa, and the Caribbean, colonialism worked in complex ways to alter perceptions about the condition of women in traditional societies. On the one hand, discrimination against the native reinforced the subordination suffered by women under patriarchy; on the other, colonial policy encouraged social reform.

In India, for example, the British opposed 'Sati' (the Hindu practice in which a widow accepts immolation on the funeral pyre of her dead husband), child marriage, and caste discrimination, although later commentators qualify the claim for social progress and gender equality under colonial rule. Colonialism had its historical demise, but racism and patriarchy do not look likely to end any time soon. Women writers continue to articulate their resistance to patriarchy, finding common cause with the struggle for self-representation by all minorities that suffer marginalization and discrimination. This section touches briefly upon examples from Asia and Africa as a comparative context in which to explore the poetics and politics of gender in poetry by women from the Caribbean.

The rhetoric of gendered writing differs from society to society. However, 'I was that Woman', by Debjani Chatterjee (b. 1952, India/UK), reminds us of a pattern of subjugation common to male authority and religiosity:

> I was that woman at whom the Vedas, the Avesta,
> the Bible and the Quran were flung;
> their God was the bogeyman
> who kindly sent male prophets
> to keep me humble in my place.
>
> (2004: 14)

Imtiaz Dharker (b. 1954, Pakistan/UK/India), in *Purdah and Other Poems* (1989), dramatizes the predicament of a woman born in an Islamic society, where the concealment of the face becomes a metaphor for a variety of proscriptions that invoke religious sanction in order to perpetuate systematic discrimination against women. Islam denies women the freedoms that are relatively commonplace in other patriarchal systems. In 'The Child Sings', 'She is nothing but a crack | where the light forgot to shine' (1989: 31). In 'Stone', 'Your history is a trapdoor | that you must struggle through | blinking from the darkness | into a shower of light' (54). When the family of a bride fails to deliver a dowry, the Indian woman is subjected to many forms of cruelty by the husband's family, including 'bride burning'. Dharker tries to ventriloquize the kind of fatalism that would accept this fate in 'blessing':

> This was the house she had been sent to,
> the man she had been bound to,
> the future she had been born into.
>
> (1989: 37)

The point of depicting a woman accepting death so passively is to make us reflect that it is we who 'shield our faces from the heat'. The volume is animated by the desire to encourage women to resistance. 'A Woman's Place' enjoins women to 'Scratch, | scratch at paper, hoping to draw blood' (33).

Dharker's second volume, *Postcards from God* (1994) makes room for a sardonic tone and a wider social awareness of contemporary India.

'In My Image' still keeps womankind in mind as 'the unquiet sea, | the resurrected shore' (51), but the frame of reference throughout the volume expands, as in 'Whim', to encompass contemporary reality as 'this | monstrous, magical thing' (10). In a manner reminiscent of Ted Hughes's *Crow* (1970), Dharker's God reflects on the mess he has made of His creation. The volume quickens in urgency as the poet tackles the issues raised for contemporary India by the ethnic violence that led to Hindu–Muslim riots in Bombay during 1992–93. More than 700 people were killed by their fellow citizens, mostly through arson. Millions of dollars worth of property was destroyed. The economic productivity of the city was brought to a standstill. Dharker insists on asking a metaphysical question about urban politics: 'Am I there | when I can't hear your voice?' (30) she asks, in 'Question 1'; did God make us in his image, or we him in our image?, asks 'Question 2' (32).

Everywhere in Asia, the metropolis is the locus of modernity. Bombay (or Mumbai, as it was renamed in an act of nationalist re-appropriation) is the financial capital and the most hybrid urban environment in a nation founded on the principle of secularism. The ethnic riots of the early 1990s illustrated the fragility of cosmopolitan secularism. '8 January 1993' remembers Mumbai as 'a scream | that never found an end' (81). 'Kite' treats concern for where Indian urban society is headed, like a set of aspirations 'launched hopefully | through the air' which float down, eventually but inevitably, 'to the few feet of earth | that shift themselves | and jostle out a space | to fit us underground' (90).

Dharker's third volume, *I Speak for the Devil* (2001), develops a variety of metaphors for presenting feminine identity through a set of negations. The self is what is left after roles are stripped. It belongs neither here nor there. It speaks truly neither in this tongue nor in that silence. It arrives at a relationship either too late or too soon. Closeness and sharing are precious, fragile, and precarious. The title sequence animates belief in possession, not in the sense of self-possession, but as in demonic possession. In 'Learning to Speak in Birmingham', going out of control feels the same as someone else taking over one's life: one moment Ella can hear the sound of her own voice, 'The next I found | his breath inside my mouth' (2001: 58). In 'Breeding Ground, Chicago', possession becomes a double displacement: roles pushing women to the sides of their lives, delirious notions of freedom stealing souls:

I'm burgling myself, and I'm so good
I won't be caught.

(56)

The poet invents women who invite the reader of 'Have you ever lost control?' to walk 'the crazy paving in my head' (62). Dharker's poems are accompanied by a handful of black-and-white drawings, whose lines etched deep, as in woodcut, reinforce the imagery of mixed guilt and glee with which dispossession is spoken of as sleeping with the Devil. 'Possession' declares:

The devil is a territory
That lets you believe you belong,
Happy when you worship
At its mirrors.

(104)

The book ends on the recognition that poetry works as a form of exorcism.

In contrast to the Indian scene of writing, the changes in social perception needed for the growth of women's writing were slow to take root in Africa. A few—like Ama Ata Aidoo (b. 1942, Ghana) or Gcina Mhlophe (b. 1958, South Africa)—use several genres including poetry, but the number of women who write poetry remains relatively small. Those who do generally turn attention away from the politics of nation to the routines of everyday living, to what needs doing from the ground up. Naana Banyiwa Horne (Ghana/USA), for instance, declares in 'A Note to My Liberal Feminist Sister (1)':

The issue for me, Sister,
is not whether I have been
knocked up or knocked down
[...]
The real question for me, Sister,
is how I am going to rise from the ground up
after I have been knocked down;
keep a song in the hearts of all my children,
wanted and unwanted...

(2000: 41)

Among postcolonial societies, the Caribbean is notable for the quality and range of poetry by women. In *I is a Long Memoried*

Woman (1983), Grace Nichols offers a litany of praise to her unremembered female ancestors:

We the women who cut
clear fetch dig and sing
[...]
who praises go unsung
who voices go unheard
who deaths they sweep
aside
as easy as dead leaves

(13)

Their lives become a source of inspiration for later women. Lorna Goodison (b. 1947, Jamaica/USA) answers the question, 'So Who Was the Mother of Jamaican Art?' with the claim, 'She was the first nameless woman who created | images of her children sold away from her' (2005: 15). The female drudgery remembered by Nichols is absorbed in a jocular affirmation by Louise Bennett in 'Jamaica Oman':

Jamaica oman cunny sah!
Is how dem jinnal so?
Look how long dem liberated
An de man dem never know!

(Donnell, A. and Welsh 1996: 145)

Bennett is amusing, but the joke wears thin in a sharper account of the escape from silence into voice, dramatized by Amryl Johnson, in 'Lookin' fuh a Voice':

Ah makin' babies since ah sixteen
[...]
But ah strange thing happen today
meh tongue feel like it have somethin' to say
lips start movin' tuh sounds comin' down
an' now ah cahn stop singin' dis song...

(1992: 15)

Such poetry disdains Standard English, affirming a local patois that rejects the language of masculinity and colonization. Such affirmations did not come quickly or easily to the Caribbean. The attempt by women to articulate a sense of poetic individuality began in a combination of diffidence and perseverance with Una Marson (1905–65,

Jamaica). Marson showed considerable enterprise on a variety of literary fronts. She founded a journal in 1928, wrote the first play by a native author in 1933, and championed a variety of causes throughout her life.

Her poems seem fated for the representative role of a woman with intimations of a freedom whose time had not yet come. Many of the early poems are feminine in tone and subject, and express feelings of loneliness and desire within a formalism that is constrained by its own decorum. At her best, however, Marson gives signs of what Louis James describes as an 'edgy fluency' (1999: 53), the result perhaps of what Denise Narain calls 'the sense of restlessness and lack of fulfillment that pervade much of her work' (2002: 9). In the frequently quoted 'Kinky Hair Blues', dialect makes a modest but effective entry:

Now I's gwine press me hair
And bleach me skin.
I's gwine press me hair
What won't gal do
Some kind of man to win.

(Donnell and Welsh 1996: 138)

Marson empathizes with the plight of women several rungs below her on the class ladder. Her vocalizations are accurate in respect to the speech habits of her subjects. However, sympathy for harsh conditions and grim histories leaves little room in which to offer plausible hope that such women might suffer less at the hands of men or society. The poetry has no clue to how such women might shape their own lives with dignity and self-respect. Yet, as Rhonda Cobham points out, middle-class writers were liable to romanticize their downtrodden subjects in the misplaced desire to celebrate the dignity of labour or the sturdiness of the working-class woman: 'At the same time, the middle class woman is reduced to a negative stereotype and made the scapegoat for the failings of the entire black bourgeoisie' (1990: 215). As with McKay (Chapter 4.3), Marson spoke in Standard English, her lower-class subjects spoke in dialect.

A more consistent and sustained sympathy for the underprivileged and the oppressed informs the poetry of Louise Bennett, whose career began with *Dialect Verses* (1942). Her stylistic preference avoided schizophrenia by choosing always to use dialect. The price she paid for this choice, though it brought her enormous popularity in Jamaica, was exile from the Caribbean literary canon, a situation that altered grudgingly only after the 1960s. Bennett's poetry provides a humane and humorous social commentary on many aspects of Jamaican society. However, Cobham points out a limitation: 'her poems tend to show women using men as surrogates for their aggression, and . . . she seems to follow the bias of Jamaican men in her presentation of women as apolitical' (217). As for her satirical technique, Cobham notes, 'in her dramatic monologues she can only be as positive about women as she thinks the character through whom she speaks is in real life' (219).

Bennett's strength is based on a robust faith in dialect. She explained to Dennis Scott in 1968: 'The nature of the Jamaican dialect is the nature of comedy . . . you can express yourself more strongly and vividly than in Standard English. . . . we find dialect all over the world . . . Our people . . . have a wonderful sanity and clarity in their language' (Markham 1995: 45, 46, 48). 'Colonisation in Reverse' (1966) exemplifies most of her virtues. It reflects on the ironic situation that confronts England in the form of immigrants from the Caribbean, who are characterized as taking an odd sort of pride in an enterprise learned from the 'motherlan'. History is turned upside down when the seat of Empire is inundated:

> Oonoo se how life is funny,
> Oonoo see de tunabout?
> Jamaica live fi box bread
> Out a English people mout.
> [. . .]
> What a devilment a Englan!
> Dem face war an brave de worse;
> But ah wonderin how dem gwine stan
> Colonizin in reverse.
>
> (Markham 1995: 62–3)

The ability to use the full continuum from Creole to Standard English within a single poem was consolidated in the late 1970s and early 1980s by Grace Nichols and Lorna Goodison. Dennis Walder cautions readers of Nichols not to mistake her engagement with specific issues related to gender as commitment to a specific ideology, because she resists 'facile identifications of her position as either "feminist" or "black"—or indeed as the "long-suffering black woman" ' (1998: 147). In *The Fat Black Woman's Poems* (1984), Nichols invents an attractive persona that subverts stereotypes of femininity with a show of cussedness that is endearing for being sardonic. The persona acquires dignity by refusing to succumb to the social pressures that reproach women for being fat or black (or both). Racial prejudice is assimilated into a wider struggle to gain freedom from ideas of shapeliness and desirability that victimize women into accepting the role of objects meant for male visual consumption, as in '... And a Fat Poem': 'Fat feels | as fat please ... Fat is a dream | in times of lean' (17).

Poetry empowers women to rupture the silence enjoined upon them by patriarchy, as in Lorna Goodison's 'Mother the Great Stone Got to Move', which asks the mother to provide witness to an unchronicled past:

> Mother, one stone is wedged across the hole in our history
> and sealed with blood wax.
> In this hole is our side of the story, exact figures,
> headcounts, burial artifacts, documents, lists, maps
> [...]
> It is the half that has never been told, some of us
> Must tell it.
>
> (1992: 138)

The strong sense of continuity from mother to daughter established by the poem signifies a resolve and strength capable of uncovering what has been repressed. Such poetry crosses the gap that separates cultures. Likewise, 'Protest Poem', by Pamela Mordecai (Jamaica/Canada), shows how a mixed register moving freely from Creole to Standard usage can negotiate between cultural differences:

> Is di ole chattel ting again: di same
> slavery bizniz, but dis time...
> we the people propose
> the abolition of you
> and us: we propose
> an acknowledgement
> of our persons and
> an alliance of poverty...
>
> (Glaser and Pausch 1994: 14)

When the diction moves from Creole to words like 'propose' and 'abolish', the slave reveals mastery over the colonizer's vocabulary, suggesting the likelihood that differences in dialect do not affect the underlying humanity.

Jean 'Binta' Breeze provides another example of a contemporary poet who moves freely across the continuum from Creole to Standard English, just as she moves fluently from the performance stage to the printed page. The poem 'caribbean woman' celebrates its subject in a comprehensive vision of someone who can cry, or kick out her man, or raise a son or a daughter, while at the same time 'cookin | washin | ironin || . . . cussing | winin | jokin | . . . prayin | "oh lawd" ':

oh man,
de caribbean woman

she doan afraid a de marchin beat
she doan care if he timin sweet
she doan care if she   kill a man . . .

(1997: 73)

A more recent poem, 'The Garden Path', drops Creole for Standard English, and asserts a determination to rid the feminine of several roles in which the gendered overlaps with the postcolonial:

I am more than colour
more than class
more than gender
I am more than virgin
more than whore
[. . .]
I cannot be framed
or torn apart

(2000: 24–5)

Contemporary women poets have expanded the scope of their writing to include more than resistance to patriarchy. In the last of 'Four Meditations on Small (the practice of precise diction)', Jennifer Rahim (UK/Trinidad) analyses the issues at stake in the rhetoric of belittlement that is shared by colonialism and patriarchy in keeping the Caribbean woman's view of herself and her islands as 'small':

String of islands,
we first learnt you as *small*
(meaning nouns) colonies
of nothingness, at best
imitations of greater places;

(2002: 27)

The poem is explicit about how colonial belittlement extends to postcolonial neocolonialism:

> Antilles lesser or greater,
> chains of the *discoverer's* passage,
> his language present
> in politician's tyrannies,
> cable t.v. culture, foreign-
> used economies and policies
> [...]
> In my language, you see,
> *small* may yet be an abstract
> (meaning mentality) noun
> that threatens sovereignty.
>
> (2002: 27–8)

The male presence of the bully and the colonizer pervades the region as the mentality of small-mindedness. Poets like Rahim bear witness to a Caribbean in which neocolonial forces are recognized and resisted with dignity.

8.3 **Postmodern practice: South Asia**

> Where do we go from here, where do we go,
> Out of the broken bottles? Pious sot!
> You have no guide or clue for you know only
> Puce snakes and violet mastodons, where the brain beats,
> And a seltzer is no answer, a vomit no relief,
> And the parched tongue no feel of water.
>
> 'Myra Buttle' [Victor Purcell], 'Sweeney in Articulo'

In this section, we are going to examine the work of a poet who highlights the role played by translation in the relation between postcolonial predicaments and postmodern techniques. In each term, the 'post-' defers to, and differs from, the noun it qualifies. 'Modernism' refers to a loose set of tendencies that found concentrated expression in European and American art during the early decades of the twentieth century; modernity was the historical realization of the European Enlightenment project of instrumental rationality, with progress as its goal, and the technological rationalization of nature and human societies as its means.

The use of 'modernism' to describe various art practices (and beliefs) creates several difficulties when transposed from Europe to postcolonial societies. First, similar to British (and unlike German) Romanticism, European 'modernism' is largely retrospective in nature. Second, the notion of the 'modern' equivocates between a denotation that is historically specific and a connotation that evokes perpetual novelty. On the one hand, 'modern' implies a link with the 'new', the 'contemporary', and 'the avant-garde'; but, as Raymond Williams remarks, 'What was "modern", what was indeed "avant-garde", is now relatively old' (1989: 52). Third, intellectuals of every persuasion, from American New Critics to European intellectuals from the Left (such as Georg Lukács and Theodor Adorno), shared the belief that aesthetic autonomy was the principal trait of 'modernism'. However, as noted by Peter Bürger in the 1970s, the post-Romantic and modernist myth of the autonomy of art inhibits analysis of its aesthetics as arising from 'an institution in bourgeois society' (1984: lii). This repression becomes particularly noticeable when modernism is transplanted outside Europe, where its role as an aesthetic principle meets with different social formations and political agendas. As remarked, more recently, by W. J. T. Mitchell, 'The very notion of art as a distinctive category of objects... is forged in the colonial encounter' (2005: 147).

Fourth, modernism is often treated as unrelated to European colonialism, even though modernist art—as many recent commentators have noted—provides ample evidence for a significant relation between the two phenomena. In Europe, the relation between modernism and modernization generated two types of reaction. One is described by Perry Anderson as 'cultural despair' (1992: 28), and exemplified by a range of writers from Max Weber to José Ortega y Gasset, T. S. Eliot to Allen Tate, F. R. Leavis to Herbert Marcuse. The second subsidized many types of utopian optimism, from Filippo Marinetti to Le Corbusier, Buckminster Fuller to Marshall McLuhan. With the transposition of modernist techniques or assumptions to postcolonial societies, the antithesis between despair and utopianism is affected by several ironies.

While many modernist writers were either ambivalent towards or critical of colonialism, modernism was disseminated to cultures and societies outside Europe by colonialism. The spirit of radical experiment central to modernism travelled to the newly independent nations of the mid twentieth century belatedly, either as imitation, or as the local re-enactment of the dialectic between modernity and modernism whose characteristics first took shape in European cultures. The European manifestation of modernist practices, as in the work of Joseph Conrad or T. S. Eliot, exposed the underside of the Enlightenment will to progress. However, the acculturation of colonized societies into the project of modernity did not permit their writers a corresponding degree of scepticism about the Utopian elements of modernity, either in terms of postcolonial nationhood, or in terms of the asymmetrical development of capitalist globalization.

While European modernism from Gauguin to Picasso, or Lawrence to Eliot, drew upon the otherness of the non-European in transforming its self-image, postcolonial modernists could hardly do the same. Instead, they ended up discovering or inventing oppositional alterities from within their own cultures. While Europe was busy imaging itself indirectly through its many 'Others', the formerly colonized were busy trying to emulate and adapt European modes and practices in colonial and postcolonial contexts. One of the ways this could be done, as noted by Simon Gikandi, was for 'colonized writers to use forms and figures borrowed from European modernism as a point of entry into certain aspects of Western culture' (1992: 15–16). Even if European modernists nursed reservations about colonialism, the influence of modernism outside Europe became complicit with a different agenda, which inadvertently fed the growth of Europe's continued neocolonial cultural dominanace.

Many of these issues are illustrated in the work of a bilingual poet from India: Arun Kolatkar (1932–2004). His poems show how modernist practices acquire different functions when transplanted to societies in which a postcolonial predicament interacts with a postmodern sensibility. Kolatkar deploys a surreal poetics to grapple with an internalized disenchantment with tradition. He writes from a social background that is rooted in the kind of Sanskrit culture invoked from a respectful distance by a modernist like T. S. Eliot. Ironically, an outsider like Eliot makes a value of that which evinces satire from an insider like Kolatkar. In a poem like *The Waste Land* (1922), the Orientalism of Eliot turned from his time and place to the Brahminical pieties of Indic culture for 'Shantih' (spiritual peace). In reverse analogy, Kolatkar berates the internal colonization practised on Indian society by Brahminical belief systems. Eliot's distraught disbelief drew grateful sustenance from Indic religions; Kolatkar derives his sardonic attitude from European models of post-Enlightenment scepticism.

Kolatkar began writing poems during the 1950s: in Marathi, English, from Marathi into English, and the other way round. Marathi is the language of the Western state of Maharashtra in India, with Mumbai as its capital, and a native speaker base of approximately 65 million. By the 1960s, Kolatkar's output had acquired a coterie reputation among poets in Marathi. This transformed into wider local and international recognition when the English-language *Jejuri* (1976) won the Commonwealth Poetry Prize. *Jejuri* remains the single most striking sequence of poems in English written by an Indian, in Amit Chaudhuri's words, 'a narrative, indeed, of semi-articulate but deep undecidedness and uncertainty about what constitutes, in language, poetic wonder, citizenship, nationhood, and in what ways these categories are in tension with one another' (2005: online). It was followed in 1977 by a collection of his Marathi poems. A long gap of over thirty years ensued before the Marathi poems of the intervening years were collected in two volumes published in 2003. The English poems and adaptations since 1977 remained uncollected for a long time, giving his career a certain throwaway quality that is not without its Dadaesque dimension. The publication of *Sarpa Satra* and *Kala Ghoda* in 2004 (in English), concurrent with the publication of another Marathi volume, marked 2003 and 2004 as the *annus mirabilis* of his career.

Kolatkar's style, in English and Marathi, is relaxed, ironic, and colloquial. His poems reveal a deeply ambivalent relation to the contemporary culture of urban Mumbai (Bombay) and the tradition of poetry in Marathi. This tradition is distinguished by a genealogy of poet-saints from Dnyaneshwar (in the thirteenth century) to Tukaram (in the seventeenth century), who promoted forms of devotion that gave voice to the plight of the underdog, and offered resistance to the caste system that still dominates Indian society. Like them, Kolatkar rebels against the inert weight of tradition; but he also subscribes to an implicit trust in rationality that finds expression in various forms of satire. His scepticism gives proof of the continued influence of post-Macaulay models of education in postcolonial India. Kolatkar's relation to the Maharashtrian past is split between admiration for the vernacular poets who championed the underdogs of society in their time, and distaste for the decayed Sanskritism of the contemporary bourgeoisie. An old and internal Indian enemy—Brahminism—is opposed with the aid of two seemingly unlikely but perfectly compatible allies: subaltern vernacular poetry, and Western modernist art practices.

Kolatkar's style is also gnomic and glancing, willing to take the risk of appearing facetious in order to avoid the semblance of earnestness, but the nonchalance barely conceals a troubled sensibility: 'not waving but drowning' as phrased in the celebrated poem of that title by Stevie Smith (1902–71). Its unsettling quality can be illustrated from 'Traffic Lights', a poem in which Kolatkar evokes the busy passage of a motorcade through an urban setting, and then focuses on a surreal emptiness that is reminiscent of the urban nightscapes of a painter like Giorgio de Chirico:

> . . . traffic lights
> that seem to have eyes only for each other
> and who like ill-starred lovers
> fated never to meet
> but condemned to live forever and ever
> in each other's sight
> continue to send signals to each other
> throughout the night
> and burn with the cold passion of rubies
> separated by an empty street.
>
> (2004b: 162)

This is both fanciful and desolate. Kolatkar's postmodernity is a matter of attitude, or rather, of what is half-concealed beneath a habit of uneasy urbanity. Implicitly, he accepts European modernity as the agent for the transformation of local sensibility. He also tackles culturally specific variations of an ethical question. This question focuses on the fate of values in a society shaped by colonial influence. In what direction are individuals and groups to shape their lives and objectives in light of their specific circumstance in time and place? Colonialism is encountered in two ways: positively, as access to new linguistic and formal techniques; negatively, as an internalized colonization that turns against an older analogue, the Brahminical imperialism of Hindu India.

Kolatkar's assimilation of modernist influence can be illustrated at the level of technique in his use of verbal collage and narrative montage. He places words and lines on the page as a painter might apply pigment to canvas. The lines and stanzas of the poem form a kind of pictogram or hieroglyph. In an interview, Kolatkar claims that typographic issues are 'a minor thing... a bonus pleasure' (Ramnarayan 2004). Yet the manner in which the miniature narrative in each poem is dramatized illustrates a conscious use of the logic of the unconscious. Oblique turns of thought reflect on, or radiate from, apparently disparate but subliminally linked preoccupations, as shown by the following poem, whose Marathi version, 'Takta' (alphabet-chart), ends the collection *Arun Kolatkarchya Kavita* (1977). I propose to examine the nuances of translation raised by this poem through a comparison of two English adaptations: one by Kolatkar, the other by the US-based academic and poet Vinay Dharwadker.

Kolatkar's poem and its plural history shows how acts of translation—literal and figurative—are acts of excess, that transform the perspective in which 'the first' is treated as a model by 'the second'. The poem also shows how modernity for India is as much a struggle with its own internal colonizations as a matter of assimilating a modernist style or mindset. Kolatkar's art dramatizes the predicament of a society whose assimilation into a rapidly globalizing modernity is marked by multiple forms of resistance. In such writing, the belated spirit of modernism can be said to prosper in direct proportion to how it is transposed to deal with the agony and the emancipation of a non-Western time and place. The transposition enables poetry to accomplish two things at once: to live with, and to shed, a sense of the 'post-' from the '-modern' as well as the '-colonial'.

In most respects, Kolatkar's English version adheres to the letter of the original poem, while Dharwadker's version is loyal to its spirit. Both versions show that there are instances where English does not provide equivalences to the nuances exploited in the Marathi poem. In such cases, Kolatkar is freer than Dharwadker in finding an English alternative to the Marathi 'original'. Here first is the full Kolatkar version:

Pictures from a Marathi Alphabet Chart

Pineapple. Mother. Pants. Lemon.
Mortar. Sugarcane. Ram.
How secure they all look
each ensconced in its own separate square.

Mango. Anvil. Cup. Ganapati. Cart. House.
Medicine Bottle. Man Touching his Toes.

All very comfortable,
they all know exactly where they belong

Spoon. Umbrella. Ship. Frock.
Watermelon. Rubberstamp. Box. Cloud. Arrow.
Each one of them seems to have found
Its own special niche, a sinecure.

Sword. Inkwell. Tombstone. Longbow. Watertap.
Kite. Jackfruit. Brahmin. Duck. Maize.
Their job is to go on being themselves.
And their appointment is for life.

Yajnya.* Chariot. Garlic. Ostrich. (*ritual Hindu sacrifice)
Hexagon. Rabbit. Deer. Lotus. Archer.
No, you don't have to worry.
There's going to be no trouble in this peaceable kingdom.

The mother will not pound the baby with a pestle.
The Brahmin will not fry the duck in garlic.
That ship will not crash against the watermelon.

If the ostrich won't eat the child's frock,
The archer won't shoot an arrow in Ganapati's stomach.
And as long as the ram resists the impulse
of butting him from behind

what possible reason
could the Man-Touching-his-Toes have
to smash the cup on the tombstone?

(Kolatkar 1993: 68–9)

And here is the corresponding Dharwadker version:

The Alphabet

anvil arrow bow box and brahmin
cart chariot cloud and compost heap
are all sitting in their separate squares

corn cup deer duck and frock
ganesh garlic hexagon and house
all have places of their own

inkpot jackfruit kite lemon and lotus
mango medicine mother old man and ostrich
are all holding their proper positions

pajamas pineapple rabbit and ram
sacrifice seal spoon and sugarcane
won't interfere with each other

sword tap tombstone and umbrella
warrior watermelon weight and yacht
have all found their eternal resting place

the mother won't put her baby on the compost heap
the brahmin won't season the duck with garlic
the yacht won't hit the watermelon and sink

unless the ostrich eats the baby's frock
the warrior won't shoot an arrow into ganesh's belly
and if the ram doesn't knock down the old man

why would he need to smash the cup on the tombstone?

(Dharwadker 1994: 116)

The differences between the two adaptations sensitize reading to how the idea of an 'original' holds possibilities of signification in latent form, which the act of adaptation can develop in this or that direction. The relation of the two adaptations to the 'original' suggests that 'meaning' is like a surplus that circulates through the porous membranes of languages, transforming the relation between the 'primary' source and its 'secondary' adaptations into three collateral versions in two languages.

The most obvious differences between the two adaptations are worth enumerating. Dharwadker retains the three-line stanza of the Marathi poem; Kolatkar's version expands the final line of each Marathi stanza into two lines of English. Generally, the extra line is devoted to clarifying nuances more economically expressed in Marathi. In terms of lexical choices, Kolatkar's English follows the exact sequence of nouns enumerated in the 'original' poem, but sacrifices the alliteration of the Marathi. Dharwadker transposes from the *phonological* sequence of Marathi to the *alphabetical* sequence of English, thus retaining the alliterative effect of the Marathi, while departing from its word choice. The tone in Marathi is casual in its abandonment of the conventions of punctuation, and Dharwadker preserves the experimental and radical aspect of this feature in his typographic presentation.

The surreal image of the 'Man Touching his Toes' from Kolatkar's English version has no counterpart in the Marathi or in Dharwadker.

The image is complex in its Indian—and Maharashtrian—contexts. First, it evokes the postures of yoga, exercise, and discipline. Second, touching one's own toes gives a curious twist to the Hindu ritual of touching the feet of one's elders as a token of respect. Third, these two associations acquire an ironic quality if we think of the Hindu fundamentalisms that have prospered in Maharashtra and India since the poem was written. Without being too fanciful, one could say that the 'Man Touching his Toes' is a portmanteau image, all the more effective for being tongue-in-cheek about the support it might, or might not, lend to comic subversion.

The poem (in Marathi or English) dramatizes several social issues. It also pursues an apparently straightforward whimsy concerning the surreal possibilities latent in a children's alphabet-chart. This familiar classroom tool introduces to children the basic building blocks of language as sounds and letters by linking them to what is a set of largely (but not exclusively) familiar objects or persons in ordinary life. Each stanza begins by mimicking a class recitation in which the nouns that correspond to the sounds of the alphabet are enumerated as a list, each sound linked for the child's benefit to an image. The resulting assortment of nouns also produces a set of random collocations, which provide the poet opportunity for playful fantasy. Nouns are placed in subject–object relations by verbs that have no care for the anarchy that results when the rules of grammar are observed without care for plausibility.

A literal translation of the first line in Marathi ('ananas aaee ijaar ani idlimbu' (1977: 130)) would give us 'pineapple mother trouser and lemon' (Kolatkar's translation prefers the Pune-English 'pants' to 'trousers'). The words in the Marathi are an enumeration rather than a sentence. The words as nouns evoke allusions that pull one way, while the logic of why those words have been selected points another way. The modernist element of the poem is revealed in how the reader is plunged into an act of interpretive challenge from the very beginning. The reader has to work out the logic of the enumeration, which follows the traditional Marathi sequence of vowels and consonants. Dharwadker replaces this 'ee aa o ou' sequence with the alphabetical series of English. The logic of 'a, b, c' as a sequence gives him licence to invent his own nouns: 'anvil arrow bow box and brahmin'. The words are unrelated except through orthographic and phonological accident. They happen to be nouns that begin with the appropriate letter of the alphabet. Thus 'b' might be illustrated plausibly and randomly not just with 'bow' or 'box' but 'buffalo' or 'brinjal', and so on.

Interesting things start happening when 'b' is illustrated by Dharwadker with 'brahmin'. In an Indian context, this choice is plausible but unlikely. Its subtle inappropriateness for the dramatic context makes it apt for the poetic context, because it prompts the reader to wonder why this particular illustrative noun has been selected. In contemporary experience, brahmins are more ordinary and ubiquitous than anvils or arrows or even buffalos and brinjals, yet those objects do not create the buzz of 'brahmin'. The word connotes caste, which is embedded deeper than class in India, and stirs associations that can be powerful and discomfiting. To introduce the basic divisions in Indian society as part of introducing the basic letters of an alphabet would hinder rather than aid teaching. Dharwadker capitalizes on the opportunity to drop the word into the verse line, like a pebble into a smooth pond, whereas Kolatkar uses the word much later, in his fourth stanza.

In any case, 'brahmin' in English is bland and neutral, unlike Kolatkar's 'bhatji', which is comic and derogatory. This cultural significance might not be readily accessible to readers outside India or Maharashtra. 'Bhatji' is both less and more than 'brahmin'. It refers to a priest who makes his living by performing religious rituals on behalf of other non-priestly brahmins. In other words, his caste has placed him in the indispensable position of mediating between the community and its religion. Kolatkar's other work is unflattering of the brahminical function, as performed in myth, legend, and history. In *Sarpa Satra* (2004), even 'the great rishis and maharishis' (holy men) are 'worried about just one thing: | how to wrangle a job for themselves' (33), each reduced to a 'mantra mutterer' (34). When the ritual sacrifice narrated in that poem is over, brahmins come in as 'hangers-on, | and assorted freeloaders' (80). In Kolatkar's poetic world, the brahmin is interloper, predator, and parasite. 'Bhatji' inhabits a tonal spectrum somewhere between jocular and rude. Ironically, Kolatkar belongs by birth to the brahmin caste. Marathi-speaking readers are unlikely to miss this irony, since Marathi surnames are indicators of caste affiliations. The irony of an anti-brahmin brahmin might be lost to readers unfamiliar with Marathi.

The derisive force of 'bhatji' cannot be rendered through the innocuous 'brahmin'. Dharwadker sharpens the effect of 'Brahmin' in English by introducing 'compost heap' in the next verse line. The recitation of an alphabet-chart is part of a system of socialization whose broader function would be compromised if one were to illustrate sound or letters with the most disconcerting nouns from contemporary society, simply because the ugly or the upsetting is as much a part of reality as the banal and the ordinary. Dharwadker pushes the playful aspects of Kolatkar's juxtapositions into a more threatening posture. Foregrounding 'brahmin' and 'compost heap' is only marginally milder than asking children to recite 'C for car-crash', or 'R for rapist', or 'S for suicide'. It induces a collusion of implications that can leave the reader wondering if Brahmanism belongs in a dumpster, since it has become an outworn and derelict institution.

The poem's satire is more evenly shared between the Marathi and the two adaptations in another respect: the pictorial convention of separating each letter and corresponding image in a box provides Kolatkar with an opportunity for mild subversion. The squares can be taken to stand for the first subliminal lesson in segregation. It becomes the first intimation, in the child's world, of the kind of classification system that created the caste system of India. Difference and deference, uniqueness and separateness thus come together in Kolatkar's playful twist to the pedagogic exercise that he mimics. The holding of 'proper positions' appears an innocent exercise, which keeps disorder at bay while introducing reason through the categories of knowledge. The issue of holding positions is reiterated in the last line of the first five stanzas, like variations on a refrain. It reiterates the need to keep position as the key to ideological integration and social stability: 'There's going to be no trouble in this peaceable kingdom' (Kolatkar: stanza 5). This is a prophylactic against social mobility. The caste system ensured—virtually came into existence in order to ensure—that such destabilization would not occur without conservative resistance.

The phrasing is richer in cultural nuance in Marathi, whereas in English, the connotations are flattened out in the interests of smoother syntax. When nouns are activated by verbs, and grammar permits random positions for subjects and objects, the semantics that gives society its order can be derailed. The poem recognizes that the conjugations that work as grammar are an analogy to the structural or ethical foundations on which society depends for its notion of normalcy and order. The poem opens up such conventions to what we might call additional, poststructuralist conjugations. These, if actualized, would wrench the orderliness assumed by the chart. In that sense, the poem first arouses, and then allays, fears of which the chart is either ignorant or deceptive. In the poem, the nouns of the chart move out of their secure containers, and once they start interacting, the resulting syntax creates a grammar whose semantics is both possible and inconceivable, or logically realizable but socially undesirable. The result is far more threatening than the linguist Noam Chomsky's 1957 example of an utterance that is grammatically possible even if otherwise implausible: 'colorless green ideas sleep furiously'.

A Shandyean child, who starts freeing nouns from their boxes in the classroom, could go out into the world and free people from their caste or station and role in life, unleashing a huge potential for fun and disorder. The poet indulges both sides of the fantasy. Thus, mothers might throw their babies into dumpsters, brahmins might abandon vegetarianism, ships collide with fruit and capsize, and so on. And of course, all these things do occur somewhere in our times, though we might not want to tell children that, or at least not when they are still in alphabet-school. The poem speculates fantastically on what is conceivable once the relations that ensure stability in society are set free of conventional codes of conduct, once a person moves out of what Kolatkar's version identifies as a 'niche, a sinecure' (stanza 3), and abandons the idea that whatever role one is assigned is an 'appointment . . . for life' (stanza 4).

The poem in Marathi and English ends on a rhetorical question that remains ambiguous: if the order the child is taught will hold, then there will be no need to smash the cup (that holds and contains) on the tombstone (that bespeaks the dead). Its open-endedness leaves the door ajar for the other alternative: what if all this will not hold? The scope for anarchy inherent, concealed, or latent in the child's world is thus given recognition with a technique that balances modernist *angst* with postmodern insouciance.

9

Recurrent motifs: voyage and translation

Overview

Colonialism bred three kinds of willing voyager—adventurer, explorer, colonist; one type of partially willing voyager—the indentured labourer; and one type of unwilling voyager—the slave. Postcolonial history adds two more types to this motley: the migrant, and the exile; in them, as in the indentured labourer, the distinction between willing and involuntary displacement is blurred. Postcolonial writing proliferates with symbolic voyages that are meant to ameliorate the displacement caused by diaspora. One kind of poet tackles the voyage in a collective spirit, as an individual rooted in imagined community, as when Walcott and Brathwaite appear to head away from home, only for their poetry to discover ways of revising their view of the birthplace. The second type of traveller suffers a more literal relocation through migration or self-exile, as illustrated by A. K. Ramanujan, Agha Shahid Ali, and Ee Tiang Hong. Their work shuttles between an emotional anchorage in a home left behind, and the attempt to grow new roots in a place that the poet strives to accept as home.

9.1 The voyage home: Walcott and Brathwaite

The heart of standing is you cannot fly.

William Empson, 'Aubade'

The metaphor of a voyage exercises a compulsive fascination for all poets who struggle to develop personal or communal identities from historical displacement. This applies with particular force to the

Caribbean, where the idea of wanting to be somewhere else seeks to appease the sense that where one happens to be is not where one would like to remain. The hope of arrival or appeasement leads to voyages that are symbolic as well as literal. The symbolic voyage points to an Africa of the mind and heart, an ancestral home for those displaced by slavery. The literal voyage takes a more pragmatic direction: away from a birthplace (that was never quite a home), toward the metropolitan centre, which provides an alternative (place-that-is-never-quite-home). With increasing frequency after World War II, the literal voyage took writers closer to publishers and readers in the UK or North America. It also took them close to the cultural capitals whose power to confer recognition outlasted the demise of colonialism. A smaller set of poets found other ways of voyaging, with different ideas of departure, movement, and arrival. It is to their voyages that we now turn.

The careers of Derek Walcott (b. 1930, St Lucia) and Kamau Brathwaite (b. 1930, Barbados) illustrate the range of possibilities discovered by poets writing on behalf of people beset by the persistent feeling that they are 'illegitimate, rootless, mongrelized' (Walcott 1998: 67). Walcott cannot forget that the nineteenth-century English historian James Anthony Froude claimed of the Caribbean, 'No people there', only 'Fragments and echoes of real people, unoriginal and broken' (1998: 68). The poetic voyages undertaken by Walcott and Brathwaite are aimed at transforming this mindset through a revised relation between self, community, place, and history. They imagine or invent a sense of home that will lighten the burden of colonial histories. The end of voyaging is to find oneself where one has dispelled the tension produced by displacement, in a stasis of fulfilment: 'This is the benediction that is celebrated, a fresh language and a fresh people, and this is the frightening duty owed' (1998: 79).

Brathwaite went to Africa in 1955 after having studied in England. He worked in Ghana for seven years before returning to England to pursue work on a doctoral dissertation, and then settled down to an academic career in Jamaica, followed by frequent trips to North America and Britain. Walcott chose for many years to stay on in the Caribbean, refusing to go to Britain, although he chose to make its culture his own, while he later shuttled between North America and the Caribbean, largely in order to make a living out of his vocation. In a symbolic sense, neither turned his back on the Caribbean.

Brathwaite made the symbolic voyage to and back from Africa the central preoccupation of his early writing, while Walcott rejected 'an Africa that was no longer home' (1998: 33). Instead, he made the voyage a symbol for a revised relation to personal and collective memory within the Caribbean.

Walcott's method of internalizing the experience of a voyage can be approached through a brief comparison between his sense of vocation and the metaphor of voyaging he applies to an admired predecessor, Eric Roach. In 1974, Roach swam out to sea off the coast of Trinidad: an act of suicide rather than accidental drowning. In 'The Wind in the Dooryard', Walcott wrote of the death:

> He went swimming to Africa,
> but he felt tired;
> he chose that way
> to reach his ancestors.
>
> (1976: 58)

Walcott chooses to treat the act of swimming out to sea as a gesture pointed toward Africa. Suicide becomes—in Glissant's words—an act of reversion: 'the obsession with a single origin' (1989: 16). The poem thus elegizes the pathos of despair as a form of tragic hyperbole. However, it is equally plausible to argue that Roach chose to die because he could voyage nowhere, because he could not fill a lack by migrating to the metropolis, or reverting to an ancestral homeland. That is how another Caribbean poet, Martin Carter, treats it in his elegy 'On the Death by Drowning of the Poet, Eric Roach':

> It is better to drown in the sea
> than die in the unfortunate air
> which stifles.
>
> (1999: 126)

In contrast, Walcott found it possible to sustain a gritty optimism held up by the ballast of a vigorously ambivalent sense of vocation. It endowed his writing with a sense of swimming with purpose—not to Africa—but to a new Caribbean, a blue basin whose history is erased, at least in the world recreated by poetry. Several years before Roach's death, Walcott addressed the issue in prose. 'What the Twilight Says' (1970) articulates a sense of the anguish and bitterness felt by the descendants of slaves who could never forget, in relation to the islands where they lived, that 'we were all strangers here', and 'there is no one left on whom we can exact revenge. That is the laceration of our shame' (1998: 10). 'The Muse of History' (1974) declares that 'In the New World servitude to the muse of history has produced a literature of recrimination and despair, a literature of revenge written by the descendants of slaves or a literature of remorse written by the descendants of masters' (1998: 37). Walcott's male grandparents on both sides of the family were white, while the grandmothers were black, keeping him connected to, yet distanced from, both sides of the Caribbean ethnic divide. His poetry acknowledges a sense—sometimes exultant, at other times, uneasy—of being at once both inheritor and interloper.

The patois used to dramatize the speaking voice of 'The Schooner *Flight*' (1979)—Shabine (St. Lucian French for mulatto)—expresses vividly what the poet might not have expressed for himself in such blunt terms:

> I had no nation now but the imagination.
> After the white man, the niggers didn't want me
> when the power swing to their side.
> The first chain my hands and apologize, 'History';
> the next said I wasn't black enough for their pride.
>
> (1986: 350)

Shabine, one of Walcott's most powerful evocations, declares 'either I'm nobody, or I'm a nation' (1986: 346). In tracing Walcott's (and Seamus Heaney's) debt to Dante's evocation of Ulysses (*Inferno*, XXVI), Maria Fumagalli remarks, 'the pseudonym "nobody" that Shabine claims for himself is the imaginative stratagem that allows Odysseus to save his life. It signifies the necessity of imagination out of which . . . Shabine has come and which plays such a crucial part in the West Indian "quarrel" with history' (2001: 113).

One of Walcott's earliest poems, *Epitaph for the Young* (1949), confesses fear that he might be 'Condemned to wander. | Without purpose' (Fumagalli 2001: 42). By 1970, he has overcome self-contempt to the point of claiming that a sense of poetic vocation empowers him to emulate the eloquence of the English poetic tradition (1998: 12). He can imagine himself 'legitimately prolonging the mighty line of Marlowe, of Milton' (1998: 28), even though he also recognizes that writing from the colonies could 'grow to resemble' the literature of England without becoming its 'legitimate heir' (28).

In 1974, the metaphor of the voyage, and its associations 'with Hebraic suffering, the migration, the hope of deliverance from bondage' (1998: 44) are mitigated by the sense of vocation that put divisive loyalties to use (without necessarily dissolving them): 'I was taught English literature as my natural inheritance. . . . I felt both a rejection and a fear of Europe after I learned its poetry' (62–3). An interview from 1983 is direct in asserting a dual inheritance: 'I do not consider English to be the language of my masters. I consider English to be my birthright. I happen to have been born in an English and a Creole place, and love both languages' (1996: 82). 'North and South', from *The Fortunate Traveller* (1981), acknowledges a role for the postcolonial poet as upstart:

I accept my function
as a colonial upstart at the end of an empire,
a single, circling, homeless satellite.

(1986: 405)

'The Hotel Normandie Pool' (1981) equates the British and the Roman Empires, invokes Ovid, and speaks of the poet's sense of himself as one 'whose ancestors were slave and Roman' (1986: 443). A younger contemporary, Stewart Brown, comments shrewdly that Walcott 'nurses a pride as bruised as history | By his art's indignities' (1999: 58).

What is the kind of voyage undertaken by Walcott? It entails two types of transformation: the Caribbean is seen afresh, cleansed of history; European culture is accessed through density of allusion, and its repertoire of idioms and styles is adapted to a celebration of the local. Walcott chose self-consciously to align himself with a formal literary tradition, and largely gave up on the resources of Creole and patois, although poems like 'The Schooner *Flight*' and 'The Spoiler's Return' show what he could do when he chose to use Standard English and Creole within a single poem. The wry 'Cul de Sac Valley' from *The Arkansas Testament* (1987) confesses that as a young man who had taken on the job of teaching Latin he found himself alienated from his charges (and also, by implication, from their linguistic affiliations):

The discipline I preached
made me a hypocrite;

their lithe black bodies, beached,
would die in dialect...

(1987: 23)

Walcott thinks of himself in the Caribbean as inhabiting the role of a symbolic Adam 'exiled | to our new Eden' (1986: 300). The motif recurs through his work. The 'Homage to Gregorias' section of *Another Life* (1973) begins with an epigraph from Alejo Carpentier's *The Lost Steps*, which declares, 'they would... set themselves the only task appropriate to the milieu that was slowly revealing to me the nature of its values: Adam's task of "giving things their names" ' (1986: 189). The last page of *Another Life* echoes:

We were blest with a virginal, unpainted world
with Adam's task of giving things their names...

(1986: 294)

'Names' invokes a time prior to the condition of being named:

My race began as the sea began,
with no nouns...

(1986: 305)

In his Nobel Prize speech (1992), Walcott rejects the idea of time as the degenerative history of nature. Instead, he stresses the happiness of the timeless in the Caribbean, the 'reality of light, of work, of survival in the landscape' (1998: 75): 'It is not that History is obliterated by this sunrise. It is there in Antillean geography' (1998: 81). The islands of the Caribbean offer 'Not nostalgic sites but occluded sanctities as common and simple as their sunlight'. Their celebration gives the poet his role and function: 'this process of renaming, of finding new metaphors, is the same process that the poet faces every morning of his working day, making his own tools like Crusoe, assembling nouns from necessity' (1998: 70).

The poem 'Crusoe's Journal', from *The Gulf* (1970), explains how the fictional Robinson Crusoe's journals provide a model for the Caribbean poet:

we learn to shape from them, where nothing was
the language of a race...

(1986: 94)

An interview from 1985 elicits the comment that 'One of the more positive aspects of the Crusoe idea is that in a sense every race that has come to the Caribbean has been brought here under situations of servitude or rejection, and that is the metaphor of the shipwreck, I think' (1996: 107). Walcott may be said to translate Crusoe to the Caribbean, virtually as an antidote to the Caribbean obsession with Shakespeare's Caliban. In the 1930s, Walter Benjamin accounted for the necessity of translation in the enigmatic image of 'Fragments of a vessel that are to be glued together... recognizable as fragments of a greater language' (1996: 260). A similar image is used by Walcott:

> Break a vase, and the love that reassembles the fragments is stronger than that love which took its symmetry for granted when it was whole... Antillean art is this restoration of our shattered histories, our shards of vocabulary, our archipelago becoming a synonym for pieces broken off from the original continent.
>
> (1998: 69)

Walcott's use of the mythic figure of Odysseus provides another instance of poetic restoration. The heroic figure from Homer is adapted from the Aegean Sea to the Caribbean, as one 'to whom everything has happened' (1993: 80). In *Sea-Grapes* (1976), 'That sail which leans on light... a schooner beating up the Caribbean || for home, could be Odysseus, | home-bound on the Aegean' (1986: 297). One of the most complex evocations of the voyage motif in Walcott's poetry occurs in 'The Schooner *Flight*' from *The Star-Apple Kingdom* (1979). Here, Walcott merges communal with personal history. His dramatization of voice mixes the travails of the character Shabine with thinly veiled autobiography. A contemporary sea passage modulates into older crossings, including the Middle Passage. The poem is a *tour de force* in which the Caribbean remains both the starting point and the destination of voyaging, in which the contemporary voyage is laden with memories of other sea crossings, including the Middle Passage. In an interview from 1990 Walcott speculates, 'maybe the whole West Indian experience is not itself—it is translated' (1996: 173).

For the more ambitious *Omeros* (1990), Walcott invents a kind of poetic amnesia, in which it is possible to claim that the narrative of the Caribbean basin was like 'an epic where every line was erased | yet freshly written in sheets of exploding surf' (1990: 295–6). The Caribbean is represented as a region whose pre-history is like 'the bridesleep that soothed Adam in paradise, | before it gaped into a wound' (42). *Omeros* treats the mythic inheritance of the Aegean as an antidote to the disease of memory, a magical 'exorcism' of Homer (294): through an analogy between the Caribbean and the Aegean, the mythic is divested of its culturally specific associations. The persons of the poem become extrapolations:

> ... I said 'Omeros',
> and O was the conch-shell's invocation, *mer* was
> both mother and sea in our Antillean patois,
> *os*, a grey bone, and the white surf as it crashes
>
> and spreads its sibilant collar on a lace shore.
>
> (1990: 14)

In the Homeric myth, the poet looks for a place of possibility, as for a potential that must be realized:

> not on this grass cliff but somewhere on the other
> side of the world, somewhere, with its sunlit islands,
> where what they called history could not happen. Where?
>
> Where could this world renew the Mediterranean's innocence?
>
> (1990: 28)

This act of aggressive transposition explains the otherwise odd claim made by Walcott in an interview from 1990, that 'the Greeks were the niggers of the Mediterranean' (1996: 183), just as he claimed of the Irish that they were 'the niggers of Britain' (1996: 59). Odysseus, for Walcott, becomes a figure for the possibility and deferral of fulfilment through which man will recover nature erased of history, and return through narrative to a place where time tells nothing, and the recurrence of the mythic can be disbanded. In Walcott's stage adaptation of *The Odyssey* (1993), Odysseus is presented as a figure of longing. His epic involvement in war is dismissed as 'A tower cracking, Troy, Troy! What was it all worth?' He would readily 'give up all this heaving for one yard of earth' (1993: 39). The significance of his long return voyage is explained to him by Athena as an equation between home and peace: 'The harbour of home is what your wanderings mean ... The peace which, in shafts of light, the gods allow men?' (1993: 159).

Walcott returns to the motif of the voyage in *The Bounty* (1997), where 'Signs' uses 'the fiction of Europe that turns into theatre' (21) to subsidize the claim that the transposition of European cultural references to other locations is a viable way of arriving at the universals of human experience. Likewise, 'The Bounty' asserts:

> All of these waves crepitate with the culture of Ovid,
> its sibilants and consonants; a universal metre
> piled up these signatures like inscriptions of seaweeds
>
> that dry in the pungent sun, lines ruled by mitre
> and laurel...
>
> (1997: 11)

Legitimacy thus depends on elective affinity. Walcott shows how he has accessed European culture, throughout his career, in order to revalorize his sense of the Caribbean. The relation between Europe and the Caribbean is not overshadowed by the history of displacement that includes slavery and indentured labour. Its burden continues to inform his vision, but it does not blind perception to how the Caribbean might be renewed in the fictions of poetry. This kind of voyage succeeds in getting somewhere whenever it sees the minutest chronotope (Mikhail Bakhtin's term for a continuum linking time and space in unique conjunctions of 'here and now') as independent of historical baggage, while continuing to do so in language richly embedded in the compost of European culture, as in 'The Bounty':

> to write of the light's bounty on familiar things
> that stand on the verge of translating themselves into news...
>
> (1997: 16)

The poet is mindful that the dual loyalty (to an English idiom pressed to service far from its native home, and to a region unaffected by the history that brought its recent inhabitants to the place) corresponds in reverse to a double betrayal (to Creoles, to the histories that brought them into being), as confessed by 'Homecoming':

> 'I have tried to serve both,' I said, provoking a roar
> From the leaves, shaking their heads, defying translation.
> 'And there's your betrayal,' they said. I said I was sure
> that all the trees of the world shared a common elation
> of tongues, gommier with linden, *bois-campêche* with the elm.
> 'You lie, your right hand forgot its origin, O Jerusalem,
> but kept its profitable cunning. We remain unuttered, undefined'...
>
> (1997: 32)

Walcott's defence, in the poem 'Manet in Martinique', reiterates his belief that poetry can make cultural resonance harmonize difference, as when the Aegean and the Caribbean become, in his world of words, 'reversible':

> In maps the Caribbean dreams
> of the Aegean, and the Aegean of reversible seas.
>
> (1997: 62)

This poet's journey, then, always keeps bringing him back to where he started from, the Caribbean.

Brathwaite charts a different route from that traversed by Walcott, although their points of arrival converge. Brathwaite's revisioning of the voyage motif occupies three volumes, *Rights of Passage* (1967), *Masks* (1968), and *Islands* (1969), collected subsequently in *The Arrivants: A New World Trilogy* (1973). The impact of Brathwaite's trilogy on the scene of Caribbean writing makes it one of the central documents of postcolonial poetry. It presents a composite plurality of voices animated by the rhythms of black music: American and Caribbean jazz, and African drumming. Like the unifying consciousness of Tiresias in Eliot's *The Waste Land* (1922), the poet holds his diversity of speech rhythms together in the role of the questor.

Brathwaite uses a flexible and generally short verse line, which enables him to break free of the iambic pattern favoured by traditional English verse, although rhyme is used freely to reinforce the orality and vigour of colloquial usage. He also uses frequent line breaks, which force the reader to pause on split words. These hyphenations accentuate the dramatic rhetoric of the verse movement, drawing attention to the half-puns and nuances latent in words. These features constitute Brathwaite's chief formal legacy to subsequent poets, and make *The Arrivants* distinctive for its oral vigour, its rhythmic inventiveness, and its capacity to rehabilitate the inhabitants of the Caribbean to their island homes through a revised relation to Africa:

> back back
> to the black
> man lan'
> back back
> to Afr-
> rica.
>
> (1973: 43)

Brathwaite drops a set of crucial questions on the Caribbean plate:

> Where then is the nigger's
> home? . . . Will exile never
>
> end?
> When the release
>
> from fear, bent
> back
>
> unhealing his-
> tory?
>
> (1973: 77–8)

The Arrivants gets its impetus from the recognition that the Caribbean as birthplace constitutes a state of dispossession: 'God- || less rock | the shock || of dis- | possession' (78). This shock has lasted throughout the history of slavery, which reduced a once proud people (largely from Africa) to crushed misery. Brathwaite's idea of a return to Africa is close in spirit to that proposed by Rastafarianism. The black man in the Caribbean has forgotten his African roots: 'the paths we shall never remember . . . The tribes of Ashanti dreaming the dream | of Tutu, Anokye, and the Golden Stool' (13). The state of shock in which the inhabitants of the Caribbean islands have lived for the last several centuries has produced fractured sensibilities, each of whose splintered aspects needs acknowledgement before the poet can gather the motive for a new journey. He writes for, and as, a multitude, adopting many speaking voices during the course of *Rights of Passage*, each of them expressing the aspirations of a dispossessed people. The poet's job is to represent them—to others and to themselves—as questors, who must travel in spirit and imagination on a voyage of self-discovery, but before they can travel, the demons that tie them to the places they were born in must be exorcized.

Brathwaite recognizes that some of his fellow West Indians might be resigned to their fate and place in the Caribbean, and dismiss the hope that subsidizes others in their Rastafarian gesture towards Africa. They might also dismiss the more pragmatic one-way ticket to England or other similar destinations: 'To hell | with Af- | rica | to hell | with Eu- | rope too, | just call my blue | black bloody spade | a spade and kiss | my ass' (29). Others inhabit the stereotypes only too common in the region: 'a fuck- | in' negro, | man, hole | in my head, brains in | my belly; | black skin | red eyes | broad back' (30); a type whose only affirmation is: 'Broad back | big you know what | black sperm spews | Negritude' (39).

Others are prone to a form of inertia in which the Caribbean is like a stone, a pebble: hard and unyielding, and dead. The poet's task is to convert the stone, figuratively, into soil, so that it can be tilled. The hope is that 'our blood . . . will create new soils, new souls, new | ancestors' (11). The dream of fulfilment imagines a time when it will be possible to say that the West Indian 'stepping | softly on the brown | loam, returns | to the firm || earth | his home' (83). The West Indian is now alone with his fate. 'O who now will help | us, help- | less, horse- | less, leader- | less, no | hope, no | Hawkins, no | Cortez to come' (10). His history includes 'not Africa alone' (as the Middle Passage from an ancestral home and a life of freedom and dignity to enslavement, colony, and postcolony), 'but Cortez | and Drake | Magellan | and that Ferdinand | the sailor | who pierced the salt seas to this land' (16).

The multitude named by Brathwaite includes many migrant selves, including the dejected ancestral figure of 'timid Tom | father | founder | flounderer' (15), and his modern American descendants, 'dark, tired, | deaf, cold, too old to care to catch | alight the quick match of your pity' (22). The American New Deal gave them little: 'This | the new deal for we black | grinning jacks?' (36). Recognition of their fate becomes the necessary starting point for the poet's collective journey. The multitude also includes all the contemporary migrants who rush to Britain 'with their cardboard grips, | felt hats, rain- | cloaks, the women | with their plain | or purple-tinted | coats hiding their fatten- | ing hips' (51). They and their progeny huddle miserably in their new places of disenchantment: 'we sweat | in this tin trunk'd house || that we rent from the rat | to share with the mouse: || Castries' Conway and Brixton in London, | Port of Spain's jungle || and Kingston's dry Dungle | Chicago Smethwick and Tiger Bay' (40).

The poet's symbolic journey offers an alternative to these false solutions. It has the purpose of ending the sense of unfulfilment that drives the descendants of slaves to their rootlessness: 'how long | O Lord | O devil | O fire | O flame | have we walked | have we journeyed | to this place . . . to this meeting | . . . in the soiled silence' (9–10). Their one question repeats: 'When release | from further journey?' (21). The release sought by the poet is accomplished by bringing the dispossessed back to where they started from, but transformed, capable of a new relation to the Caribbean. The region in geography and history will then have been transformed into the home it has failed to become for over three hundred years: 'Golden Guiana; | Potaro | leaping in light liquid amber | in Makonaima's perpetual falls' (36).

The second part of the trilogy, *Masks* (1967), is set in Africa. The poet explains: 'Exiled from here || to seas | of bitter edges, || whips of white worlds, | stains of new || rivers, | I have returned || to you' (153). Brathwaite's professional training as historian and scholar come to the forefront in placing the Atlantic slave trade in the context of the societies and cultures of the African Gold Coast, chiefly of Akan (i.e. ancient Ghanaian) origin, but including a wider range of geographical and cultural variety in its search for ancestors. Brathwaite's basic poetic strategy is to recreate aspects of African history before the slave trade as journeys.

These fictive journeys include migratory displacements as well as the movement of traders along routes that opened up cultures and economies to many kinds of exchange in the distant past that preceded and prepared for the slave trade. The allegory of the journey presents movement as an intrinsic part of the black psyche: history as the function of a migratory essence. The poet serves as the 'griot' for his pan-African community. He is the self-appointed oral story-teller, who preserves historical narrative and communal memory of the exchanges between societies, and the ceaseless search of African peoples for a home in which they can abide at ease with themselves.

The ancestors whom this poet imagines as the presiding spirits of all subsequent African diasporas travel from ancient Egypt, skirting the desert eastwards towards the regions on the West coast between the Niger and Congo rivers. Their restless movement enables the poet to embed the contemporary Caribbean and American manifestations of the search for a home within the imagined narratives of a much older and larger notion of displacement:

> Can you expect us to establish houses here?
> To build a nation here?
>
> (108)

Robert Fraser describes the structure of *Masks* as a 'two-way movement', in which 'the poet moves upwards from the coast in search of the village of his symbolic origin', while 'his own ancestors move downwards through the forest to meet him, their paths crossing at several imagined points of intersection' (1981: 10). The logic of these imagined encounters reaches for recuperation: 'the way lost | is a way to be found || again' (119). The retrievals accomplished in this part of the trilogy are evocations of the African terrain in all the poignancy of historical associations. That is a part of their ancestral history never available even for real forgetting by Caribbean people of African descent. Also lost—though recoverable distantly in poetry—are the tribal rituals that bind people together into communities. The ancestors eventually reached the coast. Starting from the coast inwards, the poet encounters his African contemporaries as distant cousins, who greet him thus:

> you who have come
> back a stranger
> after three hundred years
>
> welcome
> here is a stool for
> you; sit; do
> you remember?
>
> (124)

The poet-griot is overcome by profound anxiety: 'whose ancestor am I?' (125); 'Whose | brother, now, am I?' (126). The African coast becomes a zone of encounter between two timeframes. It is here that the Caribbean islander enters the ancestral mainland. It is also here that his ancestors sold others, or themselves, into slavery, for 'greed, love of || profit' (129). The griot laments, 'I hear || the whips of the slavers, | see the tears | of my daughters' (132–3). Meanwhile, the poet journeys inwards. He recollects the Asantehene kingdom of the past in the heyday of its glory. For Brathwaite, the heart of the problem is located here:

> My people, that is the condition of our country today:
> it is sick at heart, to its bitter clay.
> We cannot heal it or hold it together from curses,
> because we do not believe in it.
>
> (143)

Beyond that, the past has no answers for the poet. Was it pride that led Africans to slavery? Or greed? 'The years remain | silent' (150).

Robert Fraser interprets the poem to imply that the ancestral power and security of the African peoples of the West coast was destroyed by their 'lack of social cohesion' and 'the rival loyalties of warring sub-groups' (1981: 20). This, as Fraser notes, comes close to becoming an anticlimax from which *Masks* is hard put to recover, though the volume ends on a note of resolution that the poet will 'rise | and stand on my feet' (156).

The final part of the trilogy, *Islands*, brings the poet back to the New World. His consciousness has been altered by the preceding imaginative engagement with Africa. The New World inhabitants occupy the land, but they have 'lost the memory of the most secret places'; here, 'The gods have been forgotten or hidden', and 'The sun that was once a doom of gold to the Arawaks | is now a flat boom of the sky' (164). The poet invokes the gods of Africa in a new world that has forgotten to honour them. Ananse, the trickster god of West African mythology, 'squats on the tips || of our language' (165), 'world-maker, word-breaker' (167). The poet catalogues all the distortions of human impulse and desire that have ensued once the trade winds had brought slave labour to these lands: 'buying | a new world of negroes, soil- | ing the stars' (172). The world of nature awaits its proper tongue; the human world is reduced to 'shackles' (178). Mother and child are separated by the slaver: 'You gave your | beads, you || took my children' (182). The chance for a harmonious existence in balance with nature is lost for generations to come: 'how will new maps be drafted?' (184).

The poet hopes that the old gods 'can walk up out of the sea | into our houses' (190). However, history so far has not fulfilled that hope. Instead, it has given the Caribbean a series of 'bangs' (192): revolutions of the kind that brought Castro into the political limelight in 1956; the abolition of slavery, which brought indentured labour to the region in 1838; and before that, the Europeans, whose arrival in 1492 brought swift extinction to the Caribs and the Arawaks. The harsh reality of an existence in which the European Prospero reduced the transplanted African to Caliban cannot be exorcized easily. Brathwaite invokes the image of an island as a pebble to reiterate the idea that for the Caribbean to change and grow, the rock must be broken to create soil. Cricket is invoked as emblematic of the Caribbean psyche: 'when things goin' good, you cahn [can't] catch | we; but leg murder start an' you cahn fine a man to hole [hold] up de side' (201).

But the poet is determined to will a new beginning for the Caribbean, one in which he accepts that his African ancestors are 'never-returning', and his land is 'unbearably dry', waiting (like the dusty plains of North India in Eliot's *The Waste Land*) for rain (209). The post-independence period brings its own evils in the worship of Mammon: 'flowing fields of tourists for our daily bread' (214), and 'what we have to offer in the way of... baby watch me jive' (215). The 'old empire's promenades of cannon' (216) make room for hotel development.

That brings the poet abruptly to his answer. Brathwaite's solution is similar to that proposed by Walcott, although they take very different routes to this destination. The power of language to name the world anew, aided by the power of vision to see that world afresh: 'The tree must be named || The moon must be named' (217). The desert winds of Africa rise high and, on clear days, reach across the Atlantic to the Caribbean like a Christmas gift. Ogun (the Yoruba god of craftsmanship) and Damballa (god of the highway) are invoked. One of the final sections of *Islands*, 'Negus', offers a powerful exhortation and admonition, built on the incremental power of repetition as the phrase 'It is not enough' is reiterated:

> It is not
> it is not
> it is not enough
> to be pause, to be hole,
> to be void, to be silent
> to be semicolon, to be semicolony...
>
> (224)

For the first decade of Caribbean nationhood, the trilogy represents a sustained act of faith in the reciprocity between a people and a place that might make a home out of exile. Any account of Brathwaite's trilogy would be misleading if it did not register the fact that the reading experience offered by the poet is bewildering in its time shifts, interruptive in its line breaks, jagged and multi-vocal in its rhythms. That is precisely part of its originality. *The Arrivants* has little to say of women (a theme Brathwaite addressed in later volumes), or of those who came to the region from places other than Africa. The trilogy also represents one of the most sustained challenges from a former British colony to the conventions of metred and stanzaic verse, to the ideals of smoothness of style and rhythmic flow, to the values attached to coherence of monologue and authorial voice. Many poets before and after Brathwaite have essayed into free verse. Few have done so with as much awareness of what was at stake, and why, as Brathwaite.

9.2 Postcolonial exile: Ee Tiang Hong

Ithaka gave you the marvelous journey.
Without her you wouldn't have set out.
She has nothing left to give you now.

C. P. Cavafy, 'Ithaka'

Poetry written by those in exile or self-exile is characterized by nostalgia, regret, bitterness, longing, and the struggle to convert the notion of the journey into the appreciation—enjoined in Cavafy's 'Ithaka', or Auden's 'Atlantis'—of how life might be lived as a voyage, without proposing destinations as fictions for the appeasement of desire or the cessation of travel. Postcoloniality created situations that forced such recognitions on many poets, among them Ee Tiang Hong (1933–90), who was born in Malaysia, and died in Australia. Ee's case illustrates how the politicization of ethnicity often works in postcolonial societies.

Nationalist fervour aggravated by ethnic tensions led to race riots in the Malaya peninsula during 1969. Ee's sense of rootedness received a shock from which he never recovered fully, as shown by a poem written in self-exile, 'Comment':

we couldn't refuse—a way out
of the mess, out of the land
of big-time prophets and midwives
who didn't deliver.

(1994: 13)

There was no direct compulsion to leave Malaysia. 'His family had been one of the most celebrated of *Baba* families in the whole history of Malacca', notes Kirpal Singh, 'Why then, did Ee have to leave?' (1988: 227). Ee's answer:

I decided to leave Malaysia for good—but only after I was convinced that those involved in manipulating the organs of the state were bent on putting down any non-Malay who wrote in English. English was not the real target since it was obvious that for Malays, competence in English was and still is a mark of distinction.

(1988: 36)

For Ee, self-exile was based on a point of principle: 'I left Malaysia then when I could no longer accept, intellectually or emotionally, the official Malay definition of the Malayan nation and culture' (1988: 36). In 1975, he left Malaysia for Perth, and became an Australian citizen in 1977. During fifteen years of self-exile, he consolidated a new career, developed new friendships, but also brooded on three aspects of his displacement: from a place that he had regarded as his home, from a nation that he had felt was his country, and from a people he had identified with as his community.

Ee described his plight as of someone dragged 'down under' through a series of alliterative negatives: *disconcerted* and *dispossessed*, he had the choice only of *disengaging* from the *demeaning* (1985: 26). A poem, 'For Wong Lin Ken', returns to the obsessive desire to 'restate in summary' his 'dismay, disgust over the actions of a few' (1994: 3). Memories of 'Kuala Lumpur, May 1969' remained sharp:

soldiers in leopard-spot uniform, barbed barricade,
ministerial explanations of the causes of the riots,
reasons for the curfew.
[...]
As now more and more distant
bitterness, recrimination day by day subside,
ashes on flower, leaf and shoot
in the sparse valley of a memory.

(1985: 29)

From self-exile, Ee criticized the idea of nation enforced by the state in postcolonial Malaysia for its politicization of identity and its exclusionary definition of race. He argued, instead, for an idea of nation based on the recognition that races, religions, cultures, and languages interact as part of shared histories. He believed that attachments developed naturally over time towards places and peoples, fostered a sense of community that did not have to be racially homogenous or mono-cultural in order to expect mutual respect (cf. Patke 2003).

Ee belonged to the seventh generation of a family for whom Malacca (on the west coast of the Malay peninsula) was home. In

1988, he described his community, the 'Baba Malays', as drawing their sense of identity from two ethnic cultures, each vital without being exorbitant:

> My mother tongue . . . is Malay, or *Peranakan*, the Baba or a bazaar variant of the Malay language . . . I take the Chinese side of myself for granted . . . In my own case, as with most Babas, the Chinese cultural strand persisted in many forms . . . History, mythology and fiction were rendered in Baba Malay.
>
> (1988: 26–7)

Ee identified British colonial education as the crucial factor that shaped sensibilities for his generation: 'Mine was the last generation to have been educated entirely in English' (1988: 25). The British model of education involved minimal religious interference, but it introduced local youth from specific communities to English literature. The educational policy had obvious connections with Macaulay's recommendations in British India, though interest in creative writing developed more slowly in British Malaya than in India.

Ee explained that 'The school system was divided according to the language medium of instruction, namely English, Malay, Chinese and Tamil, to cater to the different racial groups' (13–14). Colonial administration was intent on keeping communities divided along ethnic lines. This policy ensured that the Malay leadership would remain ambivalent towards English before and after independence. The language was resented for having been bestowed by the British more freely on the Chinese and the Baba Malay. After independence, it was given grudging endorsement as the language of science, technology, modernity, and globalization. It could not be abandoned, but the local population was discouraged from using it for creative purposes. From 1967, Malay became the official language, and the indigenous Malay were named the *bhumiputra* (sons of the soil). The value placed on ethnic identity by the Malaysian state fell back on an assortment of familiar myths which can be enumerated in general terms:

> A myth of temporal origins: when we were begotten
> A myth of location and migration: where we came from and how we got there
> A myth of ancestry: who begot us and how we developed
> A myth of the heroic age: how we were freed and became glorious
> A myth of decline: how we fell into a state of decay
> A myth of regeneration: how we restore the golden age
>
> (Armstrong 1976: 399–404)

Postcolonial Malaysia made national identity synonymous with an alliance between ethnicity and Islam, thus reducing all non-Malay races to the level of second-class citizens, even when they belonged, like Ee, to ethnic minorities with long histories of partial assimilation into Malay culture. In 1969, the Malaysian writer Lloyd Fernando noted that before independence, 'conditions were never consciously created for encouraging a regard for the Malay language beyond the vulgarly utilitarian', and yet, 'It is one of the comic ironies of Malaysia that the English language is now being relegated to fulfilling the utilitarian role formerly endured by the Malay language' (1986: 86–7).

State ambivalence about English ensured that writers and readers were turned away from taking it seriously for literary purposes. The poet Wong Phui Nam noted, 'as a language for serious reading, English can account for no more than two or three per cent of the population' (Daizal 2001: 243). In an eloquent essay, 'Out of this Stony Rubbish' (1984), he confessed to a sense of acute alienation. He was distanced from the Chinese tradition for being a descendant of migrants; from the Malay tradition, for being Chinese; from the urban culture of the new nation, for wanting a spiritual freedom denied by the State; and from the English language, for traditions he could neither access without internal conflict, nor do without (1993: 133–44). Wong explains how cultural and ethnic diversity were compromised by linguistic nationalism:

> There appears to be a consensus that Malaysia is a multiethnic, multicultural, and multilingual society. Yet beneath this surface consensus, there are the voices of those intellectuals who present the inconsistent argument that since the Japanese speak Japanese, and the Germans German, then Malaysians should speak Malaysian, Bahasa Malaysia . . . These intellectuals would wish away writers in English . . .
>
> (Daizal 2001: 252)

Wong chose exile within Malaysia; Ee chose exile outside Malaysia. The poets who accepted internal self-exile include Ghulam-Sarwar Yousof, Cecil Rajendra, and Lee Geok Lan. Those who found it more practical to migrate include Shirley Lim and Chin Woon Ping. Each married in, and made a career for herself in the USA, becoming part of a growing body of Asian-American writers who continue to draw sustenance from the culture of their birthplace, but live away from the mother country.

Lim gives an account of her background: 'My story as a writer is also that of a colonized education in which the essential processes of identity formation are ironically the very processes stripping the individual of Asian tradition and communal affiliation' (1994b: 25). For writers like Lim, diaspora represents opportunity, not merely dispossession. They found that colonialism was reinforced in the lands of their birth by an even more deeply entrenched patriarchy. The opportunity to write in English, for an audience outside the Asian nation, gave them access to a very different myth of community. In Lim's 'American Driving', the constraining ghost who haunts, and must be resisted, appears as the mother:

> My mother's hand is reaching
>
> From fat autumn clouds. 'Where
> Are you going? Who are you?'
> She moans through windowed glare.
> But I drive on, going too
>
> Fast. If I don't make an error
> Or turn to a dead-end narrow
> Road, I drive forever.
> Or, at least, until tomorrow.
>
> (1994a: 66–7)

For such women writers, the diasporic condition sponsors a counter-myth, in which the country is always intact as a region of the heart and mind secure from the depredations of the nation-state.

Ee's poetry does not show the kind of resilience found in Lim's work. His poems continue to bear witness to the cost paid by the individual for the nationalism of a postcolonial State that abandons faith in the viability of societies with a multi-lingual and multi-racial culture. His fate also suggests that *where* one goes as a diasporic person is less significant than *how* one looks back on what one leaves behind. Regardless of whether and how such poets survive, their plight underlines the long-term consequences of a colonial legacy that continues to shape and distort the life of communities and individuals.

9.3 Postcolonial translation: A. K. Ramanujan and Agha Shahid Ali

> I have crossed an ocean
> I have lost my tongue
> from the root of the old one
> a new one has sprung
>
> Grace Nichols, 'Epilogue'

Exile and self-exile are largely involuntary; postcolonial migration often blurs the distinction between choice and necessity. The postcolonial migrant moves to a new place without shedding the trauma of having left a 'home' to which return is possible only in dreams, memory, and writing. For the migrant poet, displacement and relocation acquire the literal and figurative dimensions of translation. The poet invokes, elegizes, or commemorates the places and languages left behind from the perspective of the place and language to which migration has occurred, as part of the manifold consequence of linguistic colonialism and postcolonial mobility.

I propose to illustrate the homology between translation and migration from the work of two poets who left the Indian subcontinent for a life in the USA: A. K. Ramanujan (1929–93), and Agha Shahid Ali (1947–2001). Ramanujan moved to the USA in the early 1960s, teaching Dravidian languages at the University of Chicago until his death. He published two collections of poems in Kannada, nine volumes of translations, and four collections of poems in English, from *The Striders* (1966) to the posthumous *Collected Poems* (1995).

The relationship of Ramanujan's poems in English to his translations is antithetical, like the relation between a photographic image and its negative. The activity of translation seeks to recover from an invoked and imagined past a plenitude that is lacking in the poet's own life and times. Ramanujan translated into English from three South Indian languages (Kannada, Tamil, and Telugu, and a smaller quantity from a fourth South Indian language, Malayalam). In his own poems, a wry and sardonic tone prevails; in the translations, sacred and profane materials are addressed in tones of simple but hieratic solemnity.

Ramanujan's poetic world is the narrative of a three-part journey (cf. Patke 2001). In the first instance, the world to which the poet migrates is represented as depletion. The self feels isolated, without a sense of connectedness to a community. The second stage of this journey turns to a world compounded of memory, fiction, and desire, in order to recollect or invent a realm of possibility in which the self and all its modes of thought, feeling, and action are connected to a communal way of life. The final stage of the figurative journey entails using language to bring the remembered and imagined past to bear on the present through the activity of translation. Translation helps the individual cope with diaspora, while diaspora enables a collective past to survive and adapt through the individual.

Each stage of this figurative journey can be illustrated from Ramanujan's work. Migration represents loss in several ways. His English poems confess to distress at solitariness, as in 'The Difference': 'I, a community of one' (1995: 172). The world left behind haunts memory in forms of guilt and emptiness, whose colours can be evoked from one of the Tamil translations collected in *The Interior Landscape* (1975), 'What Her Girl-Friend Said to Him':

> ... the wasteland
> you have to pass through
> is absence itself...
> do you think that home will be sweet
> for the ones you leave behind?
>
> (1975: 56)

Ramanujan's English poems speak of the difficulty of sustaining a sense of relatedness to other people. 'Images' sums up routine days as little more than 'walking, a sleet | of faceless acquaintances' (1995: 44). 'Love Poem for a Wife and Her Trees' confesses to a sense of estrangement even within the reduced family unit, and even his wife can be reproached because, 'you never let me forget... you're not Mother' (1995: 180–1). 'Alien' expresses a sense of total alienation from the diasporic condition, 'a paper world in search of identity cards' (1995: 149).

The world to which he has migrated appears meaningful only when related to the world migrated from, in nostalgic double-focus, as in 'Extended Family', where 'the naked Chicago bulb' is described whimsically as 'a cousin of the Vedic sun' (1995: 169). In the early poem 'Breaded Fish', perception is obscured by the intrusions of memory, 'a hood | Of memory like a coil on a heath' (1995: 7). The poet complains frequently that he is trapped in the past, and bound to the biological determinism of a specific family and set of parents. 'A Lapse of Memory' finds him struggling with a paradoxical hunt for 'an amnesiac || use of memory', since there is no respite from 'his concave eye groping only | for mothers and absences' (1995: 76). 'Connect!' acknowledges the hold of the parent on the progeny, ambivalently, as a relation that binds: 'father whispers in my ear, black holes | and white noise' (1995: 178). In 'Questions', the maternal is treated as a link that cannot be severed from birth to death: 'my head's soft crown bathed in mother's blood, | wearing tatters of attachment' (1995: 131).

Migration from India to the West corresponds to translation from the classical and medieval Indian languages into modern English, or from classical to modern (or from pre- to post-colonial) eras. In this predicament, the world of classical and medieval South Indian poetry offers an antidote. 'Entries for a Catalogue of Fears' offers a self-portrait of 'a peeping-tom ghost | looking for all sorts of proof | for the presence of the past' (1995: 89). 'Waterfalls in a Bank' admits that

> I transact with the past as with another
> country with its own customs, currency,
> stock exchanges, always
>
> at a loss when I count my change...
>
> (1995: 189)

In the world of the past, selfhood thrives in the midst of relatedness, the individual in the midst of the communal.

Speaking of Shiva (1972) emphasizes a reverse relationship: 'Alienation from the immediate environment can mean continuity with an older ideal' (33). The translated world is a realm in which the personal is rooted in the communal and the historical. In it, experience is inner (*akam*) rather than outer (*puram*). It centralizes love as the core of experience, inventing for its varied embodiment a set of characters, situations, and environments. This world is evoked through a set of linguistic conventions, which provide a schematism corresponding to and transforming the world of actual persons, events, and feelings. The Afterword to *The Interior Landscape* (1975) summarizes the symbolic function of the cast of human characters: 'The dramatis personae are limited by convention to a small number, the hero, the heroine, the hero's friend(s) or messengers, the heroine's friend and foster-mother, the concubine, and passer-by' (112). The schematic world of classical Indian poetry, which Ramanujan translates into English, evokes a complex system of correspondences between landscape and mindscape. It unites diversity by expressing the unity of its human parts; it affirms consonance between the world of nature and the world of human thoughts and feelings. The Afterword to *Poems of Love and War* (1985) makes the relationship between inner and outer weather (as Robert Frost puts it) explicit:

> In the Tamil system of correspondences, a whole language of signs is created by relating the landscapes as signifiers to the *uri* or appropriate human feelings... This progression (from the basic cosmic elements to the specific component of a landscape) is also the method of the entire intellectual framework behind the poetry.
>
> (241)

The world invoked by translation adds two elements missing from the world the poet has migrated to: it balances solitariness within community; it contextualizes the profane through the sacred. The poetic traditions of the past merge opposites. They embody a principle of ancient coherence that is difficult to sustain in the life of contemporary individuation. In the world evoked by translation, oneness between two lovers, or between God and devotee, is the only true way of being. The traditions of devotional poetry absorb selfhood into Godhead, and offer relief from the solitariness of the individual self.

The Afterword to *Hymns for the Drowning* (1981) describes the central concept of devotional poetry—*bhakti*—as 'not ecstasy, not enstasy, but an embodiment; neither a shamanic flight to the heavens or soul loss, nor a yogic autonomy, a withdrawal of the senses—but a partaking of the god' (115–16). In the secular traditions that deal with love and the inner world, poetry practices the freedom of impersonality. Feelings can be dramatized without being personalized confessionally. This impersonality offers a paradoxical combination of accessibility and otherness, and becomes an emblem for the homology between devotion, migration, and translation. The devotee's relation to the deity is a version of the translator's relation to the original, or the migrant's sense of separation in relation to his ideal of being-in-oneness.

If we consider the two worlds of Ramanujan's poetry in stereoscopic vision, to have migrated is a tragic predicament insofar as it produces separation, isolation, and guilt. To that degree, the need for translation, like the need for migration, reveals lack or need. However, the activity of translation, undertaken as the re-accessing of a legacy, goes some way towards revalorizing the experience of migration. Desire for connectedness, and absence of connection: these are the two facets of Ramanujan's poetic world. The first is celebrated in his translations, the second is mourned in his English poems. The task identified by his translations is that of ameliorating the feeling that life is being lived as if it were a text without contexts. The poet translates diaspora by perpetuating a legacy. Translated, the migrant as poet learns to re-present himself as more, and other, than the restoration of a lost original.

A different aspect of the homology between postcolonial migration and translation is illustrated by the work of Agha Shahid Ali. Born in Kashmir, he began publishing in 1972, leaving for the USA in 1976, where he published several books of poetry, from *The Half-Inch Himalayas* (1987) to the posthumous *Call me Ishmael Tonight: A Book of Ghazals* (2003), and translated the Urdu ghazals of the Pakistani poet Faiz Ahmed Faiz (1911–84) in *The Rebel's Silhouette* (1991).

Ali made himself into a poet laureate of loss (cf. Patke 2000b). The poems from his first two volumes are replete with rituals of mourning, burial, and cremation. A later poem personifies this tendency as a 'Desperado || in search of catastrophe' (1991: 30). In the title poem from *The Half-Inch Himalayas* (1987), the Kashmir valley of his childhood is imaged, from a distance, through a picture postcard, 'this is the closest | I'll ever be to home' (1987: 1):

> And my memory will be a little
> out of focus, in it
> a giant negative, black
> and white, still undeveloped.
>
> (1987: 1)

From the perspective of the migrant, places and persons from a vanished past are recollected as diminution, objects seen sharply, but seen from the reverse end of a telescope. 'Snowmen' describes them as metonymies, 'heirlooms from sea funerals' (1987: 8). The poet's appetite for an irrecoverable past stretches backwards to the courtly days when Urdu poetry and music experienced a Golden Age. For Ali this age shows an accord between desire and fulfillment for which there is no equivalent in the present. Historical figures like the vocalist Begum Akhtar, the poet-emperor Zafar, and the poet Faiz Ahmed Faiz become archetypes of romantic ardour. The present becomes the mere occasion for evoking nostalgia for their achievements. 'The Dacca Gauzes' celebrated for their sheer transparency in his grandmother's youth now become the morning air pulled absently by his mother through a ring (1987: 15–16). 'A Call' is poignant with the sharpness of a paradox. Images of a home that is impossibly distant keep breaking in upon consciousness repeatedly, and unavailingly, as memory:

> I close my eyes. It doesn't leave me,
> the cold moon of Kashmir which breaks
> into my house
>
> (1987: 54)

The poems from *A Walk Through The Yellow Pages* (1987) image dereliction as the obsessive phone messages of someone desperately alone, ears abuzz with dead or distant voices, unable to reach through to the other side. Telephony is the medium that fails, providing no more than the static of its resistance to the tokens of presence that would be a voice at the other end, abridging silence.

> I prayed, 'Angel of Love,
> Please pick up the phone.'
>
> But it was the Angel of Death.
> [...]
> He answered, 'God is busy.
> He never answers the living.
> He has no answers for the dead.
> Don't ever call again collect.'
>
> (V)

Walter Benjamin invoked the fable of the Tower of Babel in 'The Task of the Translator' (1921/1923), an essay prefacing his translation of Baudelaire into German. Discussing this fable, Jacques Derrida asks:

> Can we not, then, speak of God's jealousy? . . . he scatters the genealogical filiation. He breaks the lineage. He *at the same time* imposes and forbids

translation ... Translation becomes law, duty, and debt, but the debt one can no longer discharge.

(1985: 170, 174)

Derrida reminds us that Benjamin's notion of the translator's task corresponds to 'duty, mission, task, problem, that which is assigned, given to be done, given to render' (1985: 176). The obligations enumerated by Derrida from Benjamin apply to Ali's sense of vocation. The unavailability of communion (with God) or connection (with parent, community, friend, home, or country) is like the impossibility of full translation. Reversed, it becomes a denial of univocity, and thus a sanction for plurality of speech as dialects, of poetry as translation, of exile as migration, and of guilt as restitution.

Ali's poetry is more eloquent about the cost in pain rather than the fulfilment of translation. The vocabulary of loss has many synonyms in *A Nostalgist's Map of America* (1991). It is always already too late to rescue the cities of the imaginary homeland. The poet lives in a world of ruins. Its narratives are forgotten histories. In 'Résumé', the poet is 'the secretary of memory' (87). 'In Search of Evanescence' depicts him as one of the few 'Survivors of Dispersal' (44), afraid that 'A language will die with him' (44), guilty of the 'erasure of names' (56). 'From Another Desert' discovers a natural affinity between the Muslim poet and the language of Islam, 'Arabic—the language of loss' (73). He can find no way back to his country, though another poem, 'Leaving Sonora' insists that he is 'faithful, | even to those who do not exist' (29). A later poem, 'I see Chile in my Rearview Mirror', expands the sense of being 'forsaken, alone with history' (97), and of being rendered into a 'shadow' (48) to include other alienated peoples, regions, and histories, that keep looking for recognition into the blankness of mirrors (96) and into what 'Notes on the Sea's Existence' images as blank reflections, images 'not mine' (89). The entire volume is an epiphany of being-in-loss. The one possibility that might translate this misery into hope is the restoration of the tragic to the heroic, as when the fabled love between the Punjabi pair of star-crossed lovers, *Majnoon* and *Laila*, is re-visioned by the poem 'From Another Desert' as the dedication of a 'committed revolutionary' for 'the revolutionary ideal' (65), whose union would bring back 'a god' 'to his broken temple' (66).

Faiz Ahmad Faiz was the modern master of the Urdu ghazal. In 1951, he suffered imprisonment on a charge of conspiracy against the military regime in Pakistan. Periodic imprisonment and exile under successive dictators inspired poems that have earned Faiz recognition as a poet comparable, in Ali's estimation, to 'Pablo Neruda, César Vallejo and Ernesto Cardenal in the Western hemisphere, Nazimet Hikmet and Yannis Ritsos in the Middle East' (1993: 66). Ali equates the despair of Faiz at what had happened to the Punjab because of the Partition of India and Pakistan with his own despair over Kashmir. The task of the translator acquires a special purpose in this dereliction. In 'Homage to Faiz Ahmed Faiz', the translator acknowledges that his hands 'turn to stone':

> In the free verse
> of another language I imprisoned
>
> each line—but I touched my own exile.
>
> (1987: 32)

Ali recognizes an affinity between Faiz and himself in respect to the shared sense that 'suffering is seldom, perhaps never, private' (1991: ii). One of the most sombrely moving poems by Faiz marks an air-raid blackout during the India–Pakistan conflict of 1965, 'Black Out'. The poet reacts in a stunned way to the ruins of the dream of nation. Likewise, Ali comes to the valley of Kashmir (as ruined by the notional entities calling themselves India and Pakistan) with a sense of historical belatedness. Faiz had long dreamt of an original unity, a fiction kept alive only in poetry, like a world of perpetual possibility. For Ali, the time of translation cannot hope to sustain this possibility, except in diminution. Thus Kashmir becomes a map or a postage stamp or a lost address from *The Country without a Post Office* (1997).

Ali's poems measure the difficulty of retrieval in translation. In a poem that alludes to a phrase from Emily Dickinson, ' "Some Visions of the World of Cashmere" ', the poet can still remember 'the face of a man who in dreams saves nations', but it is also the face of a man who in dreams 'razes cities' (1997: 36). The first of several poems titled 'Ghazal' and collected in *The Country without a Post Office* (1997) describes the poet as 'A refugee from belief' (40). According to Walter Benjamin, translations relate to an original by placing themselves as cognates not to the original, but to what 'is able to emerge as the pure language from the harmony of all the various ways of meaning' (Benjamin 1996: 257). In Ali's later volumes, as exemplified by 'After the August Wedding in Lahore, Pakistan', the metaphor of deterritorialization shifts its ground from Kashmir to Lahore and from Asia to Amherst: 'in each new body I would drown Kashmir' (1997: 91).

By drowning his Kashmir in the pool of many losses, the poet pluralizes loss. All specific losses metamorphose into a language of pure loss, 'thus making both the original and the translation recognizable as fragments of a greater language, just as fragments are part of a vessel' (Benjamin 1996: 260). Poetry fulfils in metaphor the task Benjamin assigned the translator: 'It is the task of the translator to release in his own language that pure language which is exiled among alien tongues, to liberate the language imprisoned in a work in his re-creation of that work' (1996: 261). Ali's poems liberate loss into the pool of languages, from Urdu to English, from Kashmir to Amherst. The sharing across languages and cultures does not diminish the loss, but it makes it participate in a wider mourning. That is the peculiar gift of Ali's diasporic writing: the translator recreating his losses in another tongue, in other places, among other peoples. If 'Translation promises a kingdom to the reconciliation of languages' (Derrida 1985: 200), the postcolonial migrant inherits this kingdom, and in his poetry the self is reconciled to loss, exile and migration to home, memory to pain, hope to despair: all translated into, and as, language.

10

After the 'post-'

Post-this, post-that, post-the-other, yet in the end
Not past a thing.

Seamus Heaney, 'On His Work in the English Tongue'

This book has been written under the premise that the currency of 'postcolonial' will meet with a natural datedness when societies shed postcolonial dependency and move closer to their dream of cultural autonomy. For the time being, 'postcolonial' retains contingent utility. It has been used in this book to refer to a dual recognition: as a shifting temporal marker, and as referring to a variety of situations that represent the literary, cultural, and socio-political consequences of colonialism. This dual sense constitutes a provisional field of literary production in which poetry can be analysed for how it shows the development of new creative possibilities and traditions from the demise of Empire.

Writing in European languages outside Europe provides the largest conceivable context within which to study the development of colonial-to-postcolonial writing. The Dutch left their legacy in the East Indies, the Portuguese in Brazil, the Spanish in the Americas and the Philippines, the French in parts of Africa, the Caribbean, and Canada. The linguistic and literary consequences of European colonialism shaped regional literatures. European languages provided the main element of continuity between the colonial past and a postcolonial future, underlining the recognition that 'language is the companion of the empire and a unifying factor of the nation' (Mignolo 2000: 12).

The role of language in British imperialism began with the spread of English as the primary language for literary writing in Wales, Scotland, and Ireland. It then extended to the settler regions of North America, South Africa, Australia, and New Zealand; and to the non-settler regions that came under colonial rule in the

Caribbean, in Asia, Africa, and Oceania. It also reverted to Britain, whose culture has been changed first by its colonial experience and then by migrations from the former colonies.

The course of settlement and colonial occupation differed from place to place, and time to time. Nevertheless, the control and influence exercised by Britain over other peoples and places, for long periods, was real and decisive. It polarized identities at the collective level. Each society affected by colonial experience acquired features unique to itself, and others that overlapped with the experience of other societies. Postcolonial literary traditions in English are linked by a number of shared features, chief among them, the challenge of putting various forms of English to local use, answering local needs. How that was done in a specific time and place helps delineate a composite picture pieced together from the distinctive features of individual poems, poets, and poetic traditions. The aim of understanding the shared as well as the unique aspects of such traditions has given this book a twofold objective.

Why the 'postcolonial' tag continues to stick to the other ex-colonial literatures, and how it might fall off, have provided the book with a third objective: to understand how poets have developed their command over language and literary conventions to the point where 'postcolonial' promises to become—or has become—redundant, either as historical reminder or as descriptive epithet. It can be predicated that there will come a time when 'postcolonial' will cease to function as a term of relevance, a time when a people will look to their colonial past as to a ground on which lives and literatures can be built, without feeling disadvantaged, disempowered, overshadowed, or constrained.

The Americans were the first to break free from British colonial status. Their history as a nation managed to avoid the appellation of 'postcolonial'. That avoidance has significant implications for other former colonies. Noah Webster proposed an American standard for language as early as 1789, and the *American Spelling Book* (1783) was selling a million copies a year by the 1850s (in a US population of about 23 million) (Crystal 1995: 80–3). These renovations were under way well before Walt Whitman's *Leaves of Grass* was published in 1855, eighty years after the American declaration of independence (and in the same year as Henry Wadsworth Longfellow's far more traditional *Hiawatha*).

The example suggests that the postcoloniality of any culture is a period of 'cross over'. However suspended or long drawn out this process might be, it is possible for peoples and cultures to conceive of a time when their crossing will be over, even if it leaves marks that remain indelible. The idea of 'postcolonial cultures' is thus contingent or provisional, like a name that is meant to become a misnomer, or a ladder that will be drawn up when the climbing is done.

REFERENCES

Acholonu, C. (1988) 'A Motif and a Theme in the Poetry of Christopher Okigbo', in E. D. Jones, E. Palmer, and M. Jones (eds.), *Oral and Written Poetry in African Literature Today* (London: James Currey; Trenton: Africa World Press), 103–11.

Adorno, T. W. (1992) 'Commitment', in R. Tiedemann (ed.), *Notes to Literature, Vol. 2* (New York: Columbia University Press).

Ahmad, A. (1992) *In Theory: Classes, Nations, Literatures* (London: Verso).

Ali, A. S. (1987a) *The Half-Inch Himalayas* (Middletown: Wesleyan University Press).

—— (1987b) *A Walk Through the Yellow Pages* (Tucson: SUN-Gemini Press).

—— (1991) *A Nostalgist's Map of America* (New York: Norton).

—— (1992) *Faiz Ahmed Faiz: The Rebel's Silhouette* [1991] (Delhi: Oxford University Press).

—— (1993) 'The True Subject: The Poetry of Faiz Ahmed Faiz', in K. Brown (ed.), *The True Subject: Writers on Life and Craft* (Saint Paul: Graywolf Press), 64–73.

—— (1997) *The Country without a Post Office: Poems 1991–1995* (New York: Norton).

Allen, L. (1993) *Women Do This Every Day: Selected Poems of Lillian Allen* (Toronto: Women's Press).

Alvarez-Pereyre, J. (1984) *The Poetry of Commitment in South Africa* [1979] (London: Heinemann).

Anderson, P. (1992) 'Marshall Berman: Modernity and Revolution', in *A Zone of Engagement* (London and New York: Verso), 25–55.

Angira, J. (1996) *Tides of Time: Selected Poems* (Nairobi: East African Educational Publishers).

Appiah, K. A. (1992) *In My Father's House: Africa in the Philosophy of Culture* (New York and Oxford: Oxford University Press).

Arasanayagam, J. (1991) *Reddened Water Flows Clear: Poems from Sri Lanka* (London and Boston: Forest Books).

—— (2003) *Fusillade* (New Delhi: Indialog Publications).

Armstrong, J. A. (1976) 'Mobilized and Proletarian Diasporas', *American Political Science Review* 70: 393–408.

Ashcroft, B., Griffiths, G. and Tiffin, H. (1998) *Key Concepts in Post-Colonial Studies* (London and New York: Routledge).

Attwell, D. (2004) 'South African Literature in English', in F. Abiola Irele and S. Gikandi (eds.), *The Cambridge History of African and Caribbean Literature* (Cambridge: Cambridge University Press), 2: 504–29.

Atwood, M. (1970) *The Journals of Susanna Moodie* (Toronto: Oxford University Press).

—— (1972) *Survival: A Thematic Guide to Canadian Literature* (Toronto: Anansi).

—— (ed.) (1982) *The New Oxford Book of Canadian Verse* (Toronto: Oxford University Press).

—— (2002) *Negotiating with the Dead: A Writer on Writing* (Cambridge: Cambridge University Press).

Awonoor, K. (1971) *Night of My Blood* (New York: Doubleday).

—— (1975) *The Breast of the Earth: A Survey of the History, Culture, and Literature of Africa South of the Sahara* (New York: Anchor Press).

Balderston, D., Gonzalez, M. and López, A. M. (eds.) (2000) *Encyclopedia of Contemporary Latin American and Caribbean Cultures* (London and New York: Routledge).

Bakhtin, M. (1968) *Rabelais and His World*, trans. H. Iswolsky (Cambridge, MA: The M.I.T. Press).

—— (1981) *The Dialogic Imagination*, trans. C. Emerson, ed. M. Holquist (Austin: University of Texas Press).

Barnes, J. (ed.) (1969) *The Writer in Australia* (Melbourne: Oxford University Press).

Barnett, U. (1983) *A Vision of Order: A Study of Black South African Literature in English (1914–1980)* (London: Sinclair Books; Amherst: University of Massachusetts Press).

Bell, A. (1991) 'The Politics of English in New Zealand', in G. McGregor and M. Williams (eds.), *Dirty Silence: Aspects of Language and Literature in New Zealand* (Auckland: Oxford University Press), 68–75.

Benítez-Rojo, A. (1992) *The Repeating Island: The Caribbean and the Postmodern Perspective* (Durham, NC: Duke University Press).

Benjamin, W. (1996) *Selected Writings, Vol. 1: 1913–1926*, ed. M. Bullock and M. W. Jennings (Cambridge, MA and London: The Belknap Press of Harvard University Press).

—— (2003) *Selected Writings, Vol. 4: 1938–1940*, ed. H. Eiland and M. W. Jennings, trans. E. Jephcott *et al.* (Cambridge, MA and London: The Belknap Press of Harvard University Press).

Benson, E. and Conolly, L. W. (eds.) (1994) *Encyclopedia of Post-Colonial Literatures in English*, 2 vols. (London and New York: Routledge).

Bentley, D. M. R. (2004) *The Confederation Group of Canadian Poets, 1880–1897* (Toronto: University of Toronto Press).

Bernstein, C. (1996) 'Poetics in the Americas', *Modernism/Modernity* 3/3: 1–23.

Bhabha, H. K. (1994) *The Location of Culture* (London and New York: Routledge).

—— (2000) 'Surviving Theory: A Conversation with Homi K. Bhabha', in F. Afzal Khan and K. Seshadri-Crooks (eds.), *The Pre-occupation of Post-colonial Studies* (Durham and London: Duke University Press), 369–79.

Bhatt, S. (1988) *Brunizem* (Manchester: Carcanet).

—— (1991) *Monkey Shadows* (Manchester: Carcanet).

—— (1995) *The Stinking Rose* (Manchester: Carcanet).

—— (2000a) *Augatora* (Manchester: Carcanet).

—— (2000b) *My Mother's Way of Wearing a Sari* (New Delhi: Penguin).

Boehmer, E. (1995) *Colonial and Postcolonial Literature: Migrant Metaphors* (Oxford and New York: Oxford University Press).

—— (2002) *Empire, the National, and the Postcolonial, 1890–1920: Resistance in Interaction* (Oxford and New York: Oxford University Press).

Boland, E. (2001) *Code* (Manchester: Carcanet Press).

Bolton, K. (ed.) (2002) *Hong Kong English: Autonomy and Creativity* (Hong Kong: Hong Kong University Press).

Bongie, C. (1998) *Islands and Exiles: The Creole Identities of Post/colonial Literature* (Stanford: Stanford University Press).

Bornholdt, J., O'Brien, G., and Williams, M. (eds.) (1997) *An Anthology of New Zealand Poetry* (Auckland: Oxford University Press).

Brathwaite, E. K. (1973) *The Arrivants: A New World Trilogy* (Oxford: Oxford University Press).

—— (1984) *History of the Voice* (London and Port of Spain: New Beacon Books).

Breeze, J. B. (1997) *On the Edge of an Island* (Newcastle upon Tyne: Bloodaxe Books).

—— (2000) *The Arrival of Brighteye and Other Poems* (Newcastle upon Tyne: Bloodaxe Books).

Breiner, Laurence A. (1998) *An Introduction to West Indian Poetry* (Cambridge: Cambridge University Press).

Breytenbach, B. (1978) *And Death White as Words: An Anthology of the Poetry of Breyten Breytenbach*, ed. A. J. Coetzee (London: Rex Collings; Cape Town: David Philip).

—— (1988) *Judas Eye and Self-Portrait/Deathwatch* (New York: Farrar Straus Giroux).

—— (2002) *Lady One: of Love and Other Poems* (New York: Harcourt, Inc.).

Brink A. and Coetzee, J. M. (eds.) (1986) *A Land Apart: A South African Reader* (London and Boston: Faber).
Brown, L. W. (1984) *West Indian Poetry* [1978] (London: Heinemann).
Brown, S. (ed.) (1984) *Caribbean Poetry Now* (London: Hodder & Stoughton).
—— (1999) *Elsewhere* (Leeds: Peepal Tree Press).
Brown, S. Morris, M., and Rohlehr, G. (eds.) (1989) *Voiceprint: An Anthology of Oral and Related Poetry from the Caribbean* (London: Longman).
Bunn, D. *et al.* (1989) *Writers from South Africa: Culture, Politics and Literary Theory and Activity in South Africa Today* (Evanstown: TriQuarterly Books).
Bunting, C. (2000) 'Behind Bars, Then Out in the Cold', *Times Higher Education Supplement* (December).
Bürger, P. (1984) *Theory of the Avant-Garde* [1974, 1980] (Minneapolis: University of Minnesota Press).
Burnett, P. (ed.) (1986) *The Penguin Book of Caribbean Verse in English* (Harmondsworth: Penguin).
Butler, G. (1994) *Essays and Lectures 1949–1991* (Cape Town and Johannesburg: David Philip).
Butler, G. and Mann, C. (eds.) (1979) *A New Book of South African Verse in English* (Cape Town: Oxford University Press).
Carter, D. (2000) 'Critics, Writers, Intellectuals: Australian Literature and Criticism', in E. Webby (ed.), *The Cambridge Companion to Australian Literature* (Cambridge: Cambridge University Press), 258–93.
Carter, M. (1999) *Poesís Escogidas/Selected Poems*, ed. D. Dabydeen (Leeds: Peepal Tree).
Césaire, A. (1983) *The Collected Poetry*, trans. C. Eshelman and A. Smith (Berkeley: University of California Press).
Chapman, M. (ed.) (1982) *Soweto Poetry* (Johannesburg: McGraw-Hill).
—— (1996) *Southern African Literatures* (London and New York: Longman).
Chatterjee, D. (2004) *Namaskar: New and Selected Poems* (Bradford: Redbeck Press).
Chaudhuri, A. (2004) 'History's Waiting Room', *London Review of Books*, 26/12 (24 June). Online edition: www.lrb.co.uk/v26/n12/print/chau01_.html. 7 November 2004.
—— (2005) 'On Strangeness in Indian Writing', *The Hindu* (October 2). Online edition. www.hindu.com/lr/2005/10/02/stories/2005100200130300.htm. 29 October 2005.
Cheney-Coker, S. (1973) *Concerto for an Exile: Poems* (London: Heinemann).
Chinweizu (1986) *Invocations and Admonitions* (Lagos: Pero Press).
Clark, J. P. (1981) *A Decade of Tongues: Selected Poems 1958–1968* (Harlow, Essex: Longman).

Cobham, R. (1990) 'Women in Jamaican Literature 1900–1950', in C. B. Davies and E. S. Fido (eds.), *Out of the Kumbla: Caribbean Women and Literature* (Trenton, NJ: Africa World Press), 195–222.

Coetzee, J. M. (1988) *White Writing: On the Culture of Letters in South Africa* (New Haven: Yale University Press).

Collins, M. (1985) *Because the Dawn Breaks! Poems Dedicated to the Grenadian People* (London: Karia Press).

—— (1992) 'Channels of Discovery: Perceptions of Culture and Sovereignty in the Caribbean', in R.W. Palmer (ed.), *U.S.–Caribbean Relations: Their Impact on Peoples and Cultures* (Westport: Praeger), 117–27.

Corngold, S. (2003) 'Kafka and the Dialect of Minor Literature', in C. Prendergast (ed.), *Debating World Literature* (London and New York: Verso), 272–90.

Corse, S. (1997) *Nationalism and Literature* (Cambridge: Cambridge University Press).

Couzens, T. (1984) 'Widening Horizons of African Literature, 1870–1900', in L. White and T. Couzens (eds.), *Literature and Society in South Africa* (London and New York: Longman), 60–80.

Crawford, I. V. (1972) *Collected Poems* (Toronto: University of Toronto Press).

Crawford, R. (1992) *Devolving English Literature* (Oxford: Clarendon Press).

Cronin, J. (1999) *Even the Dead: Poems, Parables, and a Jeremiad* (Cape Town and Johannesburg: David Philip).

Crystal, D. (1995) *The English Language* (Cambridge: Cambridge University Press).

Curnow, A. (1987) *Look Back Harder: Critical Writings 1935–1984*, ed. P. Simpson (Auckland: Auckland University Press).

Dabydeen, D. (1984) *Slave Song* (Mundelstrup, Denmark: Dangaroo Press).

—— (1988) *Coolie Odyssey* (Hertford: Hansib Publishing Ltd. and Dangaroo Press).

—— (1989) 'On Not Being Milton: Nigger Talk in England Today', in M. Butcher (ed.), *Tibisiri: Caribbean Writers and Critics* (London: Dangaroo Press), 121–35.

—— (1994) *Turner: New and Selected Poems* (London: Jonathan Cape; Leeds: Peepal Tree, 2002).

—— (2000) 'West Indian Writers in Britain', in F. Dennis and N. Khan (eds.), *Voices of the Crossing* (London: Serpent's Tail), 59–76.

Dabydeen, D. and Samaroo, B. (eds.) (1987) *India in the Caribbean* (London: Hansib Publishing Ltd).

D'Aguiar, F. (1993) *British Subjects* (Tarset, Northumberland: Bloodaxe Books).

—— (1999) Interview with Caryl Phillip. Roland Collection. www.educeth.ch/english/readinglist/daguiarf/author.html#by. 8 August 2004.

Daizal, R. S. (2001) 'A Heritage of Fragments: An Interview with Wong Phui Nam' [1998]. Rpt. in M. Quayum and P. Wicks (eds.), *Malaysian Literature in English: A Critical Reader* (Serangol Darul Ehsan: Longman Pearson Educational Ltd).

Daniel, S. (1950) *Poems and A defence of ryme*, ed. A. C. Sprague (London: Routledge Kegan Paul).

Daruwalla, K. (ed.) (1980) *Two Decades of Indian Poetry, 1960–1980* (New Delhi: Vikas).

—— (1982) *The Keeper of the Dead* (Delhi: Oxford University Press).

Das, K. (1986) *Kamala Das: A Selection, with Essays on Her Work*, ed. S. C. Harrex and V. O'Sullivan (Adelaide: CRNLE).

Daud, K. (1997) *Daud Kamal: A Selection of Verse* (Karachi: Oxford University Press).

Davis, J. (1992) *Black Life* (St Lucia: University of Queensland Press).

Deane, S. (ed.) (1991) *The Field Day Anthology of Irish Writing*, vol. 3 (Derry: Field Day Publications).

De Kock, L. and Tromp, I. (eds.) (1996) *The Heart in Exile: South African Poetry in English, 1990–1995* (London: Penguin).

De Kok, I. (1997a) *Transfer* (Plumstead, SA: Snailpress).

—— (1997b) 'Ingrid de Kok Interviewed by Susan Rich', *New Coin* online, 33/2 (December). www.rhodes.ac.za/institutes/isea/newcoin/docs/97/I97dec.htm. 10 June 2004. Rpt. in R. Berold (ed.), *South African Poets on Poetry: Interviews from 'New Coin' 1990–2001* (Scottsville: University of Natal Press, 2003), 111–17.

—— (2002) *Terrestrial Things* (Roggebaai and Plumstead, SA: Kwela/Snailpress).

Deleuze, G. and Guattari, F. (1986) *Kafka: Toward a Minor Literature* [1975], trans. D. Polan (Minneapolis: University of Minnesota Press).

Derrida, J. (1974) *Of Grammatology* [1967], trans. G. C. Spivak (Baltimore: The Johns Hopkins University Press).

—— (1985) 'Des Tours de Babel', in J. F. Graham (trans. and ed.), *Difference in Translation* (Ithaca and London: Cornell University Press), 165–207.

Dharker, I. (1989) *Purdah and Other Poems* (New Delhi: Oxford University Press).

—— (1994) *Postcards from God* (New Delhi: Viking).

—— (2001) *I Speak For the Devil* (New Delhi: Penguin).

Dharwadker, V. (1994) 'The Alphabet', in V. Dharwadker and A. K. Ramanujan (eds.), *The Oxford Anthology of Modern Indian Poetry* (Delhi: Oxford University Press), 116.

Dhomhnaill, N. N. (1990) *Pharaoh's Daughter* (Loughcrew: The Gallery Press).
—— (1997) 'Why I Choose to Write in Irish, the Corpse That Sits Up and Talks Back', in S. S. Sailer (ed.), *Representing Ireland: Gender, Class, Nationality* (Gainesville: University Press of Florida).
Donnell, A. and Welsh, S. L. (eds.) (1996) *The Routledge Reader in Caribbean Literature.* (London and New York: Routledge).
D'Souza, C. (1990) *A Spelling Guide to Woman* (Bombay: Orient Longman).
Dunn, D. (ed.) (1992) *The Faber Book of Twentieth-Century Scottish Poetry* (London and Boston: Faber).
Ee, T. H. (1976) *Myths of a Wilderness* (Kuala Lumpur: Heinemann Educational Books).
—— (1985) *Tranquerah* (Singapore: Department of English Language and Literature, National University of Singapore).
—— (1987) 'History as Myth in Malaysian Poetry in English', in K. Singh (ed.), *The Writer's Sense of the Past* (Singapore: Singapore University Press), 10–16.
—— (1988) 'Literature and Liberation: The Price of Freedom', in E. Thumboo (ed.), *Literature and Liberation: Five Essays from Southeast Asia* (Manila: Solidaridad Publishing House), 123–53.
—— (1994) *Nearing a Horizon* (Singapore: Unipress).
Elliott, B. (ed.) (1979) *Portable Australian Authors: The Jindyworobaks* (St Lucia: University of Queensland Press).
Eppel, J. (2001) *Selected Poems 1965–1995* (Bulawayo, Zimbabwe: Childline).
Ezekiel, N. (1989) *Collected Poems 1952–1988* (Delhi: Oxford University Press).
Evans, P. (1990) *The Penguin History of New Zealand Literature* (Auckland: Penguin).
Fanon, F. (1963) *The Wretched of the Earth* [1961], trans. C. Farrington (New York: Grove Press).
—— (1967). *Black Skin, White Masks* [1952], trans. C. L. Markmann (New York: Grove Press).
Fernando, L. (1986) *Cultures in Conflict* (Singapore: Graham Brash).
FitzGerald, R. (1987) *Portable Australian Authors: Robert D. FitzGerald*, ed. J. Croft (St Lucia: University of Queensland Press).
Figueroa, J. (ed.) (1982) *Caribbean Voices: Vol. 1, Dreams and Visions* (London: Evans Brothers Ltd).
Fraser, R. (1981) *Edward Brathwaite's 'Masks'* (London: The British Council).
Frye, N. (1971) *The Bush Garden: Essays on the Canadian Imagination* (Toronto: Anansi Press).
Fumagalli, M. C. (2001) *The Flight of the Vernacular: Seamus Heaney, Derek Walcott and the Impress of Dante* (Amsterdam and New York: Rodopi).
Ghose, Z. (1991) *Selected Poems* (Karachi: Oxford University Press).

Gikandi, S. (1992) *Writing in Limbo: Modernism and Caribbean Literature* (Ithaca and London: Cornell University Press).

Gilroy, P. (2004) *After Empire: Melancholia or Convivial Culture?* (Abingdon: Routledge).

Glaser, M. and Pausch, M. (eds.) (1994) *Caribbean Writers: Between Orality and Writing* (Amsterdam and Atlanta: Rodopi).

Glickman, S. (2000) *The Picturesque and the Sublime: A Poetics of the Canadian Landscape* (Montreal and Kingston: McGill-Queen's University Press).

Glissant, É. (1989) *Caribbean Discourse* [1981], trans. J. M. Dash (Charlottesville: University Press of Virginia).

—— (1996) *Poetics of Relation* [1990], trans. B. Wing (Ann Arbor: University of Michigan Press).

Goldie, T. (1989) *Fear and Temptation: The Image of the Indigene in Canadian, Australian, and New Zealand Literatures* (Kingston, Montreal, London: McGill-Queen's University Press).

Goodison, L. (1992) *Selected Poems* (Ann Arbor: University of Michigan Press).

—— (2005) *Controlling the Silver* (Urbana and Chicago: University of Illinois Press).

Goodwin, K. (1984) 'Poetry', in G. D. Killam (ed.), *The Writing of East and Central Africa* (London: Heinemann), 213–30.

Goonetilleke, D. C. R. A. (ed.) (1991) *The Penguin New Writing in Sri Lanka* (New Delhi: Penguin).

Gordimer, N. (1973) *The Black Interpreters* (Johannesburg: Ravan Press).

Gray, S. (1979) *South African Literature: An Introduction* (Cape Town: David Philip; London: Rex Collings).

Gray, S. (ed.) (1984) *A World of Their Own: Modern South African Poetry* (Johannesburg: Ad. Donker).

Griffiths, G. (2000) *African Literatures in English: East and West* (Harlow, Essex: Pearson Educational).

Gunew, S. (ed.) (1987) *Displacements 2; Multicultural Storytellers* (Geelong: Deakin University Press).

Habekost, C. (1993) *Verbal Riddim: The Politics and Aesthetics of African-Caribbean Dub Poetry* (Amsterdam and Atlanta: Rodopi).

Hampton, S. and Llewellyn, K. (eds.) (1986) *The Penguin Book of Australian Women Poets* (Ringwood: Penguin).

Harris, C. (2000) *She* (Fredericton, New Brunswick: Goose Lane Editions).

Hashmi, A. (1996) 'Pakistani Literature', in R. Mohanram and G. Rajan (eds.), *English Postcoloniality: Literatures from Around the World* (Westport and London: Greenwood Press), 107–17.

—— (1997) *A Choice of Hashmi's Verse* (Karachi: Oxford University Press).

Heaney, S. (1983) *An Open Letter*, in *Ireland's Field Day* (Derry: Field Day Theatre Company).
—— (1990) *Selected Poems 1966–1987* (New York: Farrar, Straus & Giroux).
—— (2002) *Finders Keepers: Selected Prose 1971–2001* (London: Faber).
Heywood, C. (1976) *Aspects of South African Literature* (New York: Africa Press).
Hill, G. (1994) *New and Collected Poems 1952–1992* (Boston and New York: Houghton Mifflin Company).
Hirson, D. (1996) 'Denis Hirson interviewed by Robert Berold', *New Coin* (May). www.rhodes.ac.za/institutes/isea/newcoin/docs/96/i96may.htm. 16 June 2004.
—— (ed.) (1997) *The Lava of the Land: South African Poetry 1960–1996* (Evanston, IL: TriQuarterly Books).
Ho, L. (1997) *New Ends, Old Beginnings* (Hong Kong: Asia 2000 Ltd).
Hodge, B. and Mishra, V. (1990) *Dark Side of the Dream: Australian Literature and the Postcolonial Mind* (Sydney: Allen & Unwin).
Hogan, P. C. (2000) *Colonialism and Cultural Identity* (Albany: State University of New York).
Hope, A. D. (1974) *Native Companions: Essays and Comments on Australian Literature 1936–1966* (Sydney: Angus & Robertson).
—— (1979) *The New Cratylus: Notes on the Craft of Poetry* (Melbourne: Oxford University Press).
Hope, C. (1985) *Englishmen: A Poem* (London: Heinemann).
Hopkinson, S. (1993) *Snowscape with Signature* (Leeds: Peepal Tree Press).
Horne, N. B. (2000) *Sunkwa: Clingings onto Life* (Trenton, NJ, and Asmara, Eritrea: Africa World Press, Inc.).
Hoskote, R. (ed.) (2002) *Reasons for Belonging: Fourteen Contemporary Indian Poets* (New Delhi: Viking).
Hulme, K. (1992) *Strands* (Auckland: Auckland University Press).
—— (2004) *Stonefish* (Wellington: Huia Publishers).
Iliffe, J. (1995) *Africans: The History of a Continent* (Cambridge: Cambridge University Press).
Innes. C. L. (1990) *The Devil's Own Mirror: The Irishman and the African in Modern Literature* (Washington, DC: Three Continents Press).
Iqbal, M. (1981) *'Shikwa' and 'Jawab-i-Shikwa'*, trans. K. Singh (Delhi: Oxford University Press).
Irele, F. A. (2001) *The African Imagination: Literature in Africa and the Black Diaspora* (New York: Oxford University Press).
Jackson, M. P. (1991) 'Poetry: Beginnings to 1945', in T. Sturm (ed.), *The Oxford History of New Zealand Literature* (Auckland: Oxford University Press), 335–84.

Jaggi, M. (2004) 'Fallen Idol', *Guardian* (24 April). http://books.guardian.co.uk/reviews/generalfiction/0,6121,1201833,00.html. 20 December 2004.

James, L. (1999) *Caribbean Literature in English* (London and New York: Longman).

Jenkins, J. (2003) *World Englishes: A Resource Book for Students* (London and New York: Routledge).

Johnson, A. (1985) *Long Road to Nowhere* (London: Virago Press).

—— (1992) *Gorgons* (Coventry: Cofa).

Johnson, L. K. (2002) *Mi Revalueshanary Fren: Selected Poems* (London: Penguin Books).

Kale, M. (1995) 'Projecting Identities: Empire and Indentured Labour Migration from India to Trinidad and British Guiana, 1836–1885', in P. Van der Veer (ed.), *Nation and Migration: The Politics of Space in the South Asian Diaspora* (Philadelphia: University of Pennsylvania Press), 73–92.

Kay, J. (1991) *The Adoption Papers* (Tarset: Bloodaxe Books).

—— (1998) *Off Colour* (Tarset: Bloodaxe Books).

—— (1998b) *Teeth: Selected Spoken Works* [sound recording] (London: 57 Productions).

Kay, J., Collins, M., and Nichols, G. (1996). *Penguin Modern Poets, Vol. 8: Jackie Kay, Merle Collins, Grace Nichols* (London: Penguin).

Kertzer, J. (1998) *Worrying the Nation: Imagining a National Literature in English Canada* (Toronto: University of Toronto Press).

King, B. (2001) *Modern Indian Poetry in English* [1987] (New York, New Delhi: Oxford University Press).

Kinsella, J. (1998) 'The Hybridising of a Poetry', *Westerly* 43/2: 64–7.

Kirkby, J. (ed.) (1982) *The American Model: Influence and Independence in Australian Poetry* (Sydney: Hale & Iremonger).

Klein, H. S. (1999) *The Atlantic Slave Trade* (Cambridge: Cambridge University Press).

Kolatkar, A. (1976) *Jejuri* (Bombay: Clearing House). [English]

—— (1977) *Arun Kolatkarchya Kavita* [Arun Kolatkar's Poems] (Mumbai: Pras Prakashan). [Marathi]

—— (1993) 'Nine Poems translated from the Marathi by the author', in D. Weissbort and A. K. Mehrotra (eds.), *Periplus: Poetry in Translation* (Delhi: Oxford University Press), 68–9.

—— (2004a) *Sarpa Satra* (Pune: Pras Publications). [English]

—— (2004b) *Kala Ghoda Poems* (Pune: Pras Publications). [English]

Lee, A. A., and Denham, R. D. (eds.) (1994) *The Legacy of Northrop Frye* (Toronto: University of Toronto Press).

Lee, B. and Wong-Chu, J. (eds.) (1991) *Many-Mouthed Birds: Contemporary Writing by Chinese Canadians* (Vancouver and Toronto: Douglas & McIntyre; Seattle: University of Washington Press).

Lee, D. (1972) 'Running and Dwelling: Homage to Al Purdy', *Saturday Night* 87/7 (July).
—— (1973) 'Cadence, Country, Silence: Writing in a Colonial Space', *Open Letter Series* 2/6 (Fall).
—— (1986) 'The Poetry of Al Purdy: An Afterword', in *The Collected Poems of Al Purdy*, ed. R. Brown (Toronto: McClelland and Stewart).
Lee, T. P. (1997) *Lambada by Galilee and Other Poems* (Singapore: Times Books).
Leggott, M. (1995) 'Opening the Archive: Robin Hyde, Eileen Duggan and the Persistence of Record'. In *Opening the Book: New Essays on New Zealand Writing*, ed. M. Williams and M. Leggott (Auckland: Auckland University Press), 266–93.
Leung P.-K. (2002) *Travelling with a Bitter Melon: Selected Poems (1973–1998)*, ed. M. Leung (Hong Kong: Asia 2000 Limited).
Lewis, S. (2003) 'Review of Ingrid de Kok's *Terrestrial Things*', *H-Net Reviews* (February). www.h-net.org/reviews/showrev.cgi?path=175221048835719. 17 June 2004.
Lim, S. (1994a) *Monsoon History* (London: Skoob).
—— (1994b) *Writing S.E./Asia in English: Against the Grain, Focus on Asian English-language Literature* (London: Skoob).
Lindfors, B. (1984) 'The Songs of Okot p'Bitek', in G. D. Killam (ed.), *The Writing of East and Central Africa* (London: Heinemann), 144–58.
Lindfors, B. and Sander, R. (eds.) (1996) *Twentieth Century Caribbean and Black African Writers, Third Series*, Dictionary of Literary Biography, vol. 157 (Detroit: Gale Publications).
—— (1994) *The Living Stream: Literature and Revisionism in Ireland* (Newcastle upon Tyne: Bloodaxe Books).
Macaulay, T. B. (1952) *Macaulay: Prose and Poetry*, ed. G. M. Young (London: Rupert Hart-Davis).
MacDiarmid, H. (1987) *A Drunk Man Looks At The Thistle*, ed. K. Buthlay (Edinburgh: Scottish Academic Press).
McAuley, J. (ed.) (1975) *A Map of Australian Verse* (Melbourne: Oxford University Press).
—— (1988) *James McAuley*, ed. L. Kramer (St Lucia: University of Queensland Press).
McClintock, A. (1992) 'The Angel of Progress: Pitfalls of the Term "Post-Colonialism" ', *Social Text* 31/32: 84–98.
Mahapatra, J. (1992) *A Whiteness of Bone: Selected Poems* (New Delhi: Viking).
Maja-Pearce, A. (ed.) (1990) *The Heinemann Book of African Poetry in English* (Oxford: Heinemann).

Manhire, B. (1987) 'A View of American and New Zealand Poetry', *Islands* 38 (December): 142–54.

Manoo-Rahming, L. (2000) *Curry Flavour* (Leeds: Peepal Tree).

Mapanje, J. (2004) *The Last of the Sweet Bananas: New and Selected Poems* (Tarset: Bloodaxe Books).

Marechera, D. (1992) *Cemetery of Mind: Collected Poems*, ed. F. Veit-Wild (Harare: Baobab Books).

Markham, E. A. (ed.) (1995) *Hinterland: Caribbean Poetry from the West Indies and Britain* (Newcastle upon Tyne: Bloodaxe Books).

Marshall, P. J. (ed.) (1996) *The Cambridge Illustrated History of the British Empire* (Cambridge: Cambridge University Press).

Marx, K. and Engels, F. (2001) *Karl Marx and Frederick Engels on the National and Colonial Questions: Selected Writings*, ed. A. Ahmad (New Delhi: Left-Word).

Mehrotra, A. K. (1984) *Middle Earth* (Delhi: Oxford University Press).

—— (1992) *Twelve Modern Indian Poets* (Delhi: Oxford University Press).

—— (1998) *The Transfiguring Places* (Delhi: Ravi Dayal).

Mignolo, W. (2000) 'L. Elena Delgado and Rolando J. Romero, "Local Histories and Global Designs: An Interview with Walter Mignolo" ', *Discourse* 22/3: 7–33.

Mitchell, W. J. T. (2005) 'Empire and Objecthood', in *What do Pictures Want? The Lives and Loves of Images* (Chicago and London: University of Chicago Press), 145–68.

Moore, G. and Beier, U. (eds.) (1998) *The Penguin Book of Modern African Poetry* (London: Penguin).

Morgan, E. (2000) *ScotLit*, 23 (Winter).

Motsapi, S. (2003) *earthstepper/the ocean is very shallow* [1995] (Grahamstown: Deep South).

Mphahlele, E. (1972) *Voices in the Whirlwind and Other Essays* (New York: Hill & Wang).

Mphande, L. (1998) *Crackle at Midnight* (Ibadan: Heinemann).

Msiska, M.-H. (1995) 'Geopoetics: Subterraneanity and Subversion in Malawian Poetry', in A. Gurnah (ed.), *Essays on African Writing, 2: Contemporary Literature* (London: Heinemann), 73–99.

Mudimbe, V. Y. (1988) *The Invention of Africa: Gnosis, Philosophy, and the Order of Knowledge* (Bloomington and Indianapolis: Indiana University Press).

Mudrooroo, N. (1990) *Writing from the Fringe: A Study of Modern Aboriginal Literature* (Melbourne: Hyland House).

—— (1991) *The Garden of Gethsemane: Poems from the Lost Decade* (Melbourne: Hyland House).

Murray, L. (1997) *A Walking Forest: Selected Prose* (Potts Point, NSW: Duffy & Snellgrove).

Nair, R. B. (1999) *The Ayodhya Cantos* (New Delhi: Viking).

Nandan, S. (1997) *Lines Across Black Waters* (Adelaide: CRNLE/Academy Press).

Nandy, A. (1983) *The Intimate Enemy: Loss and Recovery of Self Under Colonialism* (Delhi: Oxford University Press).

Narain, D. D. (2002) *Contemporary Caribbean Women's Poetry* (London and New York: Routledge).

Nasta, S. (2004) ' "Voyaging in"; colonialism and migration', in L. Marcus and P. Nicholls (eds.), *The Cambridge History of Twentieth Century English Literature* (Cambridge: Cambridge University Press), 563–82.

Ndebele, N. S. (1994) *South African Literature and Culture: Rediscovery of the Ordinary* (Manchester and New York: Manchester University Press).

Nemade, B. (1985) 'Against Writing in English: An Indian Point of View', *New Quest* 49 (Pune, India): 31–6.

New, W. H. (1997) *Land Sliding: Imagining Space, Presence and Power in Canadian Writing* (Toronto: University of Toronto Press).

Ngugi wa Thiong'o (1986) *Decolonizing the Mind: The Politics of Language in African Literature* (London: Heinemann).

—— (2000) 'Europhonism, Universities, and the Magic Fountain: The Future of African Literature and Scholarship', *Research in African Literatures* 31/1 (Spring). http://iupjournals.org/ral/ral31-1.html#f1. 17 June 2004.

Nichols, G. (1983) *I is a Long Memoried Woman* (London: Karnak House).

—— (1984) *The Fat Black Woman's Poems* (London: Virago Press).

Nkosi, L. (1965) *Home and Exile* (London and New York: Longman).

Nyamubaya, F. (1998) *On the Road Again: Poems During and After the National Liberation of Zimbabwe*, 3rd edn [1986] (Harare: Zimbabwe Publishing House), n.p.

Obeyesekere, R. and Fernando, C. (eds.) (1981) *An Anthology of Modern Writing from Sri Lanka* (Tucson: University of Arizona Press).

Oculi, O. (2003) 'A narrative on "shame" ', *Social Research* 70/4 (Winter). http://articles.findarticles.com/p/articles/mi_m2267/is_4_70/ai_112943744/pg_1. 20 June 2004.

Ojaide, T. (1986) *Labyrinths of the Delta* (Greenfield Center, NY: The Greenfield Review Press).

—— (1994) *The Poetry of Wole Soyinka* (Lagos: Malthouse Press Ltd).

Ojaide, T. and Sallah, T. M. (ed.) (1999) *The New African Poets: An Anthology* (Boulder, CO, and London: Lynne Rienner).

Okara, G. (1978) *The Fisherman's Invocation* (London: Heinemann).

—— (2003) 'Three Poems', *World Literature Today* (July–Sept.): 38–9.

Okigbo, C. (1972) [Interviews], in D. Duerden and C. Pieterse (eds.), *African Writers Talking* (London: Heinemann).

—— (1986) *Collected Poems* (London: Heinemann).

Okri, B. (1992) *An African Elegy* (London: Jonathan Cape).

Omar, K., Kureishi, M., and Rafat, T. (1975) *Wordfall: Three Pakistani Poets* (Karachi: Oxford University Press).

Ondaatje, M., (1998) *Handwriting* (New York: Knopf).

Osundare, N. (1983) *Songs of the Marketplace* (Ibadan: New Horn Press).

—— (1988) 'A Study of Soyinka's "Abiku" ', in E. D. Jones *et al.* (eds.), *Oral and Written Poetry in African Literature Today* (London: James Currey; Trenton: Africa World Press), 91–102.

—— (2002) *Thread in the Loom: Essays on African Literature and Culture* (Trenton, NJ, and Asmara, Eritrea: Africa World Press, Inc.).

Parakrama, A. (1995) *De-Hegemonizing Language Standards: Learning from (Post)Colonial Englishes about 'English'* (London: Macmillan).

Parthasarathy, R. (1977) *Rough Passage* (Delhi: Oxford University Press).

Parthasarathy, R. (1982) 'Whoring After English Gods', in G. Amirthanayagam (ed.), *Writers in East–West Encounter: New Cultural Bearings* (London: Macmillan), 64–84.

Parry, B. (1994) 'Some Provisional Speculations on the Critique of "Resistance" Literature', in E. Boehmer *et al.* (eds.), *Altered State? Writing and South Africa* (Mundelstrup: Dangaroo Press), 11–24.

Patke, R. S. (2000a) 'Postcolonial Yeats', in D. Pierce (ed.), *W. B. Yeats: Critical Assessments* (Robertsbridge: Helm Information), 4, 814–26.

—— (2000b) 'Translation as Metaphor: The Poetry of Agha Shahid Ali', *Metamorphoses* 8/2: 266–78.

—— (2001) 'The Ambivalence of Poetic Self-exile: The Case of A. K. Ramanujan', *Jouvert*, 5/2 (Winter). Online.

—— (2003) 'Nationalism, Diaspora, Exile: Poetry in English from Malaysia', *Journal of Commonwealth Literature* 38/3: 71–85.

Paulin, T. (1984) *Ireland and the English Crisis* (Newcastle upon Tyne: Bloodaxe Books).

p'Bitek, O. (1971) *Song of a Prisoner*, intro. by E. Blishen (New York: The Third Press).

—— (1973) *Africa's Cultural Revolution* (Nairobi: Macmillan).

—— (1974) *The Horn of My Love* (Nairobi and London: Heinemann).

—— (1984) *Song of Lawino and Song of Ocol* (Oxford: Heinemann).

—— (1986) *Artist, the Rule: Essays on Art, Culture and Values* (Nairobi: Heinemann).

Pearce, R. H. (1987) *The Continuity of American Poetry* [1961] (Middleton: Wesleyan University Press).

Perloff, M. (1998) 'After Free-Verse: The New Non-Linear Poetries', in C. Bernstein (ed.), *Close Listening: Poetry and the Performed Word* (New York: Oxford University Press), 85–122.
Persaud, S. (1989) *Demerary Telepathy* (Leeds: Peepal Tree).
—— 2002) *The Wintering Kundalini* (Leeds: Peepal Tree).
Peters, L. (1971) *Katchikali* (London: Heinemann).
Petersen, K. H. and Rutherford, A. (ed.) (1988) *Displaced Persons* (Sydney: Mundelstrup, and Coventry: Dangaroo Press).
Philip, M. N. (1980) *Thorns* (Stratford, Canada: Williams Wallace Inc.).
—— (1983) *Salmon Courage* (Stratford, Canada: Williams Wallace Publishers).
—— (1990) 'Managing the Unmanageable', in S. R. Cudjoe (ed.), *Caribbean Women Writers* (Wellesley, MA: Calaloux Publications), 295–300.
—— (1991) *Looking for Livingstone: 'An Odyssey of Silence'* (Toronto: The Mercury Press).
—— (1992) 'Why Multiculturalism Can't End Racism', *Frontiers* (Stratford, Ontario: The Mercury Press), 181–6.
—— (1993) *She Tries Her Tongue, Her Silence Softly Breaks* [1989] (London: The Women's Press).
—— (unpublished) *Zong!* Typescript courtesy of author.
Pieterse, C. (ed.) (1971) *Seven South African Poets: Poems of Exile* (London: Heinemann).
Plath, S. (1981) *Collected Poems* (London and Boston: Faber).
Postma, J. (2003) *The Atlantic Slave Trade* (Westport, CT and London: Greenwood Press).
Press, K. (2000) *Home* (Manchester: Carcanet Press).
Prince, F. T. (1993) *Collected Poems: 1935–1992* (Manchester: Carcanet Press).
Quayson, A. (1997) *Strategic Transformations in Nigerian Writing* (Oxford: James Curry).
Rahim, J. (2002) *Between the Fence and the Forest* (Leeds: Peepal Tree).
Ralegh, W. (1972) *A Choice of Sir Walter Ralegh's Verse* (London: Faber).
Ramanujan, A. K. (1972) *Speaking of Siva* (Harmondsworth and Baltimore: Penguin).
—— (1975) *The Interior Landscape: Love Poems from a Classical Tamil Anthology* [1967] (Bloomington and London: Indiana University Press).
—— (1981) *Hymns for the Drowning: Poems for Visnu by Nammalvar* (Princeton: Princeton University Press).
—— (1985) *Poems of Love and War: From the Eight Anthologies and Ten Long Poems of Classical Tamil* (New Delhi: Oxford University Press).
—— (1995) *The Collected Poems of A.K. Ramanujan* (New Delhi: Oxford University Press).

—— (1999) *The Collected Essays of A. K. Ramanujan* (New Delhi: Oxford University Press).

Ramazani, J. (2001) *The Hybrid Muse: Postcolonial Poetry in English* (Chicago and London: University of Chicago Press).

Ramnarayan, G. (2004) 'No easy answers' [Interview with Arun Kolatkar] *The Hindu* (5 September 2004). www.hindu.com/lr/2004/09/05/stories/2004090500110100.htm. 22 Sept. 2004.

Rampolokeng, L. (1999) *The Bavino Sermons* (Durban: Gecko Poetry).

Riaz, G. F. (2002) *Baramasa: Seasons of Rural Life* (Karachi: Oxford University Press).

Rickard, J. (1997) 'Studying a New Science: Yeats, Irishness, and the East', in S. S. Sailer (ed.), *Representing Ireland: Gender, Class, Nationality* (Gainesville: University Press of Florida), 94–112.

Roach, E. (1992) *The Flowering Tree: Collected Poems 1938–1974* (Leeds: Peepal Tree).

Sa'at, A. (1998) *One Fierce Hour* (Singapore: Landmark Books).

—— (2001) *A History of Amnesia* (Singapore: Ethos Books).

Sa'at, A. (2002) [Poems], in *Poetry Award Winners: Golden Point Award* (Singapore: Times Books), 3–19.

Sacks, P. (2002) 'Anthem', *Agni* 56. www.bu.edu/agni/poetry/print/2002/56-sacks.html. 28 Nov. 2004.

Said, E. W. (1978) *Orientalism* (London: Routledge).

Sanders, M. (2002) *Complicities: The Intellectual and Apartheid* (Durham and London: Duke University Press).

Scott, B. K. (1995) *Refiguring Modernism: The Women of 1928* (Bloomington and Indianapolis: Indiana University Press).

Scott, F. R. (1966) *Selected Poems* (Toronto: Oxford University Press).

—— (1981) *Collected Poems* (Toronto: McClelland & Stewart).

Schwartzman, A. (ed.) (1999) *Ten South African Poets* (Manchester: Carcanet).

—— (2003) *The Book of Stones*. Manchester: Carcanet.

Senanu, K. E. and Vincent, T. (eds.) (1988) *A Selection of African Poetry* [first pub. 1976] (Harlow, Essex: Longman).

Senghor, L. S. (1991) *The Collected Poetry*, trans. M. Dixon (Charlottesville and London: University Press of Virginia).

Senior, O. (1994) *Gardening in the Tropics* (Toronto: McClelland & Stewart Inc.).

Sepamla, S. (1977) *The Soweto I Love* (London: Rex Collings; Cape Town: David Philip).

Seth, V. (1986) *The Golden Gate: A Novel in Verse* (New Delhi: Penguin).

Sharrad, P. (2003) *Albert Wendt and Pacific Literature: Circling the Void* (Auckland: Auckland University Press).

Shava, P. V. (1989) *A People's Voice: Black South African Writing in the Twentieth Century* (London: Zed Books; Athens: Ohio University Press).
Shohat, E. (1992) 'Notes on the "Post-Colonial" ', *Social Text* 31/32: 99–113.
Shutte, A. (1993) *Philosophy for Africa* (Rondebosch: University of Cape Town Press).
Silva, P. (2001) 'South African English: Politics and the Sense of Place', in B. Moore (ed.), *Who's Centric Now? The Present State of Post-Colonial Englishes* (Melbourne: Oxford University Press), 82–94.
Singh, K. (1988) 'The Only Way Out: Sense of Exile in the Poetry of Ee Tiang Hong', in B. Bennett (ed.), *A Sense of Exile: Essays in the Literature of the Asia-Pacific Region* (Nedlands: The Centre for Studies in Australian Literature), 33–42.
—— (2004) 'At Lake Balaton', *Westerly* 49 (November): 186.
Slessor, K. (1990) *Kenneth Slessor*, ed. D. Haskell (St Lucia: University of Queensland Press).
Smith, A. J. M. (ed.) (1960) *The Oxford Book of Canadian Verse* (Toronto: Oxford University Press).
Smith, A. (1989) *East African Writing in English* (London: Macmillan).
Soyinka, W. (ed.) (1975) *Poems of Black Africa* (London: Heinemann).
—— (2001) *Selected Poems* (London: Methuen).
Spenser, E. (1934) *A View of the Present State of Ireland* [1596], ed. W. L. Renwick (London: Eric Partridge Ltd).
Srivastava, S. (1994) *Talking Sanskrit to Fallen Leaves* (Leeds: Peepal Tree).
Stead, C. K. (1981) *In the Glass Case: Essays on New Zealand Literature* (Auckland: Auckland University Press).
—— (1989) *Answering to the Language: Essays on Modern Writers* (Auckland: Auckland University Press).
Stevens, W. (1997) *Collected Poetry and Prose* (New York: The Library of America).
Storey, M. (ed.) (1998) *Poetry and Ireland Since 1800: A Source Book* (London and New York: Routledge).
Surendran, C. P. (1999) *Posthumous Poems* (New Delhi: Viking Books).
Taban lo Liyong (1971) *Frantz Fanon's Uneven Ribs* (London: Heinemann).
—— (1972) *Another Nigger Dead* (London: Heinemann).
Talib, I. (2002) *The Language of Postcolonial Literatures: An Introduction* (London: Routledge).
Thieme, J. (ed.) (1996) *The Arnold Anthology of Post-colonial Literatures in English* (London and New York: Arnold).
—— (2003) *Post-Colonial Studies: The Essential Glossary* (London: Arnold).
Thomas, R. S. (1993) *Collected Poems 1945–1990* (London: Dent).
Thumboo, E. (1993) *A Third Map: New and Selected Poems* (Singapore: Unipress).

Todorov, T. (1984). *The Conquest of America* [1982] trans. R. Howard (New York: Harper & Row).

Tuwhare, H. (1993) *Deep River Talk: Collected Poems* (Auckland: Godwit Press).

Veit-Wild, F. and Chennells, A. (2004) 'Anglophone Literature of Central Africa', in F. Abiola Irele and S. Gikandi (eds.), *The Cambridge History of African and Caribbean Literature*, vol. 2 (Cambridge: Cambridge University Press), 445–71.

Veit-Wild, F. (ed.) (1992) *Dambudzo Marechera: A Source Book on his Life and Work* (London: Hans Zell).

Walcott, D. (1976) *Sea Grapes* (New York: Farrar, Straus & Giroux).

Walcott, D. (1986) *Collected Poems 1948–1984* (New York: The Noonday Press).

—— (1987) *The Arkansas Testament* (New York: Farrar, Straus & Giroux).

—— (1990) *Omeros* (London and Boston: Faber & Faber).

—— (1993) *The Odyssey: A Stage Version* (London and Boston: Faber).

—— (1996) *Conversations with Derek Walcott*, ed. W. Baer (Jackson: University Press of Mississippi).

—— (1997) *The Bounty* (London and Boston: Faber).

—— (1998) *What the Twilight Says: Essays* (New York: Farrar, Straus & Giroux).

Walder, D. (1998) *Post-Colonial Literatures in English: History, Language, Theory* (Oxford: Blackwell).

Walder, D., Haveley, C. P., and Rossington, M. (1992). *A421 Post-Colonial Literatures in English: Study Guide* (Milton Keynes: Open University).

Walker, K. (1992) *The Dawn is at Hand: Selected Poems* (London and New York: Marion Boyers).

Wallace, A. (1990) *Daughters of the Sun, Women of the Moon: Poetry by Black Canadian Women* (Trenton, NJ: Africa World Press).

Walsh, W. (1990) *Indian Literature in English* (London and New York: Longman).

Walwicz, A. (1982) *Writing* (Melbourne: Rigmarole Books).

Watson, S. (1990) *Selected Essays 1980–1990* (Cape Town: The Carrefour Press).

—— (1991) *Song of the broken string: after the /Xam bushmen: poems from a lost oral tradition* (Riverdale-on-Hudson, NY: Sheep Meadow Press).

Watson, W. (1986) *Poems Collected/Unpublished/New* (Edmonton: Longspoon/NeWest).

Webb, H. (1996) 'Aboriginal Writing: Twisting the Colonial Super-narrative', in R. Mohanram and G. Rajan (eds.), *English Postcoloniality: Literatures from Around the World* (Westport and London: Greenwood Press), 189–202.

Wendt, A. (1976). *Inside Us the Dead: Poems 1961 to 1974* (Auckland: Longman Paul).

—— (ed.) (1995) *Nuanua: Pacific Writing in English Since 1980* (Honolulu: University of Hawai'i Press).

Wheatley, P. (1988) *The Collected Works of Phillis Wheatley*, ed. J. C. Shields (New York: Oxford University Press).

Wild, F. (ed.) (1988) *Patterns of Poetry in Zimbabwe* (Dweru, Zimbabwe: Mambo Press).

Wilhelm, P. and Polley, J. A. (eds.) (1976). *Poetry South Africa: Selected Papers from Poetry '74* (Johannesburg: Ad. Donker).

Williams, R. (1989) *The Politics of Modernism: Against the New Conformism*, ed. T. Pinkey (London and New York: Verso).

Winters, Y. (1947) *In Defense of Reason* (New York: The Swallow Press and William Morrow & Company), 431–59.

Wiredu, K. (1996). 'On Decolonizing African religions', in P. H. Coetzee and A. P. J. Roux (eds.), *The African Philosophy Reader* (London and New York: Routledge), 186–204.

Wong, P. N. (1993). *Ways of Exile: Poems from the First Decade* (London: Skoob).

Wright, J. (1965) *Preoccupations in Australian Poetry* (Melbourne: Oxford University Press).

Yap, A. (2000) *the space of city trees* (London: Skoob).

Yeo, R. (1999) *Leaving Home, Mother: Selected Poems* (Singapore: Angsana Books).

Zephaniah, B. (1992) *City Psalms* (Tarset, Northumberland: Bloodaxe Books).

—— (1996) *Propa Propaganda* (Newcastle upon Tyne: Bloodaxe Books).

—— (2001) *Too Black, Too Strong* (Tarset, Northumberland: Bloodaxe Books).

INDEX

(This is a selective index, which identifies key topics and quoted authors)